'90 ✓

D0849052

Indochina's Refugees

Indochina's Refugees

Oral Histories from Laos, Cambodia and Vietnam

Joanna C. Scott

OAKTON COMMUNITY COLLEGE
DES PLAINES CAMPUS
1600 EAST GOLF ROAD
DES PLAINES, IL 60016

McFarland & Company, Inc., Publishers
Jefferson, North Carolina, and London

British Library Cataloguing-in-Publication data available

Library of Congress Cataloguing-in-Publication Data

Scott, Joanna C., 1943–
  Indochina's refugees.

  Includes index.
    1. Refugees, Political—Indochina—Biography.
  2. Indochina—History—1945–   I. Title.
  DS550.S44   1989   959.05′3   89-45008

ISBN 0-89950-415-9 (lib. bdg. : 50# alk. paper) ∞

© 1989 Joanna C. Scott. All rights reserved

Manufactured in the United States of America

McFarland & Company, Inc., Publishers
  Box 611, Jefferson, North Carolina 28640

Dedicated to the Indochinese refugees...

A people forced to go a dangerous
drama across feats of darkness and
turbulent seas in favor of freedom.

Nguyen van Lau

Contents

Laos — Land of the Seminar Camps

Maps

Appendix: Viengxay Area Seminarists

Preface

In Bataan, three long hot hours' drive north from Manila, the Philippine Refugee Processing Center bakes and sweats under the tropical sun. The complex houses nearly 17,000 refugees from the three Indochinese countries: Vietnam, Laos and Cambodia. They are there for intensive language training and cultural orientation before going to join families and friends in the United States.

The population turns over rapidly. Every week the rickety red Philippine Rabbits and triumphantly named Victory Liners career up and down the mountain roads, trailing clouds of stinking black fumes, scattering goats and chickens and swerving their way around the rocks left on the road to protect the swatches of rice spread there to dry. They bring new refugees to the camp for training and take old ones to catch planes to their new lives.

I first went to the Philippine Refugee Processing Center (PRPC) as an official visitor in March 1985. When we were leaving, my husband and I were given a painting of Vietnamese boat people on the high seas. Hand-written on the back was the inscription, "Boat People: a people forced to go a dangerous drama across feats of darkness and turbulent seas in favor of freedom." It touched my heart and I went back to the camp looking for the artist, Nguyen van Lau.

Later I met with leaders from the Lao, Vietnamese and Cambodian communities and asked them if they would help me put together a series of stories telling what had happened in their home countries. I couldn't have sat with a more willing group.

I have divided the book into three sections, one for each of the Indochinese countries.

For the Vietnamese section I talked with people who had come illegally by boat and legally under the Orderly Departure Program. Their backgrounds vary greatly—from artist to monk, from soldier to housewife, from civil servant to Amerasian student.

The Cambodian, or Khmer, section deals almost exclusively with Pol Pot's time. This is because the refugees now in the PRPC are those who fled Cambodia in 1979 at the time Pol Pot's regime fell to the Vietnamese. They spent a number of years in first asylum camps in Thailand before coming to the Philippines.

In Laos I found my greatest challenge. Everyone knows something about Vietnam. Most people know at least a little about Cambodia. I, for one, didn't know anything at all about Laos. But the Lao were patient with me. They were very anxious to have a record made of their country's story and were prepared to tolerate my ignorance in order to do it. I appreciate their help. I learned a lot. I hope I have given their stories full justice.

I know the reader will find some inconsistencies in the section on Laos. I have done my best to resolve them but history will probably never know the precise facts. This is because the leaders, the military, the government, the educated were sealed off from each other in secured camps when the Pathet Lao took over in 1975. As a result, those escaping from Laos bring with them no definitive shared body of knowledge.

The one thing they had in common, both with their fellow-countrymen and their fellow Indochinese, was a fervent passion for freedom that overwhelmed their mourning for a lost country.

"When I come to the freedom country..." was a phrase I heard time after time.

*   *   *

These stories were told to me between October 1985 and May 1986. Each has been carefully checked with the story-teller. As far as is humanly possible, they are accurate as told to me.

My thanks go to the staff of the PRPC for their help, especially to Dr. Crispina Grospe of the Philippines, who kept me organized, and to Molina Humphrey of Cambodia and now the United States, who lent me her knowledge and amazing skills as an interpreter.

I also thank my driver, Virgilio Yu, for the good care he took of me.

Joanna C. Scott
Manila, Philippines
July 1986

Vietnam —
Land of the Boat People

In Favor of Freedom

Nguyen van Lau

Nguyen van Lau's painting of boat people was the inspiration for this book.

When I first went looking for him in October of 1985 he was in the camp hospital suffering from tuberculosis. I finally met with him in December, still weak and thin from his illness. Two weeks later he fell and broke his hip. He spent several weeks in an orthopedic hospital in Manila, one more sad grey bundle amongst a sea of beds, the stench of urine overwhelming in the heat.

When I left the Philippines to return to the United States late in 1986, he was still in the refugee camp, an ugly scar running down his left hip and upper leg, still on crutches and still in severe pain.

I am an artist and a painter and so I like liberty very much. I left Vietnam because I wanted to be free and I hope that when I am in the United States I can work to collect money to help my family still in Vietnam.

I have been married twice. The first time was for so long I don't remember how many years. We had ten children and one grandchild. I have been married to my second wife for fourteen years. I was very lucky to have married her because she had an

3

Nguyen van Lau.

Amerasian daughter and when I realized I must leave Vietnam to
practice my career we were eligible to come out under the Orderly
Departure Program.

I was a famous enough painter in Vietnam. I had sold more
than a thousand pictures before 1975. I had even had an exhibition
in the American/Vietnamese Association in Tu Do ["Freedom"]
Street in Vietnam.

I lived in Saigon and as well as painting I used to work for the
Aden Movie Corporation. It belonged to a friend of mine and I
worked for him operating the movie projector for twenty years. I
also worked in a shop opposite the movie theatre painting movie
advertisements.

Then my friend, the manager of Aden, persuaded me that I
could make more money if I gave up operating the projector and

focused my talent on painting movie advertisements. So I did. And I did very well. I earned a lot of money and had many occasions to visit famous places—Hue, Hanoi, Phnom Penh, Vientiane—on business trips.

When the Americans came to Vietnam I worked for them painting advertisements for American movies. The Americans treated me very well, even better than the French. And so I earned more money.

Now, there is a hotel across the road from the Aden Movie Corporation where I had an agreement with the landlord to hang my paintings for sale to the many foreigners who came through there—journalists, military officers, tourists—and so I became quite famous with the foreigners. I was already well known to all the movie businessmen because they used to come to Aden to borrow their movies and they wanted me to paint advertisements for them.

It was in the hotel that I met my second wife. At the time she was illegally married to her boss—he was a millionaire living apart from his first wife. She was very powerful in the hotel. She commanded all the workers and anyone wanting a job had to come to her.

This lady, because she knew I earned a lot of money every day, would come to see me often and little by little she became my sweetheart.

At the same time she had relationships with some of the foreigners—that is how she came to have had the Amerasian daughter. She knows who the father is but she didn't find him after the child was born—maybe because it was too long after he had gone back to the United States to make contact with him. All she knows about him is that he was a pilot.

The North Vietnamese troops came into Saigon on April 30, 1975. I could have left before they came. Some American journalists wanted me to get out with them but I had all my children there and couldn't decide so they went without me.

All I could do was adjust to the new life under the Communist government. If I hadn't I would have got into a lot of trouble with the authorities.

As it was, I was sent to a New Economic Zone because most of my children were former soldiers with the South Vietnamese Army. It was the rule of the new government that all relations of former soldiers must go. We were to forget any easy life for our children. Four of my sons went with me. I left my wife and her daughter in Saigon because I wasn't sure what would happen.

The New Economic Zone was a farm and I had to be a farmer. I planted rice, cut down trees, dug canals for irrigation — all the things that farmers do.

I didn't really believe in the future of this New Economic Zone and, sure enough, after a while I came to realize that the Communist authorities say one thing and do another. So I completely lost trust in the new government. Nobody in the camp trusted them. They just wanted to escape. The organization was very complicated and very bad, there was not enough food and, as everybody knows now, Communists always tell lies.

When I went there they said that they would give each person in my family two hectares of land. With me and my four sons that would have been ten hectares — sufficient to support the family. That is why I agreed to go in the first place. But what really happened was that the camp authorities told us all that we must work and the cadre would give us points — maybe five or ten a day. Then at the end of the month we would receive food according to the number of points we had been given. If anyone couldn't work he would get no points and so would get nothing to eat.

I didn't agree with that kind of evaluation so I escaped from the camp. It was easy. I just got on a bus and went back to Saigon. I was able to do this because I was not a political prisoner and was not in a high security camp. The guards were very slack and no one came to look for me in Saigon. If I had been a political prisoner it would have been very difficult to be lost by the security authorities. A lot of people were escaping from that camp. The Communists were not organized.

Back in Saigon my wife did not have her job at the hotel any more. She was selling bread to make money.

I resumed my painting but it was not like before. It was bad for the artists. The Communists confiscated all the painting materials from the businessmen and sold them to us. Then, once a picture was finished and sold, the authorities got 20 percent of the price. They put in nothing but got 20 percent. We had to pay for materials and only got 80 percent. I didn't like this system.

And then we found out that we were eligible to leave under the Orderly Departure Program because of my wife's Amerasian daughter so we made arrangements with the Vietnamese authorities and left.

We stayed in Thailand one week and then came here to the Philippines. We have been here one year and have to wait maybe another six months because I have tuberculosis. I am sixty-three years old. I don't know where we will go. I have an aunt in California whose husband is an electrical engineer but I will not go to live with her. She left Vietnam before 1975 and she is afraid of me because I come from a Communist country.

I have just finished a picture for a friend to send to America. I got fifteen hundred pesos, yes. When I get to the United States I plan to paint pictures while I still live. [PRPC, December 6, 1985.]

Saved by the Esso Company

Reverence Tam Minh

The Reverence is a little shorter than my five feet seven with the look of a man who should be solid but is thin by mistake. He has a smooth brown face with wide brown eyes tilting slightly upwards at the corners. His head is clean-shaven with a greyish blue tinge. Over his right eye is an indentation, an old wound, running vertically. His teeth are crowded and when he talks his words seem to be making their way around an obstacle. Excitement brings little specks of foam to the corners of his lips. He wears sometimes the long, brown, wide-sleeved Buddhist robe and sometimes the saffron robe more familiar to Americans.

The first time I met the Reverence I bogged my car outside his temple, climbed out ankle deep in mud and paddled my feet clean in the puddles on my way up the path through the little garden dominated by a glowing white statue of the standing Buddha against a backdrop of tropical hilltops.

The temple sits right on the edge of the mountain ridge, the main door looking towards the camp. It is a typical small Asian temple; a wide bare floor before a statue of the Buddha seated cross-legged.

At the back of the temple are the living quarters where we sat to talk. At one end is a tiny room with a wooden slat cot and a candle. There are two long trestle tables in the middle section and a primitive cooking area at the other end.

A door in the middle of the back wall looks out over a gem-green tropical valley dropping away into terraced rice paddies and rising on the other side

9

in lush vegetation broken by cleared patches and the occasional nepa hut. In the early morning the mist sits on the valley floor and in the evening the mosquitos rise up like an army. By day the flies and ginger-colored ants are constant company.

I got used to shaking the flies off my glass of hot tea and honey before each mouthful and operating my tape recorder with one hand while diving under my loose shirt with the other. The Reverence seemed not to notice these earthly things. I'm sure he never realized there were ants in my armpits. He was a nice man and very patient with my ignorance.

I am a monk, young still, twenty-seven years old. I was born on October 5, 1958, in Hue City in the center of Vietnam. My father was a warrant officer in the South Vietnamese Army. I had two brothers and a younger sister. I was the first son. My mother died of heart disease when I was eight years old.

In 1966, when I was nine years old, I left home to become a monk. I joined the old Buddhist temple called Tu Hieu in the mountains of Hue. There I was taught the Buddhist doctrines while attending the Ham Long primary school. In 1968 I went on to the Bo De Huu Ngan high school, graduating in 1974. I rode my bicycle to school each day. It was thirty minutes away, near Hue City.

In 1975 I started full-time studies at the Tu Hieu temple and I was living and working in this old temple when the Communists took Hue on the twenty-sixth of March, 1975. I was not yet seventeen.

A Buddhist disciple had invited me to escape from Vietnam with his family before Hue fell. But I was very young and my life was very happy. I did not understand what Communism was all about. I did not realize that my life would be in danger. So I turned down the offer and stayed in the temple. (This disciple made a successful escape. He now lives in San Diego with his family. I will see him when I get to California.)

I came to my senses after they had left and, two days before Hue fell, I tried to escape by myself. I left the temple and went to a village near a beach where I had arranged to pick up a boat. But the Communists came in too fast and my boat didn't show up so I had to turn back.

Between 1975 and 1977 there were many Soviet Communists in Hue and frequent security checks of the temple but everyone still lived there and in 1976 I became a full monk, entitled to be called "Reverence."

Then, in 1977, the administration of Hue was turned over to the civilian Communists from Hanoi and things took a turn for the worse in the religious community.

These people had no spirit of religion. They didn't accept it at all and persecuted the Buddhist monks and the Catholic priests and the nuns. They told the Buddhist monks and nuns to return to their home villages and towns where these young men and women had to work and labor all day. They could not study. They could not practice religion. Many of the young men, Buddhist and Catholic, were put into the army and sent to Cambodia for the war. (Two of my friends were sent to serve in the army in Cambodia. One of them escaped and came back to live in South Vietnam. He is there now. The other one is still serving the Communists in Cambodia.)

I myself was sent to a work farm in Tay Loc, Hue, and was there for about a year.

I did not cooperate with the Vietnamese Communists and in 1977 I was invited to come and join the temple in Dong Nai City near Saigon City on the way to Vung Tau. So I left Hue and entered the temple in Dong Nai to practice Buddhism.

But the Vietnamese Communists did not accept this. They constantly harassed us. They would break into our meditations and disrupt our studies coming to check on our family certificates. Or they would borrow the temple for a meeting. (It has since become a zone office.) Eventually they told me to return to Hue and go back to work on the farm at Tay Loc.

In 1978 I defied the Communists and left Hue again, this time going to Vung Tau. (Many Americans were living in Vung Tau before 1975. There was an American army base there.) There I studied Zen for several months with Master Thanh Tu before going on to the Pho Minh temple in Rach Gia, Kien Giang Province.

I was not allowed to teach during this time and in 1978 my name was deleted from the family record because the police could not find me at my old temple in Hue and they concluded that I had escaped. This meant I had no ID card and turned me into a fugitive.

When I had been living in Hue I had heard of an underground group operating out of Vung Tau through a friend who was involved in it, the Venerable Thich Thien Tan (who was a first lieutenant in the Airborne Branch before becoming a monk).

Then a friend, another Buddhist monk, talked to me about it. He said I should join up and I did.

This group had been started by Ha Xuan Hung, also known as Dai Hoang. We usually called him "Lieutenant General."

At the beginning there were only twenty-six members. These people became leaders and the group grew quickly. There were Buddhist monks, Catholic priests, some professors and many military officers from the old South Vietnamese army.

Our mission was to organize discussions and write anti-Communist propaganda. We went from place to place teaching anti-Communist ideas, talking about the new regime and how it did no good.

Very many people became followers and the movement grew bigger and bigger and bigger. It was becoming strong—a people's army. We started to prepare for guerrilla actions when we were strong enough and hoped that we would eventually be able to defeat the Vietnamese Communists. But we were to be disappointed.

In 1979 the Communists came with rifles and revolvers and rounded up the leaders, twenty-six people, and took them to jail. There was a celebrated trial, known as the "Da Vang trial" in Hue City. Da Vang is the name of a cafeteria in Hue City where our group used to hold meetings. The son-in-law of the owner was a doctor in the Army before 1975. We invited him to join the group but unfortunately he turned informer and betrayed us to the Communists. He is now working for them in the Hue hospital.

The president of our underground group, Ha Xuan Hung, was sentenced to death and shot for anti-Communist activity. My friend the Venerable Thich Thien Tan was sentenced to life imprisonment. I don't know what happened to most of the others. Maybe they died in jail. Maybe they are still in prison.

I do know about one. I had a letter from him just last week. He told me that they had kept him in solitary confinement for two years. Then he managed to escape and get onto a boat to flee the country. He washed up in Palawan in the Philippines and now he has resettled in Quebec, Canada. He was lucky.

Just last week I met Phan Sung, the brother-in-law of Phan Ngoc, one of the leaders of the movement. They were both thrown into jail. Phan Sung finished his sentence, went home and escaped from the country. He has just arrived at the PRPC. He tells me that Phan Ngoc died in the jail.

The general secretary of the Buddhist Association, the Most Venerable Thich Quang Do, had been put in jail in 1978. He was freed in 1980 and was living in Ho Chi Minh City in 1982. Then the Vietnamese Communists took him to North Vietnam to live with his mother in their village at Thai Binh City, North Vietnam. I have had news since that his mother has died. I do not know what has become of him.

I waited until the Da Vang trial was over and then I ran away and once more tried to get on a boat to leave Vietnam but I was caught and thrown into jail. It was my second escape attempt.

When the word got around that I was in jail, the Most Venerable Thich Tri Thu and the Thua Thien Buddhist Association intervened for me. At that time the Communists were still nervous about standing up to the masses and I was released after only seventeen days.

The principal of my old temple had just died and many people wanted me to replace my teacher so I went back to Tu Hieu up in the Duong Xuan mountains near Hue. But the Communists told me I was to work in the fields and not to practice Buddhism. I was not to leave.

I was there for two years and the Communists kept up a constant harassment. The police from town came every week and the zone policeman came by also. They checked everyone who came to visit and often used the excuse of wanting to check the family certificate. The family certificate is very important under the Communists. It is a listing of all members of households so that a check can be kept on where everybody is. The temple was considered to be a household and everyone who lived there was listed on one family certificate. They did not want to accept me as a legitimate member of the temple household since my name had been removed from the certificate.

They bullied me, asking many questions.

"What is happening in your family? What is your father doing? And your mother?"

"What have you been doing this last week? You must tell us everything you have been doing."

They insisted that I was with the CIA. They even wanted to keep a check on my thoughts.

Then in 1982 the Most Venerable Thich Tri Thu became president of the Vietnamese Buddhist Association. It was a very powerful position and he was able to take me with him from Hue City to Saigon because the Communists were not yet bold enough to cross him.

I lived with him at the Gia Lam temple on Le Quang Dinh Street. I worked for him at the University of Saigon writing for him in Vietnamese Chinese and, still refusing to cooperate with the Vietnamese Communists in their efforts to reeducate the people, I also taught young monks and nuns the doctrines of the Buddhists. There were many disciples who were anxious to learn.

Then the Most Venerable Thich Tri Thu died. It happened like this: He had become the most famous and also the most notorious monk in Vietnam. He had a great following of disciples — monks and nuns, Buddhist students and lay people too. They were constantly coming to the temple asking for him and they believed his teachings. He had from the first refused to accept the Communists because they showed no respect for religion and so the Vietnamese Communists hated him.

One day many policemen came to the temple in a closed van. They jumped down and surrounded the temple. Without saying anything to us, they seized seven monks and nuns, threw them into the back of the van and took them away. I don't know where. We never saw them again. Some of the policemen stayed in the temple and watched everything we did.

The Most Venerable Thich Tri Thu was very distressed. The Communists were pressuring him to leave the temple and come to their office for an interview. They sent for him but he would not go. And he was distraught over the fate of the seven monks and nuns. He couldn't eat and he couldn't sleep for worrying about them.

Finally, when they had not been heard of for a week, he became so upset that he fell ill. The Communist policemen saw their opportunity and offered to take him to the hospital in Ho Chi Minh City to be cared for. At first he refused but he became so sick that his disciples begged him to go so he went.

The police took over the hospital. I tried many times to get in to see him but they allowed no visitors and so we did not know what was happening. Then, after six days, the Communists called the temple and told us that he had died.

I was very puzzled. Before he fell into extreme distress over the seven prisoners, he had been in good health. With rest and proper care he should have recovered.

Then the Communists put him in an ambulance and brought him back to the temple. Around his eyes was violet and purple. There was blood in his mouth and on his lips, and his chin had fallen down. Many physicians, his disciples, examined him.

"It was poison," they said. "They injected it into his vein."

Many, many came to see him there, dead in the temple, most of the Buddhists of Ho Chi Minh City. They came to pay their respects.

I took him myself to the graveyard in the temple grounds and buried him there. He had been a good and simple man, my teacher, and I loved him. He had taught me many, many secrets of the Buddhists.

It was a sad day for the Buddhists of Vietnam. He had been their good friend. They came to his grave and wept.

After the Most Venerable Thich Tri Thu died, the Communist policemen set about clearing the temple. Everyone was thrown out.

So I became a fugitive in Saigon City. I grew my hair and discarded my monk's habit. I had no place to live. I became a wanderer, living from place to place, avoiding the police. I could not go to my family but they gave me some money and I bought vegetables which I cooked in the houses of my disciples.

For nearly nine months I lived in this condition. I had been oppressed and threatened ever since the Communists took over and seventeen times I had tried to escape and failed. Most times I had been invited by Buddhist disciples to come with them free of charge and for one reason or another things had gone wrong. Several times I got money from my aunt and my family and from Buddhist disciples and then was cheated by rogues. Now it was most urgent. I must leave or I would surely be caught and killed.

By this time I learned the hard way that there is a great deal of bad organization and outright dishonesty in the business of getting people out of Vietnam and many people, including myself, pay fees to rogues who cheat and deceive them.

Still, I was desperate. Three more times I tried. The first two I failed again. I made arrangements, paid my money and took a small boat — we call it a taxi — down the river. But there was no big boat at the meeting place. Twice I returned to Saigon, disheartened.

The third time — it was May 17, 1985 — I left Saigon for the last time. This last and successful attempt cost a total of ten taels [ca. 330 grams] of gold. Nguyen Nhon Thien, who calls me uncle, came with me. The organizer had arranged for a car which took us to Can Tho City, about two hundred kilometers south-west.

Then, at twelve noon the fisherman met us and took us down to the riverbank where he had his taxi. We climbed in and he jerked the cord of the motor. It started and we backed away from the shore, then turned and headed down-river.

For six hours we travelled and then we came to the Tra On District where the taxi driver began searching for the big boat. I was most anxious as we made our way through the many boats on the harbor. But this time the organizer had made a good arrangement. The fisherman was honest.

At exactly seven o'clock the taxi driver helped me onto the big boat that was to carry me away from the Communists.

"At last," I said to myself, "I have a real chance to escape."

Night had fallen by this time. The boat set off in the darkness and I slept a little on the deck.

In the dawn light I was dismayed. Beneath the deck, in the lower level, was a crowd of what seemed to be mainly women and children. Most of them were below with a few in the shelter of the wheelhousing. I did not know then how many but it was clear that there were too many for such a small boat—it was only about sixteen meters long and four or five wide. Also, it was only a riverboat and not made for the big ocean.

I prayed, "I hope I come to the freedom country."

As the sun rose in the sky the wind grew fierce and the boat slipped and jolted up and down dark mountains. In the valleys we could not see the horizon, only the water above us. As we came up, the bow of the boat broke through the mountain peaks and water rushed over the deck, soaking the people below. Then we fell away down the other side and crashed into the valley floor. The people were crying and vomiting and praying in terror to Buddha, to Fatima, to Christ.

I prayed, "Let this boat not break apart."

By the evening of the eighteenth the wind had dropped and the mountains in the sea became flat. But we had been thrown off course. We had started our journey heading for Indonesia but now we were on a course for Malaysia.

I talked to the captain. "Now we have gone this far, we had better stay on a course for Malaysia," he said. "If we turn back towards Indonesia, it will be too far and we will die from lack of food and water. We only have enough for three more days."

It was hot and smelled bad below decks from the sickness of the people. But at least we came upon no pirates. In fact, we saw no other vessels at all except some fishing boats in the far, far distance. The captain showed them to me through his binoculars.

At four o'clock on the morning of the third day I was under

the wheelhousing with the captain when he pointed and handed me his binoculars.

"Look," he said. "What do you make of that?"

I looked and saw what seemed to be a city rising up out of the ocean. I was puzzled.

"It is very strange. There is fire rising up from the city but it does not seem to be burning."

As we drew closer he handed me the binoculars again. The light was better by then and I could see that there were massive pillars going down into the ocean and the city floated above the water.

Then we realized we were looking at an oil rig off the shore of Malaysia. I had never seen an oil rig before and I was very amazed. When we told the others a great joy swept over the boat. It was the Esso Company. We knew that we were saved from the Communists.

At about six o'clock our boat came up alongside the rig and we could see many Americans and Malaysians on board. They shouted to us, giving directions as we approached the side.

I was overawed and did not understand everything I saw. I remember seeing a small plane come overhead and go down inside the rig. I remember the faces of the Esso workers calling to us. I remember the word "Horselin" on the side of the big boat belonging to the rig. There were Americans in the "Horselin." The word "Semankok" was written on the side of the rig itself.

Then four or five people came aboard our boat with food and water. One of them, an American, counted us one by one. We had not done a count before that ourselves. There were one hundred and twenty-seven persons — all were alive and no one was sick. Two out of three were women or children.

We all ate and drank and at seven o'clock in the morning the Esso workers helped us all up onto the rig. We stayed there for a day and both the Americans and the Malaysians were very kind. They gave us lunch and dinner and we slept that night on the rig. We were very grateful for their help.

The next day the rig workers took our boat far out to sea and scuttled it. They watched it sink and took many photographs as it went down. It made me feel sad to see it go.

Then the chief of the company had us all loaded onto their big boat and they took us to the Pulau Bidong Islands in Malaysia.

When I got there I would have been content to live with my fellow Vietnamese people but the U.S. delegation came and interviewed me after only one month. They told me I could go to the Vietnamese Buddhists in California so I had to move on to the Sungei Besi refugee processing center close to Kuala Lumpur.

There I received a letter from the Most Venerable Thich Man Giac. He is the brother of my teacher Thich Tri Thu who was killed by the Communists. He had heard that I was there and was very happy that I had escaped. He had also escaped by boat—in 1979—and was then in California where he had become the president of the U.S. Vietnamese Buddhists Association. He has been very good to me. He writes to me often, sends me money and is acting as my sponsor.

He wanted me to stay there in the camp a long time teaching Buddhism to the Vietnamese refugees and I did what he wanted. He also wanted me to come on and teach at the Philippine Refugee Processing Center.

So, after seven months I came here for language and cultural training and am teaching in the temple. I will leave at about the end of July and go to Los Angeles to live with him in the Vietnamese temple on South Berendo Street.

I am very happy now although sometimes I am sad when I think of my friends and family back in Vietnam.

I think of my father who was sent to the local reeducation center in Saigon for two weeks after the Communists took over and then to the New Economic Zone at Ta-Moon, Ham-Tan, Thuan-Hai [village, district, province]. Finally, in 1982, he was sent to a work camp in Casao Cay Gao, Thong Nhat. He is still there. He has remarried and has three more children. I occasionally get a letter from him. My brothers wrote and warned me not to write to him directly as he is watched constantly but to send letters through my aunt in Saigon.

My brothers, who were high school students at the time of the fall of South Vietnam, are also on a work farm in the New Economic Zone. My sister, also a student at the time and living with my aunt in Saigon, was not taken away. She is now a housewife in Saigon.

Reverence Thich Thien Tan is still in the Communist jail. He is my dearest friend and I pray that one day he will find a way to escape and join those of us working for a new Vietnam without Communism. [PRPC, April 11, 1986.]

My Father Called Me Freddy

Freddy Nguyen

One evening I wandered down the dirt track from the camp guest quarters to the basketball court in the Vietnamese quarters. The American and Filipino staff were playing, the teams an inept and enthusiastic mixture of both nationalities. On one side of the court the Filipinos and Americans cheered and shouted. The other side was lined with Vietnamese teenagers — all boys. This side was quiet, with soft, close conversations and the occasional foray along the back of the crowd of someone looking for a cigarette or a light. The row of heads, straight black hair swinging to shoulder-length under the floodlights, was punctuated by some so fair that only the shock of a remark thrown in Vietnamese or the turn of the head to reveal the slight elongation of the eyes betrayed the other half of their heritage. These were the Amerasians.

Freddy Nguyen is one of them. Though dark-haired, he is, as he says himself, "the image of America." Yet he still has that indefinable Asian quality, a kind of softness, that marks him as not completely American. He is of medium height, with front teeth that are big without being prominent. His hair waves slightly and is shorter than most of the other Vietnamese youths. He has a wisp of black across his upper lip and a very proper manner.

I went several times to his hut looking for him and he would never see me until he had pulled a shirt over his naked torso. When he came to the administration building he always wore a pair of carefully preserved tan-colored Western trousers that he kept hanging on two nails on the wall of his hut. Unlike most refugees, the wooden shutter to the window of his hut was usually closed. I never did get to see his mother.

I had a letter from Freddy early in 1987 after he had left the Philippines and settled in California. He said: "I'm now in the U.S. where I have longed for. . . . Everything is O.K. I hope it's the country I resettle forever. There is something quite new, strange to me. It takes me, I hope, not very long, a couple of months to adapt myself to the way of life here. I watch T.V. and learn a lot from it."

And by Christmas of 1987: "I'm rather busy with my school these days. It's going perfectly."

My father is a U.S. naval officer—a commander. He met my mother in Da Nang while he was serving in Vietnam. She worked as a librarian for the U.S. Special Service Library #14 from 1965 to 1973. They were married in Da Nang and I was born in 1966, my younger sister in 1968.

In August of 1967 my father was sent back to the United States. He promised to come back to Vietnam and take us all to the United States with him but he never came. He kept in touch with us at first but as time went by it was out of sight out of mind. He seemed to grow gradually indifferent to us. Later he got married.

My mother loved my father but when he wrote and told her of his marriage she stopped writing to him because she knew it was not going to lead to anything now. She let him be happy with his new world.

My American name is Frederick after my father. My father called me Freddy but that was too hard for Vietnamese people to say so after he left my mother gave me a Vietnamese name too. Until now I have always used my Vietnamese name, Hai Vu.

My family has a tradition of being anti–Communist. We don't like them. My mother's father worked with the French fighting against the Viet Minh. When the French left he worked for the Republic of Vietnam under President Ngo Dinh Diem investigating prisoners and political suspects. Then, after the fall of

Freddy Nguyen: "Me, taken last month [April 1986]. I's in the state just for 6 weeks. My skin was still dark because of Bataan sunlight still lingered around."

Saigon, the order went out to search for him but by then he was old. Maybe the Communists did not want to do anything to an old and crippled man. Whatever the reason, they did not send him to the "resting house" and he died amongst his family in 1983.

Before 1975 I lived in Da Nang, a normal, happy life. Nothing unusual happened to me. From 1972 I attended school with many other children and I was very happy there. I got on well with all my classmates. They loved me very much and so did the teacher. There was never any kind of violence at school and we lived in harmony with all the people. I was very young.

Then I remember March 28 of 1975. On that morning when I woke up many people shouted out, "The Communists are coming! The Communists are coming!" I remember the noise and the running.

The Viet Cong had began their first attack on Da Nang, shooting a lot of rockets. The people became frightened. They shouted and ran for shelter.

We ran to the river to search for a means to get to camp Tien Sah because, according to the radio news, there were U.S. ships there. (Tien Sah was used by the U.S. Navy before 1973.)

And so we left. We took everything. We ran for life. I was eight years old. At that time I didn't know anything about the Communists. My mother told me to go and I just followed her. I didn't know anything. I was too young.

We went to the harbor to hire a boat because by that time we knew there was a U.S. ship waiting there for refugees outside the coast at Da Nang.

We took a small boat to the ship in order to flee to Saigon. I remember that the ship was very big. It was called the "Sergeant Miller." According to my mother it could carry thousands of people. There were four or five levels. I remember we had to climb many stairs and people were everywhere, packed one on the other. We travelled in the back.

When we got as far as Cam Ranh Bay in Nha Trang Province we all had to get out because the ship was damaged. The refugees did not intend to do this. They were so tightly packed and congested that they could move only a little way from where they were. They could not take care of hygiene and they lit small fires all over the decks to cook their food. So before very long the ship stank from the human waste and was burning in many places. There was so much damage that they asked us all to get out while they repaired it.

But the day after we got off the ship in Cam Ranh Bay we heard on the radio that the Viet Cong were coming. We had to get out soon.

I remember that there was no means of transporting us to Saigon so we had to walk. There were many of us — several hundred — including the South Vietnamese soldiers, the Marines and Airborne, who came to help protect us. They were at our front and our back as we fled down the road. The soldiers in the front tried to find the best way for us to go and to open the road for us. Those in the rear tried to stop the advance of the Viet Cong by destroying the bridges behind us and putting up barriers in the road.

On that march I saw dead people for the first time in my life — many, many. Soldiers and civilians both were shot and died on the road.

We went on foot like this for seven days until we reached Phan Thiet, a province about sixty miles from Nha Trang. There was more measure of security there because the military was still there to protect it, trying to establish a front.

We stopped for a couple of days and everyone tried to find a way to get to Saigon. Some people went by boat. Some succeeded in hiring buses. My mother and sister and I went on one of the buses.

We finally reached Saigon but we were newcomers there and didn't know where to go. At first we took asylum outside the city in a camp for evacuees. Then my mother sent notes to a friend and to her sister who was in Saigon studying at the time, asking them to come and get us. They came and took us to their home.

It was the middle of April and Saigon was in a serious predicament. There were many rumors and a lot of talk about evacuations to the United States. On April 29 a curfew was set up for the whole day and by evening the evacuation was at its climax. There were so many U.S. helicopters in the sky.

At first we didn't know what was happening but when we listened to the news from the BBC in the evening we found out what had been going on. We heard that they were evacuating people who had close relations with the U.S. And we heard that, although the helicopters had come for U.S. employees, the press and panic of people was so great that they were taking anyone who could get onto the flat-top. And we found out where: the U.S. Embassy.

And so, on April 30 at 6:30 in the morning, we and many other people, went to the U.S. Embassy to try to get on the helicopter so that we might escape. But it was too late. I remember when I reached the flat roof of the embassy I saw the last helicopter taking off. We were left behind. We stayed on the roof a long time to wait for another helicopter but there was none. So we came back down.

My mother tried to find another way to flee Vietnam. We heard that evacuation was also taking place at the harbor. But there were three harbors in Saigon and we were newcomers and did not know where to go. We got confused and finally gave up and went home.

Many people thought that the first day the helicopters had come just for U.S. permanent employees and they would be able to get on the next day but the president surrendered so quickly that everyone was taken by surprise. Saigon fell without a fight and we had to stay with the Communists.

After the fall of Saigon many people committed suicide because they were too terrified by the Communists. For instance, in August of 1975 the new government reformed the money. No matter how much money a family had they could change it for a maximum of only two hundred dong. Many people became bankrupt. Others had their real estate holdings seized. Many people could not bear these things. One former Airborne soldier found death by wearing his uniform downtown. The police saw him and shot him.

My mother intended to attempt suicide. I remember being really afraid of that. I told her not to do so but she said, "You do not know about the Communists. They are very cruel. If they see you have anything relating to the Americans they will kill you."

I remember my uncle who was a police officer. When he was called to go to reeducation camp he got too terrified and committed suicide. He took sleeping pills and before dying he convulsed with pain. Seeing him like that made my mother afraid to commit suicide because it is too terrible.

Later the government issued the warning that if anyone committed suicide the rest of his family would be jailed and fined heavily. When my mother heard this she decided that she would stay alive, at least for a while, and search for another way to flee Vietnam.

Right after the Communists took over Saigon, there was a movement called the New Economic Zone. According to the propaganda, it was a very good place for the jobless people in Saigon and very easy to earn a living there. The government would supply everything.

Many people were deceived by this and they went to the New Economic Zone. I remember that my aunt and my two cousins, also Amerasian children, went. My mother intended to follow her later. But when my aunt got there she knew the real truth. There was nothing at the New Economic Zone. It was just a place in the forest. There was no means of making a living. No means of work. The Communists did not supply anything. Everyone had to begin from their empty hands.

My aunt and her children stayed there until the day she left Vietnam.

We were told about this New Economic Zone over the radio and by the neighborhood propagandist. Each neighborhood had a desk in charge of propaganda. The propagandist came to each house to encourage the family to go to the New Economic Zone. He told us, "You should go. If you don't go willingly, sooner or later you will be forced."

There seemed to be two reasons for setting up this New Economic Zone. First, it was for the poor and for those considered to be "bad elements" — people who had worked for the former government. The new government wanted to segregate them.

Second, it was a way of sending away as many city dwellers as possible so that there would be more room for the northerners coming down to live and work in Saigon.

But many people escaped from the New Economic Zone and came back to Saigon and became nonresidents. They had no homes, only the street. They lived on the sidewalks, earning their living by begging or hawking whatever they could.

When my mother saw my aunt she told my mother not to go to the New Economic Zone because it was very terrible there. So my mother struggled to do the best she could to keep them from forcing my family to go. They tried to make her but she did not do what they wanted. Many times they came to our house urging and persuading. "Sooner or later you will have to go because you are jobless. How will you eat if you do not go? If you were wise you would go now before things get bad for you." But still she would not do it.

And because a lot of people were escaping and coming back to Saigon where they lived on the sidewalks or the back rooms of friends' houses, the Communists eventually had to stop trying to force people to go there. After 1980 things gradually calmed down. So we were very lucky. We did not go. We stayed there in Saigon.

Because my mother thought that without education one could not do anything, she sent me back to the public school. I went back in the middle of August, 1975. But the atmosphere was very different. At that time everybody was getting rid of anything relating to America. No one dared to wear T-shirts with the U.S. flag or even with English words on them. People did not dare to be seen talking to those who had worked with the U.S. or with me, the Amerasian child.

I was the image of America. I sat alone at school, away from the rest of the children and no one would be my friend. My classmates teased me and were encouraged to tease me by the principal, the head of the school.

Some teachers still liked me, maybe because they secretly liked Americans, but they were afraid to show it and acted as though they did not like me very much at all. The principal of the school was a woman from North Vietnam. All the teachers were frightened of her so they didn't like to do anything to help me. At first I was very sad and then gradually I got used to it.

I remember that at the end of 1975 and in 1976 the anti-American movement was very high. They had got rid of the Americans and were trying to get rid of everything related to America. Everything must be got rid of. The people working for the new government were forbidden to use any foreign languages. Not so much as "Hi!" or "O.K." So they watched every word they said in terror. Books written in English were burned. Some people even brought out their TVs and radios and records to be destroyed — there was some black humor in all this.

My mother warned me, "If you go outside maybe the Communists will see you and give you a lot of trouble." So I did not dare to go out to play with the other children. I just stayed home when I got back from school. If anyone asked me, "Who is your father?" I would answer, "My father is French." I never admitted that my father was American because at that time I was very terrified by the Communists.

There were other Amerasians in the school when I first went back but, because of the atmosphere there, before too long there were no more. They left because they felt very lonely and also for economic reasons. They had to support their mothers. Many had to do very dirty work as scavengers.

Every day they would go out to look for anything that might still be useful — plastic bags, bottles — and they would pick them up, maybe from the sewer, in the muck. Then they would wash them and take them to market to sell. They could earn maybe five dong per day like this. Some sold lottery tickets on the streets, some cigarettes. For them it was a hand-to-mouth existence.

And so society forced the Amerasian children to become a naughty element. They were considered to be low class. They could not go to school so they were uneducated. They had to fight for their existence. As a result they did not behave like other people. They became tough and impolite.

In my case, because my mother could earn a living by making dresses, I was one of the luckier Amerasians who could go to school. I did not go out to work. My mother did everything for me.

When I started back to school in 1975 there were more than a thousand students in my school with only five or six Amerasians. Some Amerasians studied for a few years and but finally they dropped out. I stuck it through until my graduation in 1984.

At the end of every year there was a prize-giving with awards for the best students. I was the best student in my class all the way through elementary school and high school but I never got the first prize. They would give me third prize instead. The top places had to go to real Vietnamese.

In school there was compulsory political activity. Every student from eight to fourteen had to join an organization called the Ho Chi Minh Vanguard of Young Pioneers.

This union was established to control the minds of the students. They would like to imprint their minds so that they would think that the Communists are the best. Every student was required to be a member. But I was an outsider. I did not want to join. They told me, "If you are not a member of that union; it could give you bad trouble." But I did not join up and that was one of the reasons that many teachers did not like me.

My mother made many applications to the U. S. Catholic Conference in Washington, D. C., and to the Orderly Departure

Program office in Bangkok, Thailand, trying to get permission to leave to go to the United States. But at that time there were no programs for Amerasians so we did not receive any reply.

Then, in the summer of 1981, my mother and my sister and I decided to flee Vietnam on the high seas. We joined quite a large group under one organizer.

But unfortunately, on the way to the beach to get on the small boats which we call "taxis," the coast guard caught us. We were spread out in a long line as we came down the beach and they came up and entrapped the middle section—thirty or forty of us. The people on the ends were able to flee away.

My sister panicked. She turned and ran. They called to her, "Stop! Stop!" but she was too terrified. She kept on running and they shot her. She died immediately there on the beach. My mother and I could not take her body away. We had to cover her with the sand where she lay. She was younger than me.

All the Vietnamese were allowed to go free but I was Amerasian so my mother and I were put on a truck and taken to prison in the Baria District of Dong Nai Province. I was nearly fifteen years old.

We were there for forty days. The cell we were living in was very small—about fifteen meters by four but there were about two hundred and forty prisoners living there. Most were political prisoners who had wanted to flee Vietnam but were arrested so they loved us very much and we lived in harmony with them all. There was nothing wrong between us.

During the day we were sent out to work. Most people did hard labor—cutting wood in the forest or hauling it. I was given the lightest but the hardest and dirtiest job—cleaning the cows' stall. There were twenty or so cows and I did it with one other person. We carried the dung in our hands. By nightfall we were very tired.

It was very crowded at night when all the people were back from working. We were so packed in that we did not have space to lie down. We sat up to sleep, leaning against each other.

Every day everyone was supplied with one gallon of water for washing and drinking and one bowl of rice soup with salt. Twice a week we got spinach and once a week pumpkin.

In the prison there were very strict rules. If we were hungry we were not permitted to cook any more rice. If someone was caught in the action of cooking more rice there would be very cruel punishment.

I remember that one night one of the prisoners was assigned to go out to be cook for the others. He wanted to cook more rice for the sick people in the prison so he went ahead hastily, not reporting what he was doing to the security officer. When the security officer saw him cooking the rice soup he made him get in a very cruel position by asking him to open his mouth and then he poured the very hot soup into his mouth. His tongue was wrinkled and he could not talk properly. He stuttered when he spoke and no one could understand what he said. The guard said, "If you want to do anything you must report to the security officer first. This should be a very good lesson for you."

Then my family, my aunt and some others bribed the security officer of the village where the prison was that I might be set at liberty. The organizer of our planned escape had been there on the beach when we were surprised. He listened to what was going on to find out where I was to be taken and gave this information to my aunt. Then he acted as her go-between. She gave him money, he negotiated the deal and paid the local security officer, and so I came back home.

Shortly after this, we heard on Voice of America that Amerasians would be allowed to leave Vietnam officially under the Orderly Departure Program. It became official policy for Amerasians to leave the country. The Communists wanted to get rid of them, to get them out as soon as possible. It amused them to see the American government bearing that burden.

Many left, although some were left behind. Some could not afford the expense for the papers even though, knowing that Amerasians were very poor, the officials did not ask much. Others had no resident's book. People were classified as resident and non-resident. Only those who had a resident's book could leave. Most of those who had lived in the city. The non-residents lived in the countryside. Some lived in the Buddhist pagodas and were taken care of by the monks and nuns. Some were raised by Vietnamese families who used them as servants and wouldn't let them apply to leave.

Those living in the New Economic Zone had no one to help them. For instance one of the requirements was a curriculum vitae certified by the neighborhood security office but this wasn't done in the New Economic Zone. So, even though the official policy was for Amerasians to leave the country, it depended on the individual situation whether they could or not.

We waited for a time and then in 1982 we applied for permission to leave Vietnam. In August of 1983 we got a letter of introduction from a Mr. Donald Collin in Bangkok telling us that we could leave. We were very happy, thinking that a letter of introduction would mean we could leave sooner. But it turned out not to be such a good thing after all. In fact, it brought us a lot of trouble.

The officer in the Immigration office where we took the letter thought that an Amerasian with a letter of introduction must be very important to the U. S. government. So, while many Amerasians without a letter went on to the United States, they held our application up. It finally took us twenty-one months to get the permit and then fourteen months later to get the interview. Thirty-four months in all. Other people it took only one year. Of the three Amerasians in my neighborhood, I was the last to leave.

It was not until after the interview that they told me that we had been accepted that I began to believe that I was really going to be able to leave Vietnam. I left with my mother in January of 1986. We took a stop in Thailand and then came on here to the Philippines.

I have only my mother here but my aunt and her two Amerasian children have been waiting for us in America for nearly one year. She will be my sponsor. She is in California, in San Francisco. Although she is very poor, she would like to sponsor me if my father won't.

I don't know how many Amerasians are in this camp but it is a lot — maybe a few hundred. Most of them are teenagers — born from maybe 1963 to 1975. I have a black Amerasian friend who is twenty-two.

We Amerasians tend to like each other best. We all came from the same type of situation and we knew each other back in Vietnam. There is no discrimination between white Amerasians and black Amerasians.

In Vietnam they told us that in the U.S. there was very violent racial discrimination. They said that the black people have to sit in the back of the bus and they cannot go into the same restaurants. And all Amerasians are considered to be colored people. There is no difference if they are white Amerasians or black. They taught me that in school.

In the camp here they tell me that there is no racial discrimination in the U.S. now and I don't know whether that is true or not. I hope so. They say that there is no racial discrimination in Vietnam but if a full Vietnamese and an Amerasian work in the same office any promotion is given to the Vietnamese not the Amerasian. It's not that the Vietnamese could do the job better but promotion must be given to him before the Amerasian. So in their words there is no racial discrimination and many foreign people believe it but in fact it's quite different.

I have also heard that there are a lot of Vietnamese Communists in the U.S.A. If you do something against the Vietnamese government they will come after you. They kill a lot of people and no one knows anything about it.

A friend of my mother saw an officer of the Vietnamese government one day when she was out shopping. He had worked in the Ministry of Interior and she remembered him very well from when she was arranging for her permit to leave. In that job he would easily have been able to leave under the Orderly Departure Program himself.

It is very difficult to tell about the future. But when I am in the United States I will continue my studies. I will work my way through college and the rest depends on my situation. If we have the money I will study longer but if not I will study for five years and then go out to work. I have been told that there is a very good university in San Francisco—Berkeley. I would like to go there.

I don't know what will happen about my father. The Joint

Voluntary Agency office was able to find out where he is now and I have written him at his address in Florida. Maybe he has his own family now so I think that what he does about us is up to him because we don't want to do anything that will make problems for others.

If he is kind and he thinks of his son in Vietnam he will sponsor me and if not I don't care about it because maybe his wife will not allow it.

I have lived in Vietnam without a father for seventeen years so I think that whether I have a father or not doesn't make any difference at all. It would be good of him to sponsor us but if not — it's up to him. [PRPC, April 23, 1986.]

The Hope of Ho Chi Minh Is Fallen Now

Mr. Le

Mr. Le told his story in almost perfect English, in a voice so soft I strained to hear. His eyes glistened with tears behind silver, wire-rimmed glasses when he spoke of how his son would be educated as a spy against his family.

He is a gracious, gentle man with a humble manner that disguises a strength of purpose and forcefulness of personality that made him a leader amongst his countrymen and a man known by name to every one in the camp administration.

I saw him frequently around the administration building, coming and going to meetings, organizing and pleading the cause of other Vietnamese who needed special help.

His wife and son had been left behind in Vietnam but early in 1988 he wrote to me from Alhambra, California:

"I'm now so busy of welcoming my wife and my son. They are now in Palawan camp [a first asylum camp in the Philippines which houses many boat people]. They have been accepted by the [U.S.] Immigration and Naturalization Service on the last December 1st. I hope they will come to U.S.A. very soon."

After graduating from the Institute of National Administration I served my country as a public administration manager for eleven years.

Later, I was called to the army and graduated from infantry officers' school. So I was a former government official and a former officer of the South Vietnamese Army.

After the collapse of the Republic of Vietnam, all former government officials and officers of the South Vietnamese Army were put into Communist jails and reeducation camps. I spent almost seventy months in reeducation camps before I was released.

These reeducation camps are nothing more than hard labor camps and we were just hard-working prisoners there.

Every day I had to perform hard labor in the jungles, clearing dense forest for cultivation or in the fields digging great canals. The work was all done by manpower. It was very hard. The prisoners had only a little food and no medicine when they were sick. We got thin and weak. Each month and sometimes each week there were deaths in the camp.

In my last camp there were about one thousand three hundred prisoners of all kinds—former government officials, former officers, new political prisoners (insurgents after April 30, 1975), murderers, thieves, corrupt officials, pickpockets, prostitutes and narcotic drug users. There were men and women, old and young, even minors who had been caught stealing in the market.

After spending almost seventy months in reeducation camps, I was released with twelve months' confinement at home.

During my time of home confinement I earned some money by doing watch repairs and then by repairing locks. I taught myself how to do it. But I was supporting three people, including myself, and I could barely earn enough for our daily necessities.

My wife had been an English teacher in a high school in Can Tho City under the former regime. But when I was put in the Communist reeducation camp she was dismissed from her school because she was the wife of a former government official. She tried to earn her living by selling second-hand things in the market.

I have only one child. He was very young then—about eight years old. Because he was still so young he was only attending primary school and although we haven't had any urgent problems with him yet, I don't like him being educated by the Communist regime because they thrash the children about the head. They indoctrinate them with beliefs quite strange to our culture and traditions. They teach them hate instead of love and piety. Eventually they turn them into spies to follow their parents at home and into fanatic Communists capable of gunning down their own fathers.

Truong-Chinh, president of the Socialist Republic of Vietnam, was a famous example of this fanaticism. In 1953 he killed his own father because he was a landowner. By doing this he showed his dedication to the Party. It is an inhuman kind of knowledge my son will learn. It is very dangerous to have our children educated by the Communists.

My life under the Communist regime confirmed what I had learned in a politics course that I had taken at the Institute of National Administration in Saigon. It is an inhuman regime. The Communists never observe human rights and so people have no way to protect themselves. They are simply put in jail if the authorities want it.

In my case, because I was a Catholic, a former government official and an officer in the South Vietnamese Army, I was always in danger when arrests were being made by the local authorities. And so I lived with constant fear and suspicion until I realized that I could no longer live under this inhuman regime and I decided to escape from my home country.

But it is difficult to escape from Vietnam because all movements, all comings and goings of the people, are severely controlled by the authorities. Even if I just wanted to go to the next village to see a friend I had to have a permission paper from the local authority.

So I worked out a careful plan. After I had finished my confinement at home, I asked permission to go to Saigon City to find a job and it was granted. So I went to Saigon and worked there, every so often coming back home to renew my permission paper.

Meanwhile, my wife arranged for my escape with an organizer and several other people. She wouldn't tell me how much it cost her — just that she had arranged to pay when I reached freedom.

Then, one time when I left Saigon to go back home to have my permit updated, I managed to get permission from the Saigon security authority to visit one of my friends in a village along the way. I took advantage of this occasion to join the other people at the rendezvous. And so I escaped on a small boat with some other refugees. I left my home country on March 9, 1984.

The boat was maybe ten meters long with an engine and thirty-seven people on board. We spent four days and nights on the sea and we were robbed three times by pirates. I think they were all Thai fishermen because they caught fish on the sea and their fishing boats were very nice. On each boat there was a radio.

They destroyed our engine too so we had to sew some mats together to make a sail. The weather was very fine and there was no wind but eventually we came near the coast of Thailand and there was enough wind for us to sail until we were washed up onto the shore.

We arrived in the south of Thailand very near the Malaysian border in a district named Saiburi in Pattani Province. We came to the beach at midnight and stayed there three or four hours waiting for daylight.

Very early the next morning some villagers were going to fish and they saw us and I asked them to inform the local police. After maybe half an hour the local police chief came to see us and asked us some questions about our situation. He put us in a residence near a Christian hospital that was close by. He also promised to report our case right away to the Ministry of Interior and to the United Nations High Commissioner for Refugees office in Bangkok. Then two American ladies — maybe they were nurses in the hospital — came to see us. They told us that they had watched our boat coast in and they gave us candy, cigarettes and aerograms. These were the first people to help us in the free world.

The next day a UNHCR official drove to see us. He brought gifts and made a list of our names to take back with him to the office.

After two or three weeks there in Saiburi we were sent to Songkhla camp, still in the south of Thailand. We stayed there about three months and I was elected as camp chief. Then we were transferred to Sikiew camp which is north and east of Bangkok.

I stayed there almost one year and worked at the UNHCR office doing administration.

I was accepted by the United States delegation on July 22, 1985, and on August 14 I was transferred to the Panat Nikhom transit center near Bangkok. Then, on September 17, I was transferred to Manila and the next day I came here to the Philippine Refugee Processing Center.

When I reach my destination in the United States I will try my best to reunite my family. I will find whatever work I can to earn my daily living and to make sufficient money to sponsor my wife and son out of Vietnam under the Orderly Departure Program as soon as possible.

I don't know exactly how much it will cost. When I get to the United States I will study that very carefully with friends and relatives there. My wife's brother is in New York State and he has promised to help me.

I am convinced that one day my country will be liberated. The lesson of the Israeli people is a very precious example for us. I know we shall overcome the Communists. Maybe it will take a long time but I believe we will have victory. My beliefs are built on the following considerations:

Communism doesn't go with the Vietnamese culture and tradition. The Communist regime in Vietnam was built on lies and oppression. Then, when hundreds of thousands of North Vietnamese as well as hundreds of thousands of South Vietnamese were trying to escape from their home country, carrying their lives in their hands, the Vietnamese Communists couldn't lie any more. So only oppression remained. But oppression always ends in defeat.

By forcing the unification of the South to the North, the Vietnamese Communist Party swallowed a poison into its body which is taking effect now. The Vietnamese Communist members are feeling contemptuously cheated by their leaders because when they came down and saw the reality of the South they realized that the nationalists had successfully provided the people with a life more abundant and happy than the life of the North Vietnamese. So they have started sending their membership cards back to the

Party as a sign of their indignation and urging changes in the leadership. This was told to me by cadres in the camps. I also knew some who lived in Saigon who had lost their jobs as a result of their protests — especially the intellectuals.

The old, backward-looking and power-loving leaders of the Vietnamese Communist Party want neither change nor evolution because they are afraid of being gradually eliminated. But any regime that cannot keep up with natural evolution will be overcome and left behind. The Vietnamese Communists will surely collapse under the opposition coming both from within the Party and also from the Vietnamese People's Resistance supported by the Vietnamese refugees abroad.

And this is the second purpose of my escape — to contribute my part to the liberation of my native country by the Vietnamese themselves.

*   *   *

This was the second time I had escaped from the Vietnamese Communists. The first time was about 1947 or 1948 when I was a little child. My family is Catholic and when the Communists took over my village in the North they killed my Catholic priest and they didn't allow catechism classes for the Catholic children. So my parents decided to leave my village — to escape from Communism and go to the Nationalist area in the South. My father joined the Nationalist army to fight against them. But now he is dead. My mother died too, when I was very young.

I have two brothers living in Vietnam. The older brother is a former officer like me. The younger brother is an agricultural engineer but he doesn't work for the Communists. He stays at home and earns his living by repairing clocks. They have tried to escape but it is very difficult for them to do. My older brother has a big family and life is very hard now so he hasn't enough money to pay for the trip. But he writes to me that he always thinks of escaping. He cannot live under the Communist regime.

I do get mail from Vietnam. Letters sent to my village take a long time to reach home especially when they get to Saigon. They stay there a long time and then take maybe one or two more months from Saigon to the province. But when the letter is from Vietnam to me it is very quick — maybe as little as ten days or two weeks.

In Vietnam and I think in all Communist countries the mail is controlled by Secret Security. We understand that we cannot speak directly of some matters so we talk around the point and say things that only members of the same family understand. For example, my younger brother wrote me that he's "trying to visit Uncle Six." But our Uncle Six is in Canada now. So that means he's trying to get out. It is unbearable for him to live there.

I hope and I firmly believe that in the future the Communists that are living now will fall down and collapse because this regime was based on lies and on oppression. It is nothing to lie to the people so the people don't trust them.

In the beginning, Ho Chi Minh said that when the Vietnamese Communists had victory over the Americans our country would be ten times better. But our country becomes poorer and poorer. It is poorer now than it was thirty years ago. And it is very dangerous to live there. The Vietnamese Communists are more fanatic slaughterers than leaders and administrators. Their failure to provide a prosperous life for the Vietnamese people has demonstrated once more that Communism cannot bring easy circumstances of life, liberty, prosperity or happiness. The hope of Ho Chi Minh is fallen now. [PRPC, October 23, 1985.]

Finally It Was All a Lie

Name Withheld

*This story is one of the few told to me by a woman. There were a number
of reasons. For the most part the men spoke better English. Some had done
military training in the United States. Some had worked in U.S. embassies
or with U.S. military programs like the Strategic Hamlet Program in Vietnam. Others learned the language at school. Some of these men also spoke
French, so my high school French came in useful when their rusty English
failed them.*

*Whereas the men came to me of their own volition, the women tended
to be much shyer and I had to actively search them out. Also, all the ethnic
community leaders were men and it was with their group that I first put for-
ward this project.*

*The teller of this story was typically shy and asked to have her name
withheld. Although she was learning English at the camp, she was too
overawed to practice it on me so her story was told entirely through an interpreter. She wept when she was given her copy.*

Before the revolution in Vietnam I was a school student. We
lived in Cho Lon village and our life was good.

My father was a carpenter and he would go to the forest to get
lumber to work with. My mother was a housewife and I had three

brothers and three sisters. We owned two houses. They were small houses—just one level, made of stone and about ten meters long by four meters wide. One belonged to my grandfather and one to my father.

Then in 1975 the Communists came in and my father could not go to the forest any more. He started to work with machines and things started to get bad for my family. My older brother—he was sixteen—had to leave school and go to work. He worked with machines also and when he was paid he would give the money to my mother.

Under the new government the money changed. For one hundred dong we could only buy what we used to buy with ten dong. The businessmen could not stay in business. The government controlled it all. They said, "You have your own shop? This is not yours. This is a government shop. We must keep control—all the control."

Then the Communists took the business to the country and turned it into agriculture. They took all the businessmen away and made them work on farms. They had to plant things and labor in the fields. They did not buy and sell any more. This was very bad for the people in the cities. There were few goods for them to buy now, they were more and more expensive, and there were not enough jobs for all the people to support their families.

My father was not taken away to the country because he was not in business. He was just a worker. But in 1976 he lost his job working with machines. He found another job making shoes but the salary was not enough for my family and we had to sell all the things we owned—the television, the refrigerator, our clothes.

Then in 1978 my brother turned eighteen and the government called him to military service. My father did not want him in the Communist army so he planned to help him escape from Vietnam by boat but the owner of the boat failed.

The organization that helps people to escape is like a company. People pay them gold—three ounces and six grams for every passenger. Of that, the owner of the boat keeps one ounce and two grams and the rest he must give to the Communist Vietnamese. The owner of this boat failed maybe because he didn't give enough to the Communists so they didn't let my brother go and we lost our money.

By 1978 many, many people had left by boat. But in August of that year the government decided that too many people were escaping so they said, "O.K. We will plan that." But they didn't want the public to know.

They would say, "You give to me more gold than the company, O.K? You give them three ounces. You've got to give me five ounces. Give me more gold and I will let you go. But don't tell anybody about this. Just go."

My brother had to give them a lot of gold — twelve ounces. It came from the savings my mother and father had before the revolution.

So my brother escaped and washed up in Malaysia safely. And in 1979 my sister escaped. She was sixteen years old. She went alone and came safely to Indonesia. Then my aunt's family escaped also but they are all of them dead. Their boat sank and they drowned.

By this time my family had no more money. They had used it all to help the others escape. And so we became very poor. My father had to work hard and things were very expensive. I did not go to school any more. I worked. I stopped school in 1980 when I was fifteen years old after spending the last five years being educated under the Communists.

I used to like school before the revolution. The students were taught a lot of good things including English and Chinese language. But after 1975 it was not like this any more. The Communists taught politics. There was a little English and Chinese still taught in the higher grades but in the low grades it was all politics — politics every day.

They talked about the history of the community — what it is like now and how it will be so much beter in the future. And they said it was very bad in other countries. They always said bad things about the United States and about France. They said the Americans and the French never love people, never help people, always want to rob the people. In the newspapers also they always told about things that were wrong with the United States.

They taught us how to be good Communists. They would say, "Look at our great Vietnamese Communist leader. His name is Ho Chi Minh. Ho Chi Minh loved people, helped people, never robbed from people. And so the Communist policy is to love people. We love people. And every day we make good plans for our people."

But the students didn't believe and they didn't like to go to school any more. Some students whose families worked for the government believed but none of the Chinese believed and many Vietnamese didn't either. I am Chinese—Vietnamese Chinese.

When students get through high school now they are only allowed to go on to university if their families work for the government. The professors are all part of the government also.

Then, when they graduate from university, they must work for the government or for a government factory. But their salary is very low. They only get enough to pay for breakfast. So government workers have to have two jobs in order to get enough money to feed their families. Many of them operate tricycles—the pedal ones—and carry passengers around after office hours.

There are few foreign visitors—mainly from France and Hong Kong but no one from the United States. Of course, there are many Russians in Vietnam now. Some are professors in the universities. Some are engineers helping in the factories. I never saw any military troops.

My brother got to California in 1979. He quickly found a job and sent some money back to our family in Vietnam. He had found a man in the United States who dealt with the Vietnamese black market so he gave him a thousand dollars to send to us. The man sent the money through his relatives. They gave our family only seven hundred dollars but at least we had some money and so for a time we could buy things and we saved some too.

Another time my brother sent a package—some clothes and fabric, some medicine and some flashlights—but when we went to the airport we had to pay the Communists very high taxes before they would give it to us. My brother also sent money to us through a Vietnamese Communist bank but the Communists held all the money.

They said, "If you need to buy something from us and you pay tax then you can have the money."

So we took that money and we bought a refrigerator, a radio, a television and other such things because if we didn't buy those things the money would stay with the Communists.

On the television we could watch only Communist programs. They had news and sometimes cartoons and shows and songs. It was all Communist propaganda.

We got the news from Russia. Every program they would tell us that in the capitalist countries there were no jobs and no goods to buy, the companies were failing and the factories closing down. About Russia they said good things. They showed pictures of Russians. They said that life in Russia is very, very good and some of the people are very wealthy. The Russian people are so smart. The Russian space program is so good. The Russians are so proud of their country. Everything is good.

They also gave Vietnamese news. They talked about the government's plan for the citizens. They said that they were trying to plan something good for the population. They were there to help the population.

But finally it was all a lie. It is just not true what they say. The population is low, low and dying. Some people lost their jobs and some people the government cast into jail and then beat them until they died.

People are thrown into jail for many reasons. Sometimes they have said something wrong about the government or maybe they have tried to escape in a boat or been caught selling medicine. If they do and they are caught they are sent to jail. If they have money and pay they are let out but if they have no money they are beaten to death. If they are not beaten to death, then they starve.

Many people from my village were killed in jail, especially the leaders in the community and the people who worked for the old government. Not my father though because he was just a worker.

When my brother had enough money he sent a sponsorship to the family to bring us out under the Orderly Departure Program. So we applied to the government. We had to wait three years to get an exit visa to leave Vietnam and after one year more we were interviewed by the United Nations High Commissioner for Refugees (UNHCR) and the American government and they agreed to give us a visa to enter the United States.

We had to wait another year to get a departure visa to leave Vietnam so altogether we waited for five years. And right before we left we had to pay more money — another ounce of gold — because the government wanted us to pay tax for leaving.

My father and another brother had both been working but every three months in Vietnam you have to pay tax and you also have to pay a bribe to the government official. If not, they find some story. They say, "The taxes you paid were not enough. You have to pay some more." So my father had a hard time finding more money to pay the departure tax.

When we finally got onto the departure list, a man from the government asked my family, "Do you want to take Air France or Air Vietnam? If you want to take Air France you must pay me some money and I will arrange it for you."

But my family didn't give him any money and so we took Air Vietnam which is very uncomfortable and hot. They didn't give us anything to drink and only one little biscuit. But the trip was only two hours and we got to Thailand safely. There were about a hundred refugees on the flight. I came with my mother, my father, two sisters and two brothers. My grandfather was ill and because he is so very old we had to leave him behind. But he has been approved to leave and we want to get him out as soon as we can earn the money to sponsor him.

We landed at the Bangkok airport and took the bus to the transit center nearby. There we were fingerprinted and had ID photos taken. Then we went by bus again to the Soun Phlu Camp and stayed for seven days. We had medicals and more fingerprinting. We had two meals every day — cabbage soup — at seven o'clock in the morning and four o'clock in the afternoon. Not enough but we didn't mind that.

After seven days we flew on to the Philippines and came by bus here to this camp where we are being taught English and other things to get us ready to go to the United States.

I am happy now. I can study English again and many people

help me. I am an assistant teacher and I have been taught how to write a resume and how to fill out a job application. Usually we have enough to eat. We are going to leave at the end of November to meet my brother and another aunt and uncle in San Jose, California. [PRPC, November 7, 1985.]

They Came to Rob and Kill

Thich nu grac Huong

Thich nu grac Huong is one of many clerics who have fled Vietnam. She is a Buddhist.

I also met Sister Hue, a Catholic nun, in the refugee camp. She came to visit me in Manila — a frail-looking little woman with a fierce heart. She offered to act as go-between for me with her brother, a Catholic priest still in Vietnam, to get up-to-date information on what was happening to the church.

However, before she had time to contact him, she had a letter from her family. In August of 1986 she wrote to tell me:

"Dear Maman,

. . .My younger brother. . .is still prison about 2 months ago. He was arrested due to teaching Catechism without permission from Communist government.

Oh! Maman!

It's rainy and I'm crying. If my family has money for them [the government officials] they will let him free. If not, he will have 1-6 years in jail. . ."

I am Le Thi Hoa and I am from a rural town in the Duy Xuyen area. I was born in 1948. My father died when I was very

51

young and left my mother with six children. There was one boy and five girls. I was the second youngest.

By the time I was eleven years old I was going often to the temple. I don't understand why, but I liked to be there. Maybe Buddha had called me, maybe it was my fate.

I asked my mother for permission to become a nun but she refused. When I asked her why, she said, "Why? Because your father died early and I don't have anybody to help me. Your brother and three of your sisters are already married and I need someone to help me and your little sister." I tried to explain to her. "Mother," I said, "Buddha is calling me. He wants me to be in the temple." Many times I tried to persuade her but she was adamant. "No." At last I could not resist the compulsion inside me. I decided to go without my mother's permission. I would run away from home and go to the temple.

We all used to sleep together in one bed, my mother in the middle, with my sister on one side and me on the other side. One night I waited until my mother and sister were asleep and carefully got up from the bed. I left the house and set out in the darkness for the temple. I would make my way to the road by walking along the beach by the river.

As I stepped out onto the beach the moon came out and the sand shone white in its light. I thought that the Buddha was giving me light but, no, the light was against me. Some men from the village security group were doing their rounds and they saw me. "What are you doing here? Where are you going?"

"I don't know," I replied, hoping that they would go away. But they watched me so I pretended to be going home until I saw them go away. Then I turned back.

But again I was unsuccessful. I met a man who knew me. "Why are you so far from your house? You are too young to be out so late at night. It is too dark."

"But it is not dark," I said, "Look at the beautiful moon."

"No, no." He was very stern. "I have to take you back home because you cannot go out except in the light of the sun." And so he took me back.

I waited until he had gone, determined to try again, but our maid had heard us and came to see what was happening. "Where did you come from?" she demanded. "Go to bed at once."

But I couldn't sleep. I lay there a long time. Then, in the early morning, I got up. I wrote two notes. "Goodbye Mother. I love you very much but I must follow what the Buddha calls me to do."

One note I put under the bed and one I put on a top shelf. I hoped that one day my mother would find them and understand. I went quietly over and looked down at her as she slept. She did not stir. I turned to go.

But the maid caught me again as I was about to open the door. "Where are you going?"

Our house was very small and there was no bathroom inside, so I lied. "I have to go to the bathroom."

I made my way to the highway, about one kilometer. There I waited until a bus came and took me the thirty kilometers or so to the temple at Gwa Nam where I arrived in the early morning.

There was one monk in that temple and two nuns. I told the monk I wanted to be a nun and asked him to shave my head but he said, "You wait."

So I waited there for two days and two nights. Then the monk came to see me and told me that my mother had been trying to find me. My older sister had been inquiring after me in the temple market. My brother was looking all around for me too. He had asked our friends to help. They knew that I was in a temple somewhere because my mother had found my letters.

I was sad that I had made my family worry about me and I cried to be away from my mother. I was still so young. But I had given my heart and my life to the Buddha and I could not do otherwise. I wanted more than anything else to be a nun, so I turned my mind from regrets.

It happened that another monk had arrived on a visit from Saigon on the day that I came to the temple and when his visit was finished it was decided that I would go back with him.

There was also another young man who was to come with us. He carried a bag of woodworking tools and at first I thought he was a carpenter working at the temple but then I found that he also had come there wanting to be a monk. Later, when I got to know him, I discovered that he was a cousin of mine.

So we set out together on the long drive to Saigon. It turned out to be a three day trip because it was the time of the floods and also we got a flat tire on the jungle road and had to spend the night there.

We had no spare but even if we had we could not have done anything about it until morning as it was very dark and there were tigers, big ones, many of them, attracted by the lights of the car. So all we could do was wait, watch the tigers around the car and try to sleep. In the morning my cousin walked into the next village to get a new tire and we continued the trip.

When I arrived in Saigon I asked again to have my head shaved but the supervisor of monks said, "Not yet. After three months, if you are still with us and you have not changed your mind, then we will do it. But for now I want you to go back home and ask permission from your mother. When you come back we will agree to let you stay."

"But I am sure that if I go back home my mother will never let me go again. Please accept me."

So the supervisor of monks became my teacher. He gave me a new name, Thich nu grac Huong. He gave me lessons every day and I worked very hard around the temple, cleaning and scrubbing, everything that needed to be done except cooking. I was still too young to have learned to cook. I missed my mother less now, being so busy.

Because I was so diligent, my teacher came to like me very much. He was an old man — sixty years — but he was very patient with me and loved me like a father. And after three months they shaved my head in the manner of a young nun, leaving a small section long at the front above the forehead. This meant that I must forget every bad feeling, every upset, and forgive anyone who tried to make an enemy out of me.

And so I was a real nun. I had a photograph taken and sent it to my family. As soon as my family knew where I was they sent a telegram, "Your mother is very sick. You must come home."

I talked to my teacher. "You must go," he said.

"But I am afraid that if I go I will never come back. What can I do? My mother might die and I will never see her again."

He took pity on me. "We will send someone with you to take care of you." And so another nun, an older woman, went with me to see my mother.

But when I got home, there was my mother, perfectly well. She had lied to me. "Now you must stay with me," she said. "I need you to help me."

When I became a nun I had promised my life to helping others, so how could I go back to the temple now? I would have to stay for a while at least.

I stayed for seven months and in that time my mother did all she could to persuade me to give up my calling. "Now," she said, "you grow your hair back. I will go to the temple and ask Buddha to release you. Don't eat vegetarian foods. You eat meat with us just as though you are no longer a nun."

She tried hard. If my sister gave me vegetables with no meat, she would say, "No. Don't give her that. I want her to eat meat."

But I said, "No Mother. I'm sorry. I am already committed to the Buddha. I must keep my oath." So I continued to observe the ways of a nun and wore the gray nun's habit all the seven months.

Then I said to my mother again, "Mother, I cannot do as you ask. Let me go. I will come back to visit you during my vacation. If you keep me here and I have to run away another time you will never see me again."

Finally she decided that she had lost and must let me go. But she was very upset and cried a great deal.

After I got back to the temple, the teacher asked me how I had done at home. I told him that I had not done anything wrong, that I had observed all the customs of a nun. "So," he said, "you pass."

And they sent me to a Buddhist university in Saigon where I studied the Buddhist Bible with one hundred and fifty other young Buddhist nuns. As well as religion we studied Vietnamese characters seven days a week — they have characters something like the Chinese. There was no more manual work now but still we worked hard.

I graduated in 1968 when I was in my mid-twenties. I had

been studying for more than ten years, four years in the temple and six at the university. Before I joined the temple I had been to Vietnamese school for three years.

After I graduated from university my supervisor said, "Now I am going to send you to another temple where your supervisor will be an older nun because now that you are grown up you cannot stay here." So I went to another temple.

At university I had studied only religion so now I went back to high school level where I took general subjects for a Vietnamese high school degree. I worked hard physically again in this temple while earning my degree. Then I started work on a second bachelor's degree, this time in general subjects.

I also requested a teaching assignment so they put me to work in an orphanage. There were other Buddhist nuns and monks as well as Catholic sisters working with the children there and life was very happy.

Then, in 1975, the Communists came. The city went into a panic. The word went around, "The Communists are coming from the north." Great crowds of people ran through the city to the south but there they ran into crowds crying, "They are coming from the south," so they rushed back towards the north. There was screaming and crying and commotion. Many people, terrified of the Communists, ran to the temple.

That same day I saw an American helicopter land in the street near the temple to pick up Vietnamese who had worked with the Americans. People were running and pushing and trying to get on. At last it took off, loaded. But its propeller tangled in the overhead electric wires and it fell back into the street and exploded amongst the crowd of people underneath. There was a great fire and many people were killed and burned.

By that time the Communists were already twenty kilometers or so inside Saigon. They came into the city sitting on their tanks, many of them. The people crowded to see and we stared at their strange uniforms and the leaves stuck in their hats as they rode slowly through the streets.

Someone called out, "Hey sir, I have some questions."

They replied, "Well, go ahead. Ask."

"We heard that when you got through to our area you would seize women with long fingernails and pull them out. Is that true, sir?"

They said, "No, it's not true."

Another question: "We heard that pretty South Vietnamese women will be forced to marry handicapped North Vietnamese men. Is that true, sir?"

There were many rumors. They answered very nicely, "No, none of these things are true. They are rumors. There is no truth in any of them. We came here to help you, to save your lives. We came to get the Americans out of here because they are so bad for you. We came to get things straightened out and to make things fair for you."

When the people heard these answers they didn't know whether to believe them or not. It was all so new. They just gaped. I was there in the crowd.

I lived under the Communists almost ten years and I found that the answers they gave to the people that day were not true. They said they had come to save our lives. That was a lie. They came to rob and kill and to treat the people cruelly. They brought to South Vietnam a very, very hard time, the complete opposite of what they had told us as they rode into the city on their tanks.

When they first came, shooting rockets and causing all the panic, I had said to myself, "These Communists are Vietnamese too." I didn't think that once they were in power they would be cruel or kill people. I had no idea then of what was to come.

To us the Communist supervisor of teachers under the new government said, "Religion is propaganda and slows down the Communist political advance." He wanted to get us out of the orphanage so that we would not influence the children. Then he told us, "If you want to teach and come to education meetings, you must not wear your uniforms."

This was easy for the Catholics. When the sisters took off their uniforms they still had hair, but we Buddhists had no hair. When I went back and reported this to my supervisor, she said, "OK then, we will have to give you a wig and civilian clothes for teaching and going to meetings."

I felt so awkward in the wig and so shy in the skirt and blouse. It had been a long time since I had worn anything but the nun's habit.

One day, at a meeting, they called on some people to talk. They said, "What do you think, how do you feel since we have been here with you?"

And everybody was afraid. They said, "Oh, fine — nice."

But one old lady said, "O.K. everybody, be quiet. I have something to say." So she got up. "Oh, thank you for coming here," she said. "Now we don't have any more rockets from the Viet Cong."

The Viet Cong in charge of the meeting was taken aback. "Oh, that's O.K. That's O.K. You sit down." The old lady didn't understand about the so-called liberation of South Vietnam or the Viet Cong. We were very embarrassed for her.

One meeting, some Catholic sisters and I talked to them, saying, "You know, our uniforms are very important to us. We wear them because we love and believe our religion."

I had my own temple by that time and after that meeting, whenever someone did something against the government, if that person was a Buddhist, they would call together all the leaders of the Buddhist religion, nuns and monks, and say to us, "Did you teach them that?"

"No," we would say.

"Yes! You have taught them to do this thing. You have taught the people to go the wrong way. If you continue to teach them like this and we catch them, then we will punish you for their wrongdoing. You will go to jail. You are responsible."

If they found someone of the Catholic religion acting or speaking against the government, they would call all the priests, the sisters and the fathers together. And it would be the same. "You have taught them this."

If they suspected a priest or a nun of working against them they would call a meeting of all the people, and they would ask them, "What do we do about this?"

The people would say, "Put them into jail!" because they were afraid. And they would do what the people said. But if they had real evidence that one of us was working against them, they didn't take it to the people. They would just come to the house at night and take that person away. I didn't know where.

I became more and more uncomfortable and finally so upset with the way we were treated that, after three months, I resigned from the orphanage. I had no freedom and I could see that there would never be any freedom for religion with the Communists.

And the people had come to mistrust each other. Each three houses watched each other. If one family was eating well and saw someone from another family watching they would be afraid that they would be reported to the authorities. No one trusted anyone.

Everybody was trying to leave the country, not because there was not enough rice or food or other goods but because there was no freedom. The Communists gave them no freedom at all. Talking, meeting, everything was under their control. I knew I could not stay.

I tried many times to escape. I tried again and again to get on a boat out of there but every time I tried they caught me and I could not go. The last time I tried was in May of 1985. My brother-in-law had heard that an escape was being planned. He came to me, "Do you want to try again? I think I can help you." And this time I was successful.

The first day at sea the wind was high and the ocean was rough but by the next day the wind had dropped and for three days the weather was calm and the sea flat.

But on the fifth day the wind whipped up again and the seas began to roll. The boat's engine broke down and we ran out of water. There were seventy-seven of us on a boat nine meters long and about two and a half wide.

We met a pirate boat. They took all the men and tied them up. They were planning to rob us so we started to negotiate. "We don't have much wealth but what we have we will give you if you will please give us some water and some food and let us continue on our way."

They held us right through the night and then they agreed. So we gave the pirates our gold, our clothes and our watches. In return they gave us water, fish and rice and let us go.

Shortly after that we noticed two big fish in the water, one on each side of the boat. They had fins on their backs and went up and down through the water beside us. And there was a single gull. It flew just ahead of the boat and showed the way while the big fish went beside us all our journey.

Even though the pirates had given us water, it was not enough for all the people on the boat so whenever it rained I put on all my clothes and stood out in the rain until they were soaked. Then I went down into the boat and squeezed them out, catching the water in a pan. I went back and forth doing this all the time it rained. There was a priest on the boat and I worked with him. I would collect the water and give it to him to give to those who needed it most. I tried to pray. When the people were suffering from thirst I prayed for rain.

We met pirates again. They were from Thailand. They took from us everything that we had left and then they turned on the women. But the people called to each other and said, "Thailand is Buddhist. Maybe they will listen to grac Huong. Maybe she can save us from them." "Please do something," they begged me.

So I took out my yellow uniform and put it on. And when the pirates saw me they said, "Oh, in this boat there are Buddhist monks." They thought at first that I was a monk.

Then they talked amongst themselves, "We must not rob these people. Everything we have taken we must give back." So they gave back all they had taken and let the women go.

Then they asked, "Does anyone speak English?" A number of people did so they spoke to me through an interpreter. "Have you had anything to eat lately?"

"No," I said.

"O.K. We will give you this big pot of rice and some fish for your boat." And they showed us the way to go.

When we came to the coast of Malaysia the two big fish and the gull disappeared. Now, when I rise early in the morning and go out to feed the birds in the courtyard of the Vietnamese temple here, I think of the gull who went before us to freedom and I give thanks. [PRPC, April 17, 1986.]

Americans Missing in Action

Mr. Champamay

Mr. Champamay is a big man, tall and powerfully built, with a broad, strong face that is belied by his gentle, unassuming manner. He is very serious.

His father-in-law brought him to meet me when he first arrived in the camp. During that meeting he spoke no English at all and gave no indication of understanding what I was saying. His father-in-law acted as interpreter. Two weeks later I came back to him with a draft full of questions. We sat alone together for an hour or so and, with the help of some sign language and improvised sketches, managed to resolve almost everything.

When he was leaving, I said, "Tell me, how did you manage to improve your English so much in such a short time?" He looked at me with solemn eyes. "I study very hard, ma'am."

His real name has been withheld at his request.

I am a Lao. However, what I have to say mainly concerns Vietnam and information I have gathered on Americans said to be still in concentration camps there.

I was in the military, a first lieutenant working in the headquarters Security Command in Vientiane. After the Communists took over in 1975 I was sent to Camp 03 at Long Kai in Xieng

Khouang Province with my wife and children. (There was also a Camp 03 in the Viengxay area.)

The Long Kai camp was seven kilometers east of Ban Ban and then one kilometer south of the road. I was there for six years and had two more children.

Then, in December of 1981, I escaped to Thailand and became a refugee at the Na Pho camp in Nakorn Pnom Province.

One week after I arrived, the Thai seconded me to work with them gathering information about the situation in Laos. It was important to their national security to have this information and I was happy to help. And so I came to be in a position to learn many things.

During this time I listened to Voice of America and other international radio and television broadcasts and heard about the disappearance of American military personnel during the Indochinese war. I became very interested. These men had fought to keep Indochina free of the Communist regime and I resolved to help them.

And so I made it my business to gather all the information I could on American prisoners still living in Indochina. I kept this information separate from what I was collecting for the Thai. I saved it for the Americans. The Thai didn't want any American officials to come to see me. They wanted to keep me to work only for Thailand.

Until now, the only American I have given this information to is a man in the United States consulate in Udorn City, Thailand. I think his name was Jim Brono but I am not sure. I talked with him on a number of occasions but I only called him Jim.

He told me not to give anyone else this information as it could put my life in danger. He said, "Don't give anybody this information. You must keep it secretly."

I told him I had already given it to my father-in-law, who had translated it for me. He said, "O.K. Only your father-in-law but no one else."

He also said it was not safe for me to carry copies of the statements out of Thailand with me. I must leave them all with him. So I gave him the originals of my written statements. I do not know what action he took on the information.

Until today, I have only discussed this with my father-in-law. I had sent copies of the statements with him when he left Thailand to come here to the Philippine Refugee Processing Center.

*   *   *

There were two people who were especially helpful in providing me with information on what might have happened to Americans missing in action. One was a Mr. P. The other was a Mr. V.

Mr. P. is from Van Vieng, my home town, in the Vientiane Province of Laos. He was studying foreign trade in France when the Communists took over Laos. Then, in 1978, he returned and went to work for the government as a trade expert. He was assigned to the Lao consulate in Da Nang, Vietnam, in 1982 and worked there as a trade advisor until November of 1984 when he was arrested and thrown into jail as a secret enemy agent.

He escaped and fled to Thailand in December of 1984 and it was there that I met him in the Na Pho refugee camp in Nakorn Pnom. Mr. P. told me:

> During the month of February 1984, a meeting was held in the consulate of the People's Democratic Republic of Laos in Da Nang. It started at 19:00 hours. There were thirteen other men present: six Lao representatives, five Vietnamese representatives and two Vietnamese journalists. I was there as the Laotian trade counsellor.

> After the meeting ended the participants had a small party. During this party I had the opportunity to talk with the mayor of Tam Ky City in Kuang Nam Province, Vietnam. We talked about Tam Ky factory development and operation.

> He said that many factories in Tam Ky had had a lot of problems because they were old and the equipment had originally come from Western countries, mainly America. He said that they needed technicians and specialists from Western countries to operate and maintain the engines properly and to develop factory procedures.

> The factory situation had been becoming critical due to this lack

of operating and maintenance expertise. They urgently needed Western specialists. So the city committee decided to get some American prisoners with a specialty in operating those types of factories and put them to work. They did this and, with the Americans there, the factories ran well and continuously.

As soon as the mayor of Tam Ky started talking about American prisoners, I became very interested. I had been collecting information on this subject for some time and had learned a great deal since I had been in Vietnam. I was very anxious to learn more. How many were there? What location were they from? I wanted to ask many questions but I dared not press him as I was afraid that the others would criticize me as an enemy. So I had to cut off the discussion with my questions unanswered. The party ended at 21:00 hours.

Mr. P. told me that these prisoners were still working in the factories at the time we were speaking together — February of 1984. He gave me a great deal of other information he had gathered about Americans in Vietnam, and also gave me his opinions on the relation between the Vietnamese Communists and the current Lao government:

The Kaisone government is simply following Vietnamese policies. Kaisone himself is under the command of Hanoi and must accept its orders. He must get authorization from the Vietnamese "experts" in Laos before undertaking any actions. All leadership positions in Laos, whether in the administration, in associations, organizations or out in the provinces are under the control of these "experts."

Laos will soon be integrated as Vietnamese territory. The Kaisone government is simply a political instrument to make Laos a colony of Vietnam. However, the Lao people are suffering heavily and I think their hatred for the regime can be used to break it.

Mr. V., the other man who gave me information, was originally a native Vietnamese.

He was born in Khe Kien village near Tuong Yuong City in the Ngeting Province of North Vietnam. He did military service in Ngeting Province, attaining the rank of master sergeant. After the Communists took over the North, he escaped from Vietnam and went to Laos. His father later lost his job in city administration as a result of his son's escape.

Mr. V. lived in Laos from 1958, working first as a salesman in Pak Kading. Then, after marrying a Laotian girl, he went into business with his father-in-law in Pak Sane City. In 1961, the South Vietnamese military attache to Laos asked him to come and work with the embassy in Vientiane doing military reconnaissance and he agreed. After the South Vietnamese Embassy in Laos became defunct in 1975, Mr. V. took a Lao name and lived as a Lao with his family in Ban Sikeut.

Then, in February of 1979, he had the opportunity to go to visit his parents in North Vietnam. It was during this visit that he heard about American prisoners of war still in North Vietnam. This is what Mr. V. told me:

> In February of 1979 I put in a request and was authorized to travel by truck to visit my parents, brothers and sisters in Khe Kien village in the Liu Kien area of Tuong Yuong City in Ngeting Province, North Vietnam. My travel orders were given to me by Mr. K., the Lao Assistant Minister of Commerce. He gave me special consideration because his wife was a Vietnamese from the same city as I was and my father had taken care of her family. When I arrived in the homeland, I found my father still living at the age of eighty years. Both he and my nephew told me that there were many hundreds of American prisoners in Ngeting Province at that time — about three hundred in the Xadoui prison camp and about five hundred at the Ben Heui camp, most of them Air Force and Army.

> My father had been told this by a police major who worked in the camps. My nephew was in the Marine Corps and he had seen the American prisoners with his own eyes and could provide details.

Mr. V. had been very interested to hear this. Part of his job in military reconnaissance was to collect such information.

Then, talking to old friends who had been in seminar camps in Vietnam — they have seminar camps in Vietnam also, like in Laos, for political prisoners and South Vietnamese military officers — he also learned that they had been told in lectures by the Communists, "Laos is ours," meaning, "Laos is our territory."

In November of 1981, Mr. V. was arrested by the Lao Communist government and sent to the That Dam jail in Vientiane, charged with sending food and rice, arms and ammunition to the enemy—the Lao Liberation Front. Then, on November 18, 1981, seven police from the Ministry of Interior found five kilograms of explosives in a Mr. T.'s house, a friend of his. Both men were charged with planning to blow up the Vientiane airport fuel stock.

On the 12th of April, Mr. V. was sent to repair the police office in Vientiane. During the noon lunchbreak he fled, swimming across the Mekong River to Sri Xieng May in Thailand. From there, he was sent to the Na Pho refugee camp where he continued to work for the Lao Liberation Front. He also worked with the Thai police collecting information on Laos until October 1984, when his health became too frail for such work.

It was in the Na Pho camp in Thailand that I met Mr. V., during the time we were both working with the Thai collecting information on Laos.

When I was sent to the Thai refugee transit center in Panat Nikhom, I asked as many people as I dared about these P.O.W. camps. There were many Vietnamese there and I tried to seek out people from Ngeting Province who would know more. I had to be very careful not to talk openly to too many people because I was afraid that the Vietnamese authorities would hear that I was asking questions and send someone to kill me.

However, after all my investigations, I have come to the conclusion that, with one exception,* there are no American prisoners of war still in Laos. Those captured in Laos were taken to Vietnam and are now in Xadoui or Ben Heui.

With the information I have gathered I have been able to put

---

*There is one American prisoner in Laos. Mr. Area [sic] is his name, although Thai documents also refer to him by the code name Dakong. He is an American Greek who used to be a pilot in Vietnam. He was one of a private group operating out of Thailand looking for American POWs in Laos. A Mr. Jimbocris [sic] was their leader, although I only saw it written in Thai letters so I am not sure how to translate it into English. I learned of Mr. Area's arrest in Thailand in July of 1985 from my agent for the Vientiane capitol. He reported that, in 1982, Mr. Area had been arrested and put into political jail in Ban Phonethan village in the Saphanethong District of Muang Kay Setha, in the south-east part of Vientiane City. He is still there, and, as far as I know, Mr. Jimbocris is still in Thailand. —Speaker.

together thumbnail sketches of these two camps. There is good reason to suppose they are still housing American prisoners of war.

In describing them I use the present tense [March 1986] in spite of the fact that I cannot be absolutely certain that they are still in use. Mr. V.'s theory is that there is now one camp only, the Ben Heui camp, and that the prisoners from Xadoui, the mainland camp, have at some time been transferred there.

This sounds plausible. Ngeting Province is very hard to get into. It was the home of Ho Chi Minh and is a very special area. It can only be entered on official business.

As for Ben Heui, it is six kilometers or so offshore and the Vietnamese government doesn't allow anyone to go there. American prisoners of war would be hidden very effectively on this island where it is almost impossible to go without being noticed and where enough food can be raised for large numbers of prisoners to be self-sufficient.

Xadoui P.O.W. Camp

The Xadoui camp is located northeast of Vinh City on the coast of Ngeting Province in Central Vietnam. Before 1975, this was the central camp for high ranking Vietnamese political prisoners. After 1975 it was used for Americans arrested in Laos and Vietnam during the Indochina war. There were reportedly about three hundred American prisoners in 1979.

The camp is in an open area. It is about two kilometers square and surrounded by a barbed wire fence. The buildings cover about five hundred square meters and are surrounded by a concrete wall six meters high and forty centimeters thick. There are electric wires running along the top of the wall. These function twenty-four hours a day. There is only one gate, located on the west side.

There are about one hundred concrete buildings with flat roofs about twenty centimeters thick. Each building has fifteen rooms. The even-numbered rooms have ankle irons that automatically open when the doors are opened and lock when the doors are closed. These are to lock the prisoners in at night.

Camp Schedule (approximate only)

700 hours — Vietnamese National Anthem
700 to 1100 hours — Work
1300 to 1600 hours — Work
1700 to 1800 hours — Political lecture
1800 to 2200 hours — Political and work discussion,
    rest
2200 hours — Sleep

Rations

To a value of .25 dong per diem for a Vietnamese prisoner.
To a value of 2.5 dong per diem for a U.S. prisoner. Weekly meals:
1 day — rice with fish sauce
1 day — rice with salt
1 day — rice with pork
1 day — rice with fish
3 days — rice with vegetable (leaves from the morning
    glory plant)

The rice allotment is 500 grams per person per day.
Americans also receive 500 grams of sugar per person per month
and cigarettes. The cooks are prisoners who have worked well.

There is a hospital, or rather a dispensary, in the camp.
Patients with aches or pains are taken care of by their group leader,
a fellow prisoner. Serious pain and surgery is attended to during
work hours. If a patient becomes seriously ill during the night he
must wait until the next day for the doctor to arrive. Principal
disorders of prisoners are skin diseases, paralysis and tuberculosis.

There are loudspeakers throughout the camp. Contact with
outsiders is prohibited for Americans. Vietnamese who have made
good work progress are allowed some contact with the outside.

Ben Heui P.O.W. Camp

The Ben Heui concentration camp is on an island in the Gulf
of Tonkin about five kilometers off the northeast coast of Ngeting

Province. Before 1975 this island was used as a prison camp for Vietnamese officers, NCOs and troops that were causing big problems of one sort or another, especially discipline problems. It was a long-term camp. Anyone sent there knew that he was not going to leave in a hurry. After 1975 the camp was also used for American prisoners. There were reportedly about five hundred Americans there in 1979.

The island is about six kilometers in diameter. The camp itself covers only about one square kilometer. There are one hundred and fifty buildings for housing prisoners. They are roofed with fibro-cement tiles and house twenty men each. There is also an administration building, a lecture building, an exercise yard and an electrical installation.

Camp Schedule (approximate only)

> 400 hours — Wake up and exercise
> 500 hours — Daily report (to identify illness or inability to work)
> 700 hours — Vietnamese national anthem
> 700 hours to 1100 hours — Work
> 1300 to 1600 hours — Work
> Political study
> 2200 hours — Sleep

The work is growing food and raising animals. Goals and amounts to be produced are given by the camp commander.

Rations

There are two meals a day. The food budget allows .25 dong per day for Vietnamese prisoners and 2.5 dong for American prisoners. There are 500 grams of rice per person per day. Clothes are distributed twice a year.

There is a hospital with doctors, dentists and nurses. A doctor is on duty 24 hours a day. There is a speaker system throughout the camp. No visitors and no mail are allowed, with some strictly controlled exceptions for Vietnamese prisoners. There is Vietnamese television on Saturdays and on Sunday night visiting Vietnamese shows.

There are about one thousand guards to ensure camp security, ten trucks, six eighty-two millimeter mortars, six thirty-seven millimeter anti-aircraft guns, spotlights and radio communications.

The American prisoners work outside the camp raising crops and animals for maybe one, maybe two or three, days at a time. Then they return to camp. [PRPC, March 19, 1986.]

Even the Lampposts

Nguyen Thi Yen Nga

*Nga stands maybe five feet four but her nervous energy somehow makes
her seem taller. She has a wide smile and one tooth missing on the right. Her
hair falls in rich, dark waves to her shoulders and she wears large, almost
round, gold-rimmed brown-tinted glasses. She dresses in a variation on the
traditional Vietnamese pajamas — western slacks and a loose blouse. She
speaks English well.*

*Amongst the heat and dirt of the camp, she always managed to look clean
and pressed and so did her four children, the pride of her life. Tumbling over
each other in their tiny hut — six people living in a space maybe twenty feet
by eight — the love between them was almost tangible.*

*Twice she stayed with me at my home in Manila. The first time she
brought her eleven-year-old daughter, Minh. We had just adopted three small
Koreans and they fell in love with her. With Minh having lived most of her
life in refugee camps and my new children having come from poverty and an
orphanage we had a four-day riot of undisciplined wallowing in Western
luxury.*

*American bureaucrats being what they are, when it was discovered that
one of their refugee charges had had a weekend of unbridled fun, the rules were
tightened and it was forbidden for them to leave the camp for such frivolity
again. Soon after, Nga showed up at my gate. I said, "How on earth did
you get out of the camp?"*

"They can only keep us there because we want it," she replied.

Nguyen Thi Yen Nga.

"We are all experts at escaping. That's how we got there in the first place."

Before 1975 I was a stewardess with Vietnam Airlines. I lived at 479/8 Vo di Nguy Street in the Phu Nhuan district which was then an outer suburb of Saigon (it has since been absorbed into the

Nguyen Thi Yen Nga and her family.

metropolitan area). Our house was near the Tan Son Nhut international airport which was where I worked. The house was very large and beautiful and I had my own car to drive to work. I had three servants and lived there very peacefully with my husband, three small children and parents-in-law who helped us by taking care of the children while we both worked.

I had earlier given up the opportunity to go overseas to study in favor of my younger brother. My elder sister had gone to France in 1964 and it was my turn next but the family could only afford for one of us to go at that time and my brother was in danger of being drafted into the army.

The long war was very far away and, apart from denying me the chance to study overseas, it had very little affect on my life despite the fact that my husband was a captain in the South Viet-namese Army and in charge of wounded soldiers at the Democratic General Hospital — a military hospital close to the airport.

Gradually I came to see the results of the war.

As the Communists advanced from the North, they so frightened the people that they fled before them, leaving their home provinces and coming to Saigon. They rushed to the airports in Da Nang and Nha Trang, carrying a lot of money with them. Only the ones who had gold with them could get onto the airplanes and even so, they had to muscle their way on. They were frantic to get out of their own provinces and escape to Saigon. Those who had their money invested in businesses or in savings accounts could not liquidate it in time to escape.

When they got to Saigon it was very miserable for them. They had had to leave behind their homes in the provinces. Many of them had used most of their money for the trip. Those who could went to their relatives for help but those who had no relatives in Saigon had to live on the pavements — many, many of them. They were all over the city.

The scenes at the airport were terrifying — so many people and so frightened. I was advanced in pregnancy with my last child and what I saw made me frightened also.

Sometimes they came alone. I saw a father with a very little baby of only six or seven days come down the stairs from the plane. I received him when he reached the bottom. "Where is the baby's mother?" I asked.

"I am alone. I lost her in Da Nang. She was very weak after giving birth and was pushed aside in the crowd jostling to get onto the airplane. I was clinging to the baby and so no one pushed me. I got the baby safely onto the plane — but now he has no mother."

He was very upset but he knew that whoever could save the baby had to do it. He knew that it was going to be a very bad time under the Communists. The baby cried and cried very much so I had to help him. I took him to the cafeteria and got a cup of milk and fed it to the baby.

I had been offered a flight to go abroad and my husband wanted me to get out of Vietnam with the children while I could. He could not come with me because he was in the army and had to stay in Saigon in order to fight the Viet Cong and protect our country. But I was frightened by the scenes of panic I had seen at the airport. I was afraid of the crush of people and I kept thinking of the father with the baby and no mother. I dared not leave my husband and so I stayed with him until the last minute.

But at the last minute no one understood anything because they knew the Viet Cong army was coming and we were leaderless. The army was in disarray. The president, Mr. Thieu, had already escaped and so had some of the generals and other top military. (Thieu's sister was married to the head of Air Vietnam and, at the end of March 1975, the whole family used Air Vietnam aircraft to escape from the country.) We had no one with the power left to command us. Everyone did what he thought best, without any orders. It was a very miserable time. We were in disorder. We went this way. We went the other way. We didn't know what to do or what would happen to us.

In the end my husband forced me to agree to leave him in Vietnam and go with my children while I could. "You must go," he said. "It is easy for me to get away on a plane at the last minute if I am alone. If you stay with me we will all be trapped."

So I applied to have my name put on the flight manifest. It was easy for me to do so because of my job. My number — 248 — came up for the night flight leaving on April 28.

On that day I went to visit my parents before I left Vietnam. But there was a big rainstorm and because I was pregnant I dared not go out in the rain in case I should catch cold or get sick. I did not get back to my house until five o'clock. However, I had a pass to go into the airport whenever I wanted and the curfew was not until seven o'clock so at six thirty I left my house with my husband and the parents of some friends who were now in Canada. I was to travel with them.

But that day a bomb had destroyed the house of President Thieu and the airport had been bombarded with rockets and they had closed it up. Even though I had a pass, they wouldn't allow me to go in, and so I missed my flight.

The next morning, on April 29, my husband waited at the gate until noon and, when he saw that they were letting people with passes go in, he came back home and asked me to show my pass and go in and ask for information about a flight. When I got inside the airport I was told to queue up because there were helicopters coming to pick us up and take us to a boat outside.

But I had gone there with my husband only, without any children. I could not leave them alone because it was for their future that I had to get out, not for myself alone. So I had to go back home to get them, pushing through the many people crowding outside the airport. They had rushed there when they heard about the helicopter flights but were not allowed in.

At home I had to look for my children and by the time I got back to the airport it was too late. They wouldn't let me in. They only let the official U.S. Military Airlift Command–Vietnam buses enter after that. The workers from USAID, from the U.S. Embassy and from U.S. companies used them to rush to the airport.

So I was obliged to come home, very upset. But I was consoled by a friend of my husband. "Don't worry about it," he said. "Our government has made a pact with the Viet Cong that they will take South Vietnam only down to the line north of Saigon at Han Dan and Phan Thiet so you need not worry. It's OK to stay here." He was a captain and had taken pilot training in the United States and I let myself be persuaded by him because my only other option was to escape by boat.

There were many people in Saigon who had fled from the Communists before. When they had taken over the North these people had fled to the South. They had had personal experience with the Communists and in fact had told us many frightening stories about the Viet Cong. So it was that the northerners resolved early to get out of Vietnam before the South was also swallowed up. They were the first to flee and many of them were successful.

Many, many people went to the Saigon River to escape by boat. They were there very early in the morning. But the boats didn't leave because they were overcrowded. The owners waited, knowing that eventually some of the people would grow impatient and go home.

And sure enough, around six o'clock, many people became hungry and went home to eat. These were the southerners. Having had no direct experience with the Viet Cong, their resolve left them when they got hungry and while they were gone the boats left with the northerners who were too afraid of the Communists to let hunger stand in their way.

After I had failed to get onto a helicopter my husband had been wanting me to escape by boat so I had gone down to the river to see what it was like but I was frightened by the tumult of people. Being a stewardess, I knew that when I was six months into pregnancy I could not go by plane without the permission of a doctor. Going by boat would be a much longer and harder journey and my three children were so very young—the oldest was only three. What if something happened to me and I died, who would take care of them? I decided it was better for me to stay.

Saigon fell on the thirtieth of April. The Viet Cong came in without any fighting. The South Vietnamese Army just surrendered to them because the troops had no generals to command them.*

The troops said amongst themselves that President Thieu had

---

*The country had been divided into four quarters. The first was in the north—from Quang Tri to Hue. The second was in the middle—from Bamethuot to Kontum Plei Ku. The third was from Saigon to Bien Hoa. And the fourth was in the south—from Vinh Long to Can Tho.

There was a general in charge of each quarter but there were conflicts between them and President Thieu and he had had them imprisoned in the Democratic General Hospital. They said they were sick and needed rest but in reality Thieu didn't want them to control the army. After Saigon fell one of these generals being held at the Democratic General Hospital committed suicide because Thieu had surrendered to the Communists. We had no news of what happened to the other three.

Thieu's replacement was General Duong van Minh. He was very weak on the Communists. — Speaker.

left them and they thought it was better for them to have a Communist government. (It may be that some of them were Communists too — the ones with relatives in the North.) But when the Communists were there and they came to know them better it was very terrible for them and by then it was too late. There was nothing they could do.

On that day the people were running this way and that way. We didn't know what to do. We didn't know how to react to the Communists. We didn't know what would happen to us and we were very confused. We were afraid that they would kill us because we were workers under the former government. We had often heard that the Communists would not let us live any longer unless we accepted whatever they ordered us to do. We were afraid. I stayed in my house on this day. I dared not to go out because I was pregnant and so frightened.

My husband had to report to his office at the hospital and was given the duty of keeping the Communists in charge of the hospital informed on the wounded and other hospital matters.

Then all the army materials — clothes, blankets and everything issued to the soldiers by the former government — were thrown onto the road and the Communists set fire to them.

They burned all the things from the USAID — except what was stolen by the poor people who ran to the USAID offices and took the lamps, the fans, everything they could possibly carry. My mother saw this happening from her house, which was very close by.

Everywhere across the city military supplies from the U.S. government were burned. Anything that had been provided to help the military — clothes, blankets, shoes, ID cards. People were afraid for the Communists to see that they had worked with the United States.

These Communists didn't know how to control the whole city yet because they were so poor. They didn't know anything about administration; they only knew how to struggle. The first thing they did was to publicize a reeducation program.

When my husband had been called back to duty at the hospital he had been given a certificate to show that he had worked with the Communists after the revolution. This was supposed to help him at the reeducation camp but he was deathly afraid.

First the noncommissioned officers were ordered to come to reeducation camp, bringing with them food for three to five days.

Then, on I think the fifteenth of June, they ordered all high-ranking officers to report, bringing with them thirty days' worth of food.

On June 23 and 24 it was the turn of the captains. They had to prepare for themselves food for ten days. My husband was so afraid that he joined on the first day.

The twenty-fifth and twenty-sixth were for the lieutenants and the twenty-seventh and twenty-eighth for the second lieutenants.

We all thought that the noncommissioned officers would only be away for three to five days, the junior officers for ten days, the high-ranking officers for thirty days and so on. We based this on the number of days' food supply they were told to bring. If the Communists had let it be known that they would be there such a long time, no one would have shown up.

My husband left me on the twenty-third and I gave birth to Minh, my last daughter, the next morning, June 24. I gave birth in the Tu Do obstetric hospital. My sister had been a midwifery teacher there but she had left on Flight 136 on April 24 so I was helped by her friend. The birth was normal and I stayed in the hospital for seven days.

Then I went to my parents' house, leaving the three other children at home with my parents-in-law. My mother took care of me and the baby for a month, hoping that my husband would come back and take me home. I cried so much because after ten days I didn't see my husband come back and I was very disappointed.

And I quarrelled with my younger sister. She said that, because I had been pregnant, I had not heard the rumors from the outside. She had gone around the streets and heard that the way it really was under the Communists was that people never came back from the reeducation camps, or at least not for years.

I said to her, "You do wrong to speak ill of the Communists," because I still hoped that my husband would come back. And to myself I said, "Because we have never done any harm to anyone, he must come back very soon." But I was deceiving myself.

I waited for a month in my parents' house and then I went home to wait for him there. I had to wait for him a year and a half before he came. I cried too much during those days.

Now, the local Communist government held a meeting every night to teach the citizens in Saigon and the head of each household was required to attend. It was at this meeting that my father-in-law was told we must have Communist soldiers living with us.

In this area, most of us were Catholic, but my parents-in-law were Buddhist. There was a Catholic church behind our house and they pretended that they wanted to observe the Catholics but they just wanted to billet with us in order to control our activities. Also, they wanted to have a look around because the street we lived on was all big houses. Ours was very luxurious with a big, lush garden.

I begged my father-in-law, "Please don't let them come into our house. They will keep it and chase us out. Don't let them do it."

He said, "You don't know anything. It's better for us to let them come and it's better for your husband. It means he will be able to come back as soon as possible."

We had no choice but to follow their orders.

More than thirty soldiers arrived all at once, bringing with them big bags of rice and peas and other food provided by the government. I was afraid of them at first and kept in my room but gradually I got used to them and I had pity for them. And for them it was very beautiful. They took care of my children. In the evening, when they had no work, one would take the baby on his knee, the others would take care of the other three. They lived with me for more than six months. I stayed on the first floor and they lived on the ground floor. It was not the same with all of the Communists but the ones who came to live in my house were not bad people.

At first they asked me for information about my neighborhood but I didn't know anything. They asked me, "Why don't you know anything about your neighbors?"

"I have my own job," I answered them. "I have to leave the house in the very early morning — at four thirty when everyone else is still sleeping. I come back before one o'clock and eat and have a sleep. The next day I leave the house again at one o'clock for another shift which doesn't finish until nine o'clock. When I come back home I have my own privacy. I don't know anything about the people around me."

They said, "In the North we know all about each other. We even know how many cans of rice our neighbors have in their houses."

"It is different here in the South. Here we respect the privacy of other people. We only know our own houses and maintain our own privacy. We don't look after other people's business. That is the way it is here." Eventually they believed me because they watched the way I lived and so they knew that what I told them was true.

Early in May an old friend of my father-in-law had come to our house. This friend had left South Vietnam after the declaration of independence from the North in 1945 and joined the Communist Army. Then, after the fall of Saigon, he came back to the South representing the Communist government. He was very powerful.

As soon as he arrived he had come at once to seek out his old friend. He reassured us, "Do not be upset by the Communists. Their only purpose in fighting has been to bring peace to the whole country. They want to bring only good to the citizens of Vietnam. During war it is impossible to bring happiness to the people, but now that the South has been freed and there is peace the new government can bring a better life. So do not worry. Little by little they will bring a peaceful life to everybody."

He really believed that at first but at last, before we left him, he admitted that he was very disappointed. He told us that, in the North, they had always been told that in the South the people were very miserable. They were under the control of the Americans and forced to do very hard work. The women had to sell their bodies in order to earn a living and the children had to scavenge for food.

He and many like him were convinced that they were the ones

who could free their countrymen and solve their problems. But when they arrived in Saigon they were astonished by the buildings. And they didn't know how to use any modern appliances — not even a toilet. They put fish in it and when they pushed the lever and the toilet flushed they said, "Someone has stolen my fish!"

I was told that, when they first used the shower, they didn't understand the hot and cold water. They got in and turned on the hot tap and were burned. Then they said, "Even though the Americans have gone, they will still destroy us." Even the pads that we used during our menses they would use to put on their heads as sweat bands.

We wanted to laugh but we dared not. They didn't know anything and, because we were so afraid of them, we did not dare to say anything. But there were a lot of jokes going around at their expense.

For instance, they said, "In the North, we have everything."

And we said, "Do you have Hondas? Do you have Suzukis? Do you have Kawasakis?"

"Oh, yes! In Hanoi we have a lot of motorcycles. Hondas, Suzukis, Kawasakis — everything."

"Do you have TV in Hanoi?"

"Oh, Yes! Yes, of course! Many, many TVs. They are on all the roads!"

They were very anxious to show us that they had had a better life than us, these soldiers from the North. I talked to many of them who stayed in my house.

I still had my job at Vietnam Airlines until July 1976 because I was sponsored by the friend of my father-in-law. I called him uncle and we were very fortunate to have him to help us the way he did. He was not a relation, only a friend, but he was a very good one.

It was because of him that we could trust the Communists. He was willing to help us with anything. He brought us the food that the government gave to him. He would help any way he could.

At that time I had only forty-five dong for one month. This was the salary from the North. The money was changed during 1975. (Since then there have been four more changes in the money — in 1979, 1980, 1981 and September of 1985.) They took all the old dong and issued new dong in their place. Before that I had earned more than 40,000 a month. After Independence Day we all had to have the same salaries, North and South.

The prices dropped at first too, to make us the same as the North. We could buy two and a half kilos of rice for one dong so people started to trust the Communists because our cost of living had dropped and for a while we thought that after all it was going to be better for us to live under the Communists. We were cheated.

In spite of the comfort I got from my uncle I was always frightened because my husband had not come back. I had to live day by day and take care of my children even though there was always a fear behind, inside my heart, but I dared not show it. I had to get used to it as a way of life. We were so frightened because we had worked for the former government. We dared not mention it even in our own privacy and we were careful to obey every order we were given.

The soldiers disturbed us very much intruding on the family but we dared not say anything. And sometimes they frightened us. They wanted to control us so they could do anything they liked. One day one of them went to the airport and went through the trash cans where all the things from the former government had been thrown away. He got some string that had been used on rifles, for hanging them from the soldiers' belts, and brought it home and used it to hang mosquito nets.

Another one of them saw this rifle string and came to me, saying, "Do you have any weapons in your house?"

"No. I have no weapons in my house."

But they didn't believe me. They searched through the house, looking in all the drawers and closets. They were convinced that I had a weapon hidden there somewhere. Then they asked, "Does your husband have a weapon?"

"No, no. He doesn't have any weapon. The only weapons in the house are children's toys." And I showed them my children's toys — things I had had the air hostesses buy for me in Hong Kong and Japan.

They didn't believe me and searched through the drawers again in the night when I was asleep in my room. They didn't say anything else but they watched me and I became very nervous. At last the one that took the string from the garbage told them where it had come from and then they believed me.

Once we had a chicken to eat and we had to dig a hole outside and bury the feathers to hide them from the soldiers. In the North they almost never got chicken to eat. They only ate rice. When they were in battle in the forest they didn't even have rice. They had to eat the leaves from the trees. There was nothing else.

But they were driven by a purpose. They had to do all this in order to save their countrymen in the South from the Americans. They believed all the Communist propaganda. They thought that the South was controlled by the Americans who treated the people harshly. They believed all the stories about women being forced to sell their bodies in order to get money and children being forced to go from one trashcan to the next to find something to eat. They didn't know any better at the time.

They had been told, "The Thieu government is not a good one and the Americans only give because they want to get something. They only support the South because there are a lot of natural resources under the ground, kerosene for instance. They want to control the country so they can have these resources for themselves." But once these northerners had occupied South Vietnam for a while they started to change their minds, to realize that what they had been told had been lies.

They never talked to me about this. They just said that they were having some initial difficulties administering Saigon but in the long run everything would be in order. They never could get everything in order.

As soon as they came in 1975 they took all the rich people and put them in jail. Then they took all their properties and forced them to sign a paper agreeing to go out into the countryside. They would only let them out of jail if they signed this paper. And the Communists from the North came and lived in their houses. Saigon is full of North Vietnamese government officials. There are many Soviets in Saigon too — mainly technical people. They have taken over the Majestic Hotel on the Saigon River for them to live in. We were not allowed to have anything to do with them. When we saw them in the streets we looked down. We did not want to have anything to do with them for fear of being sent to prison.

My parents-in-law were rich. Before the revolution my father-in-law had operated a horse-racing business and had made very good money. My mother-in-law had also been a business-woman. She had sold fabrics in the market and made a lot of money. In fact, they had made so much money that they retired from business with enough to live on for the rest of their lives.

It was only because of my "uncle" that we did not have to go to jail. Instead we had to have the soldiers living in our house and searching through our things. They knew that in the house there was only me with my parents-in-law, who were very old, and my children, who were very young. They had nothing to worry about from us. We were no threat to them.

In 1976 I was given permission to go visit my husband in the reeducation camp. It was very far — more than a hundred kilometers from Saigon. The trip there took a whole day so I had to ask permission for time off from work. I asked my supervisor for three days and he granted it. But when I came back they chased me out because I was the wife of a captain and they didn't trust me. They chased out all the wives of the officers of the former government. They had not known about me before that but I gave myself away by telling them why I wanted leave.

My uncle could not help me then. It was the policy of the Communist government, he explained to me. In the old days before 1975 Air Vietnam had had a lot of flights to and from Saigon. After the revolution we had one flight from Saigon to Hanoi, maybe twice a week. The only other flight was Air France to Bangkok to Paris taking the French citizens back to France once a month. How could we go on with the work in the airport with so little work? The staff must be cut down.

After I lost my job I did nothing but cry. I always cried because I had never encountered a difficult situation like that before. I reacted in a passive way — always crying. My parents consoled me, "In some ways it is better to have a hard circumstance like that in order to learn from life. And you have nothing to worry about because we can feed your children. Come back and live with us. We will take care of you." But as a married woman I dared not go back to my parents' house and disturb them. I had to earn my own living.

Every day I would make rice soup and go down to the railway station and sell it to the passers-by. Later, I joined my aunt-in-law at the market. She made girdle cake* and I was the one to take the dishes to every shop and window, asking them to buy from me. They had pity on me and were ready to take one of everything in order to help me because they thought I was one of those who had to bear the Communist condition. They regarded me as part of the intellectual group that was maltreated by the Communists so they helped me by buying everything that I had for sale. Then they asked me to bring them lunch because they could not go home for it. And so I did.

Before 1975 I had never had to cook my own meals but now I had to cook rice and other food at home and put it in two very big baskets. Then I carried it to the department stores. The guards there helped me by letting me in when the doors were locked at lunch time so that I could serve lunch to the salespeople. Instead of bringing their lunch to work with them they would buy it from me. Everywhere they helped me like that. So with their pity and help and my own hard work I made enough money to live on.

For a year and a half my husband worked very hard in the reeducation camp in order to show that he was a good person. They had to go into the forest and cut trees to make the camp and everything in it — the beds, everything. It was just like a concentration camp. They had to do everything for themselves. And then my uncle sponsored him and they agreed to let him go. But before he could leave he was forced to sign an agreement not to stay in the city but to go to the countryside to work because there were no jobs in the city.

All the wives of the men in the reeduction camps had already

---

*A large, thin rice cake like a pancake, boiled and rolled up with chopped meat inside. — J.S.

been forced to go out into the countryside. I had not had to go because of my uncle but all the wives who were suitable for doing hard work had had to go. If they could get a permit from their native provinces, they were allowed to return there and their husbands coming back from the reeducation camps could join them. If not, then they had to go to the New Economic Zone.

This New Economic Zone was the area around the city but far out, maybe sixty kilometers, where the land was undeveloped. The men who had been in the former government were forced to go there first to cut the grass and clear the land and make houses. After that their wives and families went to join them.

Fortunately, my husband's aunt had some land at Long Binh in Bien Hoa Province about forty kilometers from Saigon. We decided that he would go there but the local government would not agree and I had to beg them. I cried and said, "He doesn't want to move like this but he is forced to so why don't you help me?" And I cried again. I felt as though I was some kind of disease that all of them were afraid of us.

Then the official from the local government took pity on me and he signed the paper allowing my husband to come to Long Binh. That was luck for me. As soon as my husband had this paper the authorities in the reeducation camp had a meeting and, because he was being sponsored by our uncle, they agreed to let him go. So he was able to leave the reeducation camp much earlier than he would have otherwise. I went to get him there and took him home to visit with me and his parents.

He was very happy to see the family again but became sad when he discovered how hard things had been for us without him. Until then he had thought that I was still working with the airlines. I still had the letter of introduction from Air Vietnam and had gone on using it to visit him. I hadn't let him know that I had been chased out because it would have made him very miserable. So when he came home he was very disappointed.

When he had been in Saigon for one day, the local government (the men who had stayed in my house were now the local government) took pity on my situation and asked him to stay there temporarily. But he dared not. He said, "I signed an agreement

when I was in the reeducation camp that I would go to the countryside and work."

He was afraid that, even though the local government wanted
him to stay, the central government would disagree and they
would come by night and take the whole family to the New
Economic Zone. He thought it was better for him to go alone and
to let me and the children stay in the city. So he went and worked
on his aunt's property.

The Americans had been planning to set up a military base
nearby and my aunt had wanted to build a laundry to service all
the American soldiers. She had bought the land with that in mind
but because of the revolution she had not been able to go on with
her plans. So there was nothing there when my husband first arrived. He had to make himself a hut to come to at night and then
he had to start clearing the land.

My aunt's husband was there with him. He was very old and
couldn't do much. He had come there because it was a way to
escape from the city and not have to listen to orders and to lead
a peaceful life.

But my husband was different. Because he had just come from
the reeducation camp it was better for him to show that he could
adjust to the situation and show that he had learned something
from the reeducation camp.

The land was not suitable for farming and we had to spend
a lot of money in developing it. We had to hire a machine to plow
it up and we had to buy the manioc plants and hire someone to help
in pulling the grass and in growing the crops.

They had taken from my husband all the rights of a citizen
and he was considered as someone who had brought harm upon
the citizens of the South. He had no right to vote. (We did have
elections but the names on the voting ballot were chosen by the
Communist government so really we had no right to choose our
leaders.) He had no right to come back to Saigon to see his family.
He had no papers, no ID card, and without papers he could not
move from one place to another without asking the permission of
the local government. They even took his paper of release from the
reeducation camp.

And, despite all the work and money we had invested in the farm, after one year we had nothing at all because the local people came at night and stole everything from us. They were poor and starving and so they had to steal from us in order to live. As workers of the former government we dared not say anything or they would cut our throats. Also, if my husband could not show that he could adjust to the situation, maybe they would take him to the reeducation camp once more.

All during the time my husband was in the countryside I had to visit him twice a month to take him dried food and rice to support him while he was there. In Saigon we had nine kilos of rice for each person per month and he was a farmer and had no kilos of rice at all. But fortunately my children were very young and did not eat all their rice allowance so I could take it to my husband to feed him.

He had to stay like that until 1979 when he asked for his citizen's rights to be restored. Then at last, because of our good behavior, they agreed that he could have his rights back.

As soon as he had his papers he tried to escape from the country by boat but he was caught by the local government of Ba Ria near Vung Tau and put in jail. They took everything away from him, even his clothes, leaving him with only his shorts. He wanted to escape but was afraid that it would be another mistake on his part. So he talked to a young man who was in the jail with him. "Why don't you escape?" he asked the young man.

The young man replied, "I cannot. I am a drug addict. My family is in this area and as long as I stay here they provide my heroin for me. I cannot go away where I would not get it. But, as for you, did you have gold for your escape with you when they took you?"

"Yes," my husband replied, "Six taels [562½ grams]."

"Then you should go. If you stay here they will send your papers and everything you had in your pockets to the central government. They will hold an investigation when they find you were carrying so much gold. They will find out that you were trying to get out of the country and it will be bad for you. But if you escape from jail then the local official will steal your gold and destroy your papers. That is the best thing for you in your situation."

So my husband decided to escape. A young man came that night to guide another man who had been supposed to go on the same boat as my husband. He also helped my husband to get out.

It seems that there was an agreement between this young man and the local government. For a share of the fee they would turn a blind eye if he wanted to help prisoners escape from the jail. As long as he took the road to the right outside the prison he would go unchallenged. The road going the other way was watched. They waited there ready to catch "illegal" escapees.

Unfortunately my husband turned to the left because he didn't trust the guide and he had to dive into a stream and swim from six o'clock in the afternoon until three o'clock in the early morning. If he had walked on the country paths the dogs would have barked and he would have been caught.

When he got to the Ba Ria market he saw a truck carrying charcoal so he asked the driver to help him. He told him all the truth about what had happened and the driver pitied him but he could not take him to Saigon. His truck only went to a town ten kilometers away. So my husband offered to sell his wedding ring to the co-workers of the driver in order to get money for the trip to Saigon. No one had the money to pay what the ring was worth so he sold it for only ten dong.

With ten dong he could come back to Saigon but he dared not come to our house so he got in touch with his niece and told her to let us know that he had been caught and had escaped from prison. Then he came to the house of a cousin and hid there for a while. It was very dangerous. If the government had found out, the whole family would have been chased out and sent to the New Economic Zone.

Because of the paper shortage we did not have any copies of my husband's papers in case of loss or theft. (There was very little paper stock on hand by a year after the revolution. Copying was severely restricted and there were long queues.) I would have to get them replaced so I went to Long Binh and told them that he had met with an accident and someone had stolen his wallet and all his papers with it. I said that he had hurt his leg and couldn't walk so I filled out the form applying for duplicates. But they didn't replace them. All we had was the report we filled out saying that he had lost everything.

After that, in 1980, my father-in-law died. He had never known that his son was hiding in Saigon. I had to hide everything like that, even from my parents-in-law.

I applied to the local authorities in Saigon for my husband to come back from Long Binh to be the head of the house because his mother was very old and sick and our children were very young.

It was the ones who had stayed with us in our house that I asked and they gave him permission to stay. They knew that he was a good man because in 1976 they had asked him to stay and he had insisted on keeping to his agreement to go to the country-side. But now our situation was very different and they were will-ing to help. This was in 1980 and he was given the temporary right to stay with us until 1983. They gave us papers. They were only temporary but with them I applied for an exit permit.

We had to go to the local government offices in Phu Nhuan to ask for an interview. We bribed the official and I also asked help from the secretary there. She had worked for the U.S. in the Third Field Hospital and understood our difficult situation. I said, "You must help us. The Communists do not trust us. We have no right to apply for an exit permit so you must help us." And the secretary was very good. She helped us.

From 1981 to 1983 we waited. During this time we taught my children to swim because we never knew how we would eventually get out of Vietnam. If we went by boat then we must all know how to swim. My husband took them to the public swimming pool in Saigon long enough for them to learn but then we had to stop the lessons because the pool was very dirty and people were catching eye infections.

However, they could swim well enough and, because we had very little confidence that we would ever be allowed to leave legally, we tried to make arrangements to leave by boat. But we were cheated over and over again by the pilots, by the taxi drivers, by the area supervisor. (The area supervisor has to grant permission

for people to move from one area to another. The escape organizer
has to bribe him so that he can bring groups of people through.)

In March 1985 I was interviewed by the American group from
the UNHCR and after that they took all our applications to
Bangkok where they investigated our application.

I was feeling more confident that we really would be allowed
to go by this time so I took my children out of school, saying that
I was sending them to another school, but in reality I sent them
to intensive English language classes. They were taught by a man
who had had his training in the United States before 1975. He was
allowed to take up to ten students — after he bribed the local
government. My husband took the children to his class every day
and I also had a tutor come into the house in order for us to prepare
for our life in the United States.

Our sponsor was my sister in the United States and she had
pleaded our case well, explaining that my husband was a captain
in the South Vietnamese Army before 1975 and I was jobless
because we were workers of the former government.

Then, on the first of December 1985, the Americans let the
Foreign Affairs Ministry in Vietnam know that they had agreed to
take us. Our names were written on the flight list for the thirteenth
of February and at last we could escape from Vietnam legally.

My parents had left Vietnam in 1982. They had applied at the
same time as me under the sponsorship of my brother in France
but when they were told that they had been approved to go they
were very distressed. My father said, "I cannot go. How can I go
and leave my daughter alone with no one to help her?"

I said, "You must go. It is better that you go now while you
can and I will follow very soon."

Before they left they sold their house. (People could do this
from time to time. Sometimes it was legal. Sometimes it wasn't.
This is the way of the Communists.) The house was bought by the
head of the local government for that district so my parents got
some gold and they gave it all to me to pay for my escape. My sister
in France had sent me some money by a kind of illegal transfer in
1979. She gave francs to a friend who sent it to her parents in Vietnam. Then the father who was in Saigon brought me a tael of gold.

From these two sources I got the money that I used to pay for our escape but it was not until 1985 that we could follow my parents.

When I wrote and told them that I had been approved, they were very happy and left France to visit my sister in the United States to wait for me there.

However, we could not go straight there. We were told that we must first go to the Philippines for language and cultural training. I could not persuade them otherwise even though all the family speaks English and we had worked with the Americans before 1975. We tried to get the time shortened but it was no use and now my parents' tourist visa to the U.S. is due to expire and they will have to return to France without seeing us.

My husband and I were so happy when we reached Bangkok but when we reached the Philippine refugee camp we were very disappointed. I had had so many modern conveniences in my home and there I had to learn how to light a charcoal fire to make the food.

Now the rains are coming. There is not enough food. The fish they give us is spoiled. The rice has stones in it and it is not enough. Charcoal is in short supply. We get water only one hour in the morning and one in the evening. There is no milk for the children and it is almost impossible to get a pass to shop in Manila.

I am one of the lucky ones because of the support of my sisters. Others in the camp are very badly off because of the insufficient and bad food and the maltreatment by the Filipinos. We are all made to work very hard under the hot sun. The huts are too hot to stay inside and there is nowhere to shelter in the heat of the day. There is no ice or anywhere to keep food cool.

The Filipinos teaching us American cultural orientation have never been in America and don't know anything about it. Many refugees have visited America and lived there to study or do military training. When they tell the Filipino teachers that they are mistaken in what they tell us, the teachers fly into a rage.

They skim off the food. For instance, if a family should have eight cans of rice, the person delivering will keep one. This goes on all down the line. By the time the food gets to us it is very bad and very little.

However, we have to understand that the Filipinos are also very poor and need to feed their families. At least, when we have suffered through our time here, we will go to the United States. We have hope. They have none, so we can only pity them.

Recent arrivals in camp tell us that the situation in Vietnam is getting worse all the time. The Communists try to keep Saigon as a showplace to convince the world that South Vietnam is doing well but under the show the reality is poverty and cruelty and starvation. Prices are going higher and higher. Only those who have relatives abroad can afford anything. Many people have starved. They are still starving.

Taxes are 80 percent of the rice grown on the farms. The Communists claimed they were going to export what they collected from the people but the rice harvests in the North have been so bad that all they are doing is exporting grain to the North.

Saigon, the showpiece, is actually supported by overseas relatives — mainly Americans — who send packages and money to their families. And the families are made to pay very, very high taxes before the packages are handed over. It can take as long as eighteen months for a family to actually receive a package.

All this has happened to us because the people in the North really wanted to help the South. They believed the propaganda that was told to them. But when they came to the South they found that, with all the comforts and the luxury, the way the South lived was very different from what they had been told. There it had been a very good life — better than in the North. So they discovered that they had been told lies by their government. When they realized this it was too late. There was nothing they could do.

Even if the United States had decided they wanted to win the war it would have been a false victory. It would have been impossible to govern the country afterwards and the whole thing would have started up again. This is because the northerners were convinced they were helping their fellow citizens and because the southerners gave in without a fight. It is always easy to persuade poor people that Communism will be better than the government they have because they will always believe the promises about redistribution of wealth. Also, they had relatives in the North.

Minh's first birthday in freedom. Her mother, Nguyen Thi Yen Nga, is in the foreground. Joanna C. Scott is seated, center.

Even the Communist officials knew that what they were doing was all wrong. My uncle, a powerful man in the government, told me privately, "It is a bad idea, sending everyone out from the cities to work on farms."

And now that people know what living under Communism is really like they wish the Americans would come back and help them. But it is too late. Now all of them wish to go abroad.

When the relatives who escaped from Vietnam and resettled in the United States started to send packages to feed the ones still in Vietnam, they realized that the better life is in America. We are all relatives. Everyone has some kind of relation who has already gone. Even for the Communist workers, the dream is to go to

America, although no one dares to say so for fear of who may be watching and listening. They just long for freedom and for America in a passive way.

We have a saying in Vietnam, "If we were allowed to go abroad freely, even the lampposts would get onto the boats." [PRPC, May 12, 1986.]

It Is Lost, My Country

Tran van Xinh

Tran van Xinh wore wire-rimmed glasses issued to him by the medical authorities at the camp. They were too loose and he had to push them up on his nose every time he bent his head. Behind their lenses his eyes shone wet when he spoke of Vietnam.

The title of his story reflects the emotions of many refugees. They think of the homeland, not as a country fallen under an alien government, but as one lost, never to be seen again.

I went to a concert put on by the refugees in Manila. A young man sang, standing under the spotlight like a lost child, his dark hair brushing the shoulders of a pale, shimmering blue, high-necked tunic. The song was "Vietnam" and, though I understood only that one repeated word, his agony at home lost swept the auditorium and trembled in the air.

As the slight figure sang out his sorrow, the audience held its breath and when the sound faded with the fading spotlight a great sigh went up.

———————————

I am free now and many of my countrymen too. But we remember and we are full of sorrow for Vietnam because it is lost, my country.

My name is Tran van Xinh. I am the Vietnamese Inter-Neighborhood Council chairman here at the Philippine Refugee Processing Center. I would like to tell about why I left my country.

Scenes at the Philippine Refugee Processing Center.

Before 1975 I was a first lieutenant in the Army of the Republic of Vietnam and principal of a high school in Kien Luong in Kien Giang Province. I worked with the American Army helping to run the education program for strategic hamlets. I worked with a Major White.

In 1975 when the Communist regime took over they said that I was CIA and put me in jail in the Ha Tien district of Kien Giang Province. After six months they released me but they took my house and all my possessions. They said that, because I had worked for the Americans and the former government, these were the possessions of the population, not mine.

Many other people had their property taken away just like me, especially the old government officials. They all lost their houses and possessions to the Communists.

I had to move back to Long Xuyen, my native village, with my family. It is a medium-sized village — about 5,000 people — and I worked there as a farmer on some fields that I got from my father. He had only one hectare of land so the Communists had not taken it away, although they taxed him heavily on it. I was under the control of the village chief.

The village chief is the head Communist in the village. Each week I had to present myself to him and give an accounting of everything I had done over the past week. He gave me a schedule for the seven days and I had to write on it everyone I met, everyone I talked with. He kept track of all my actions, everything I did every day.

All officers had to record and report their schedule like this after they were released from jail. We were considered dangerous to the new regime. They gave each of us a worker classification — A, B or C — according to how dangerous they thought we were. An A classification worker was considered the most dangerous to them and he would be followed. No one was told his classification. We could only leave the village if we got permission from the chief. This was very difficult to do. He knew everywhere we went and everything we did.

During the time I lived under this regime I got to know the Communists very well and I learned that they don't have even the basics of freedom. The man who has no freedom is like a slave, like an animal.

There is no freedom of speech. Nobody can speak in a public place unless under the guidance of the Communist Party.

There is no freedom of religion. Many priests have been arrested by the Communists. They say, "There is no God! Only Communism can make people happy! Only Communism can help you and your people!" But I say the Communist regime doesn't help anybody.

There is no freedom of assembly. No individuals or groups can organize a meeting except the government. Anyone wanting a meeting must put in a request. But if it is a group of farmers, for instance, they won't give permission. They give permission only if the government is doing the organizing. We had to obey. They watched us. There were no secret meetings.

There is no freedom of the press. When I worked with the Americans they taught me great arguments. I learned how the free press can present controversies. In the freedom world people discuss things with each other. There should be a right hand and a left hand. But under Communism there is no controversy. It is all Communist ideology. The press is controlled. There are only government opinions and Communist orders.

In Vietnam there is one national newspaper. It is called *Nhan Dan*, which means "new paper of the population." Each province has one bulletin but this bulletin is an echo of *Nhan Dan*. Only the members of the Party can publish in it. It doesn't give the people any information about the outside world — only Communist and Russian information.

If any news is about the freedom world it is propaganda. They only tell about mistakes in the freedom world and they say that when the United States is friendly towards another nation it is only because it wants sovereignty over that nation.

The people can't listen to radio broadcasts from the outside either — only broadcasts from Hanoi. If the Communists hear anybody listening to the Voice of America or the BBC they say, "This is propaganda from the outside, from foreigners."

So the Vietnamese people are cut off from the outside world.

A life of oppression, slavery and suffering has been imposed upon them. They live amidst blood and tears in an atmosphere of darkness. It is a government of jails and killings. People's lives are of no value. They simply vanish with no trial, no justice. There is only one freedom. This is the freedom of hard work — hard work from day to night. And the world does not know about the cruelty and the wicked intention of systematically destroying the nation's traditions and culture.

In the last ten years a million people have left their country. They endured suffering until they could bear no more and accepted the risk of death to seek freedom. Tens of thousands of Vietnamese lie at the bottom of the deep sea. Some drowned and some were killed by pirates. Tens of thousands died in deep mountain forests. Some starved and some were killed by Cambodian bandits when they tried to escape across the border.

Yet despite the risks of the high seas and of jungle banditry the Vietnamese exodus continues. A deep desire for freedom has made them accept suffering and brave death.

In 1980 the Communist Party caught me again. They accused me of being dangerous to the regime and sent me to the U-Minh reeducation camp in the forest near the border between Minh-Hai and Kien Giang. There were about 4,000 people there.

In this camp I worked from six o'clock in the morning to five o'clock in the evening. I had no tools for working. I used my bare hands. I ate only one bowl of rice for lunch and one for dinner. We had to plant rice and prepare rice fields, pulling out wild grass with our bare hands. It was very sharp and after one week our hands bled all the time.

The camp was in two parts. One part A and one part B. I lived in part A, which was for former officers and government officials. Part B was for soldiers and criminals. From time to time the Communists would organize a meeting in the evenings. They would discuss what all the workers had done since the last meeting — who had worked well, who had worked badly. Sometimes there were orders from the Communist government and sometimes they talked about Communist ideology. I lived in this camp for eight months and for eight months I longed to escape.

Then one day, having worked hard and finished my work before the others, I came back first from the fields. I looked around and didn't see anybody there. I had some clothes hidden in my barracks in case I should get the opportunity to escape so I took them and went away.

I walked about one kilometer and changed into them so that I would not look like a prisoner. Then I saw a small boat. It was going up-river to the market in another village so I paid some money and they took me. They thought that I was a resident. When I came to the market I changed to another boat, and another — many boats. In that way I got to the Tan-Hiep district of Kien Giang Province and came straight from there to Saigon.

I didn't have any official documents so I had to move around from place to place to keep from getting caught. I was on the run in Saigon for two years. Some of the time I worked for an old friend. Other times I bought and sold clothing. Then I said to myself, "I love my mother country but I think I have to escape."

And in 1983 I left my native country. I took with me my wife, my two sons and my four daughters. For this I give my thanks to an old student of mine who helped me and my family arrange the escape. We went at night and in the morning our boat came onto the high seas. But after two days the engine broke.

Then we were robbed by pirates. They were Thai fishermen. They came near to our boat and when we hid they called to us through a loud hailer. They offered to give us food and water. They said that they would help us get to Malaysia. Then they boarded us and called all the men and the boys to one side and the females to the other side. They searched our boat looking for gold and money and any dollars we had. And they took it and all our precious things.

They took nine girls onto their boat and raped them for eight hours. When they returned them to our boat they were exhausted. Some didn't know anything any more — they had lost their minds. Some were only fourteen years old. The oldest was twenty-five maybe.

The men were beaten. One former commander of the navy, they beat him and he fell down in the sea. I pulled him out again.

Scene at the Philippine Refugee Processing Center.

They beat me but I pulled him out. All the pirates that attacked the Vietnamese on the high seas were Thai fishermen. I know this because later, when I was president of the Vietnamese in three camps, Songkhla, Sikiew and Panat Nikhom, I asked all the residents, our fellow-countrymen, about the pirates. They said they were Thai fishermen only.

After our suffering the wind blew our boat to shore in Songkhla Province in Thailand and there we were robbed again by Thai villagers. There were about a hundred of them. They were hidden near the shore and when they saw our boat wash up they ran out and took everything that we had left.

Then the police came and helped us to get to the Songkhla refugee camp, where we lived for a month and a half until the UNHCR transferred us to Sikiew camp near Nakhon Ratchasima, about three hundred kilometers northeast of Bangkok. We lived there for a year and a half. On July 4, 1984, the United States delegation accepted my family and on September 27 they moved

The Vietnamese temple at the Philippine Refugee Processing Center.

us to the Panat Nikhom camp near Bangkok. On June 12, 1985, we were moved here to the Philippines.

Now we are studying English and taking a cultural orientation course to prepare us for a new life in the United States. When we get there we will contribute our part to make the United States more and more prosperous. We will complete our duty as residents and citizens. We will be self-sufficient in our lives.

But we will also have to think about our native country and our people there who are still suffering under the bloody hands of the Communist regime. We want to liberate our nation. There are two things we must do. First, we must preserve our ancient Vietnamese philosophy, which teaches that all Vietnamese are equal. And so we must love each other. If we follow this philosophy we will be in unity.

I don't have enough words to describe this philosophy but if you read some of the works of the American Vietnamese philosopher Kim Dinh you will understand that the ancient Vietnamese philosophy is based on two things—unity and love.

If our past leaders had ruled in accordance with the spirit of the Vietnamese race, our country would have seen peace and prosperity. The ancient kingdom would have not fallen to invaders no matter how wickedly strong they may have been. But the ancient kings strayed from the original Vietnamese spirit and now the kingdom has fallen under slavery and is at risk of extermination.

And so I think that the Vietnamese people should organize Vietnamese schools to teach the ancient philosophy to the younger generation so that they can win back Vietnam by the Vietnamese spirit in their blood and in their hearts. Vietnamese ideology will destroy Communist ideology by reuniting all the Vietnamese that are still inside with those who are outside. We are planning to organize classes in the evenings, on weekends, on holidays and in the summers. It is very important.

If we are brother and sister we will love one another and sacrifice for each other. Those of us who are free will take it as our duty to work for the freedom of our suffering countrymen. We can help the people inside with money and we can contribute intellectual power by working and by writing.

And then we must fight. That is the second step. I think that if we are united by a strong ideology and if we can just get some arms we can fight with the Communists. We can take back our nation.

I think that Americans because they are former allies, can help us to fight with the Communists — not the Vietnamese people but the Communists. And I think that other freedom nations can help if we work out a good way to take back my country. But first of all we must help ourselves. We have to be self-sufficient.

I know the United States is the melting pot, it is the land of the migration and we will learn many different ways there. But we must keep our culture to save Vietnam. And we must fight. And maybe twenty or thirty years from now we can take back our country. As for me, if my country needs me to come back, I will come back to my country. [PRPC, October 23, 1985.]

Cambodia—
Land of the Killing Fields

All the People of Khmer Were Very Troubled

Ven Yem

The refugee camp is built along the top of a mountain ridge that runs down to the sea. The little village of Morong sits between the camp and the sea and, on the nights I stayed over, I would often go walking on the beach in the glow of the tropical sunset, watching the fishermen as they dragged their canoes out into the golden water and sat patiently waiting for the light to fade before they cast their nets.

The golden glow cast on the village turned it into an idealized picture postcard of native huts and palm trees. But the reality behind this beauty was sad. Though the refugees lived a life of considerable hardship, the villagers, looking at the neat camp provided by the Philippine government with its United States funding and Japanese medical equipment, felt like the poor cousins. At first this threatened to be a severe problem until measures were taken to provide the villagers with free medical care at the camp hospital and to give them special trading privileges at the camp markets.

This was enough to keep ill feelings under control but not enough to bring prosperity to a rural Philippine village suffering from the general poverty of the country and so there continued to be problems like village children coming into the camp to beg from the refugees.

My name is Ven Yem. I am Khmer. I want to tell about what happened in my country and why I decided to leave.

Pol Pot's regime occupied Cambodia in 1975 and all the people of Khmer were very troubled. The towns and the cities were full of Pol Pot's soldiers and they displaced all the people from the cities and the towns to live in the countryside. They divided them into three groups, men, women and children, and set them to build big canals and to work in the rice fields.

I had been a farmer and a goldsmith. I had my own farm, about 30 *rite* (one *rite* is 1,600 square meters), and I grew rice. Pol Pot's Communists took away my farm. They took me away, far away from my village and from my family. I heard that my farm is now a reservoir.

For a long time then I lived with Pol Pot's regime. And I was very troubled. I had no freedom and no hope. By 1977 there was no food to support all the people. For three years the Khmer people ate only boiled rice. Into one big pan they would put just one can of rice to feed twenty or thirty people.

So they found it very hard to do the work, very hard. All the people were tired, very tired. Some died in the rice fields and some were accused of being spies and killed. I got sick because there was not food enough to eat, just boiled rice, boiled rice for a long time. I was so very tired.

We had to work very hard making a farm and digging drainage and growing food for the Communists. Sometimes we had to get up and start work very early in the morning while it was still dark—as early as three o'clock—and sometimes we had to work right through the dark night. We never got more than two or three hours' rest. There was no food in the morning until eleven o'clock, then one cup of water with some rice in it. We had the same again at five o'clock in the afternoon.

After the evening rice we had to do other work near the camp. I worked growing vegetables—cabbages, potatoes, tomatoes and also sugar cane. This food was not for us. It was for the Communists. The chairman of the village ordered it.

We lived in huts. In some huts there were thirty people, in some one hundred, in some two hundred. There were no soldiers

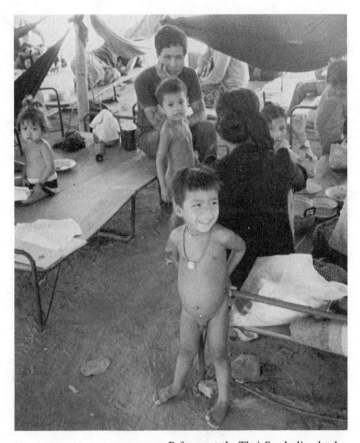

Refugees at the Thai-Cambodian border.

in the huts. There was a group leader. He answered to the chairman of the village.

We could not run away. They said, "Do not try to escape. We will see you. We have many eyes, like a pineapple."

They had an action army — spies. They were chosen by the village chairman. Some were Communists who came from outside and some they recruited from amongst the people in the camp. They lived amongst us. We did not know who they were. They watched us and knew all that we did. So we were afraid.

If anyone tried to escape or if they did not work hard enough they would accuse them of being enemies of the new regime. And they would be killed. The village chairman would order it.

They kept us all together. This was so that they could have meetings with us, many meetings. There were meetings every night. They told us all we must make a new regime. We must forget the old regime. They told us we would not have monks any more. There would be no more Buddhist religion. The people were not to respect the monks. They said the monks were like leeches, sucking the blood. The Communists did not believe in religion. They wanted to do away with it and with the monks too. But the people were worried about sin.

While I was in Pol Pot's camp, my wife had been working for the Communists also. She was growing vegetables for them in our home village. There was no school for the children. They had to work in the fields too. They cut grass, piled it up and hauled it.

Then after the Pol Pot occupation of my country, it was occupied a second time by Heng Semrin and the Vietnamese soldiers. They said that the soldiers of Vietnam had come to help us but I knew that Vietnam and Cambodia were not friendly. My parents and grandparents had told all the children that the soldiers of Vietnam would take the heads of Khmer people to boil their tea water. They would cut off the heads of my people and take three of them and put them on the ground in a triangle, like stones. Then in the middle they would make a fire and on the heads they would support a pot of water to boil. I think these stories were true.

And so I decided, and all the Khmer people decided, to try to escape from our country because all the people in my family and my country were afraid of the troops of Vietnam. I ran away and found my wife and we made a plan to escape from my country because it was unbearable to live there. Then we ran away to the border of Khmer and Thailand.

I left my country in 1979. When I left I had five children. With my wife and myself there were seven people in my family. We came by walking and my small children I carried.

All the people were leaving my country. They did not go by the roads because the soldiers would see them. They went through the fields and through the forests.

Refugees at the Thai-Cambodian Border.

We went from our village, from Sousey Village in Battambang Province, and walked about five days until we reached the border of Khmer and Thailand. There we met UNHCR organizers. They had a big truck and I was very happy because they took us into Thailand's country and the Khao I Dang camp.

I stayed there for a long time and had two more children. At first I worked in construction. Then I worked in food distribution to the people that lived in the camp. And after that I worked in the United Nations warehouse for three months. I was glad to do that.

After that they took me and my family and all the Khmer people to the Chunburi camp in Thailand. We stayed there two months and after two months they took us all to the airport in Bangkok and we went to Manila town. I stayed in Manila town one night and after that they took me by bus to the Philippine Refugee Processing Center camp.

I arrived in the PRPC camp August 17, 1985. I have been here about two months now. I am an assistant teacher in the evenings and in the afternoons I work in the Inter-Neighborhood Council chairman's office.

When I finish studying here I will go to the United States. I have a sister in San Francisco and I will go to San Francisco too. When I reach there my sponsor will help my family and I will find a job. I don't know yet what I will do but I must work hard to earn money for my family because now I have seven children. If I can find work as a goldsmith or on a farm I can do it. But I will do any work and I will work so hard to make America a good country for my family.

Above all, I desire and I want to drive Vietnam out of my country. I want to help my country displace the Vietnamese soldiers because all the Khmer people love their country so much but now the Vietnamese soldiers occupy all of our Cambodia. So I hope to organize all the countries in the world that love peace to help my country. [PRPC, November 6, 1985.]

My Mother, My Sister

The Story of Samol Him*

A generation of Indochinese youth sits in American schools side-by-side with Americans, flipping hamburgers in McDonald's when school lets out and rapidly becoming indistinguishable from their American peers.

But for this generation growing up in America there will always be a difference: the memories of childhood. While our children will remember Christmas trees and new bikes, Halloween candy, yellow school buses and Mom with the station wagon, their Indochinese counterparts will remember beatings and death, starvation and mortal fear.

They were born in labor camps and refugee camps, they watched their parents weep over dead brothers and sisters, their mothers weep over dead fathers. They will remember the suffering of untreated illness and the taste of rats and cockroaches. They will remember running and hiding and scratching in the ground for food. And they will remember the long months and years spent in the limbo of statelessness waiting for the grinding bureaucracy of "the promised land" to determine if they had earned their dream.

He was only ten years old when he lost his father. He was killed by Pol Pot's soldiers during the time when things were

*Told by a Filipino staff member at the Philippine Refugee Processing Center.

in a great mess in Cambodia. Families were separated. He was separated from his mother and his younger sister and he was put with what they called a "mobile team." His mother and sister were put in another group and then assigned to different small camps.

So he was there and he couldn't do anything about it. He knew that they were under a difficult system now so he compromised. He did only what he was supposed to do.

But then in the evenings they would hold meetings. They had a cadre leader who would ask them questions about the old regime and what they wanted to do now and what they thought of establishing a new regime and what they expected. It was a soft way, actually, of observing who were the intellectuals in the group.

And he being quite intelligent and outspoken tried to air his views. They were hearing news of the killings of the intellectuals in some areas and he deplored what was happening. Then the rumor went around, "Hey, you'd better watch what you are saying, because they're going to mark you."

But he said, "Why should I? I am going to stand for what I believe in." And so he continued on being outspoken.

One night they held a big meeting again and he had a feeling that something was going to happen to him if he didn't move. So that very night after he had said his piece he packed up his things and he went through the forest.

He didn't know which direction to go or what camp he would go to but he just kept walking until he came to another camp. He went into this camp and made up a story about how he had lost his way looking for his mother and his sister. And this was partly true.

He was very gracious and kind and an old woman who was there took pity on him and recommended him to her daughter who was a leader in the camp. So he got a kind of formal welcome and was given a job which he did very well.

A few weeks later another person slipped into the camp. It was a friend from the first camp. He said to the boy. "You know, you were so lucky that you made up your mind to go because that night they searched your hut and looked everywhere for you. You were to have been killed." And the boy made up another story and his friend also got incorporated into the new camp.

Since he was showing leadership and responsibility in the camp they came to trust him. Then, one day he told the lady in charge that he really was looking for his mother and his sister and he wanted some kind of official permit to travel through the forest.

So the lady said, "OK, I'll give it to you. You go look for their camp but that's all there is to it. You're on your own." And so she gave him a pass.

A month passed by before he finally decided to make a move to go out. He had got to know more people and was also known by others so he had more confidence to be on his own. There was no guarantee that nothing would happen but at least there were some people who knew him.

So he went and luckily he came to the right camp where he saw his mother and his sister. And his sister was very sick at that time. Since he had a pass, the leader of that camp said, "OK, you can visit your folks here." And then he convinced his mother that they had to escape. He made a plan. He would carry his sister on his back. He would go through the forest and his mother would slip out of the camp very quietly. Fortunately they were not so keen on watching these old folk.

So they left and went back to the second camp where there was more food. And he took care of his sister until she was well and they lived there together in the camp. He told me what happened later:

In 1979, when the Vietnamese Communists took over, we got the chance to go back to live in the city. We could not go to our home town but went to Battambang instead.

I felt a lot better as we expected that we would have our freedom and be able to make a better living. However, we missed having the family around so after a while I decided to leave my mother and sister there and go looking for our relatives. I found them in a village in the Trang district, about five miles from the town, so I went back and got my mother and sister and brought them there to live with the family again.

We were there for a couple of months but by then our food was exhausted and we had no way to find more except by going into the forest to the farms and rice fields left by the Pol Pot regime. But everywhere we went was a dangerous place and we had to travel by foot, having no other transportation.

In mid-1979 more and more people started leaving Cambodia heading for the border camps where they could survive by exchanging gold for Thai money that they could use to buy things from Thailand.

The situation in Cambodia became tougher and tougher. All my relatives were worried. We had no choice at all but to escape to a border camp.

I took my sister and left, leaving my mother behind for the time being because she could not walk fast and I was not sure of the way. It was the right decision as we had a very difficult trip through the deep woods, avoiding robbers, mines and battles between the Khmer Liberation Front and the Vietnamese military on the way. However, we made it to the border camp and I went back and got my mother.

A month later we were taken to the Khao I Dang refugee camp in Thailand by the UNHCR people. That was in December of 1979 and I spoke no English at all.

Six months later I still spoke no English because I was spending all my time trying hard to make money for the household by smuggling.

Then one day I met an old friend of mine who was walking on the street talking with an American. He was surprised and excited to see me and introduced me. The American said, "Hi!"

I could not even say "Hi!" at that time. I just nodded my head and turned to ask my friend," "Who is he?" in Cambodian. "He's a doctor," answered my friend.

Then the American started asking me about my life and what had happened to me. He had to use my friend as interpreter. That inspired me to start learning English.

From that day on I decided to give up smuggling and try to survive on what was provided by the UNHCR while I studied English. I didn't have enough money to pay an English teacher so I would stand outside the classroom and listen to the teacher and then copy from the others until I found a friend who would teach me at night.

My English got better and better and I was so happy to get away from such ignorance. Also, I was able to get a job in the hospital as an interpreter and had been working there for a little more than a year when I was called for an interview for resettlement in the United States.

My family and I were moved to the Panat Nhikom processing center in Chunburi, Thailand. I got a job there as a nurse assistant and also as an interpreter in the Family Center where they took care of

Khmer at the Philippine Refugee Processing Center.

psychiatric cases and people who had been crippled by leprosy, and also did general family counselling.

I was there for fourteen months and then I left for the Philippines.

I met him here in the Philippines [continued the Filipino staff worker]. By then he was a young man of about fifteen or sixteen but he was very mature. I remember he told me about a time when they were still in the Khao I Dang camp.

There was a man who was interested in marrying his mother. He said to me:

I know that I am only a son. I can never be a husband to my mother and she has needs that I can't fulfill. But when I met this man I had a feeling that he would not make my mother a good husband. I told her about it but she insisted. She was lonely and getting old, so she got married.

But sure enough, after she became pregnant and delivered the baby, the man didn't care for her at all. He only wanted the child.

So I fought for that child. I went to our neighborhood leader and I said to him, "What can this man do for this baby? A baby needs milk. How can this man nurse this baby? . . .

That is the argument he used for that baby. So he brought the child here also and he was a father to his younger sisters.

He was very hard working. He was one of those who when he worked with me would not be at all conscious of time. He would work in the evening, the morning, whatever . . . anything that needed to be done. He would volunteer sometimes for the hospital in his free time. He had a deep compassion for his people.

He's now in Massachusetts and he writes me back. He's working in a factory part-time and also studying. He is still in high school. He tells me his plans. He has a car now and he says he has no problem at all adapting to the new country. He likes it very much there. It's free and he can do a lot of things. But still he tells me: "Even though you think that now it is possible for me to forget the time of isolation and suffering under a dreadful regime, I know I will never forget it. It has gone deeply into my brain and my heart and become as a bitter memory that will last the rest of my life." [PRPC, October 24, 1985.]

They Liked Only
the Stupid People

Him Mao

Before the Philippine revolution, I had always driven myself up to the refugee camp but, with the nervousness that then pervaded the foreign community, I was persuaded to have my driver take me. Until then he had been unaware of the presence of Indochinese refugees in the country, even though Morong, the little town neighboring the camp, was his mother's home town.

He became fascinated with these newcomers and, while I went about my interviews, he would sit in the heat under the shelter of the makeshift wooden stage in the main square of the camp, surrounded by the hulks of Vietnamese boats, and talk. Being half Chinese himself, he was tickled when he was taken for a Vietnamese.

One afternoon he met me with the car, looking very down in the mouth. I asked him was was the matter. "They are lucky, so lucky. They can go to the United States. We are poorer even than they are and we cannot go."

I am Him Mao, Cambodian citizen, and I lived near Phnom Penh in Poursat Province before 1975. I was a schoolteacher.

In 1975 Pol Pot's soldiers seized power from Lon Nol. That was on March 18th. Then, on April 17th, all the people were forced to go out from the cities to live in the country to make communal farms.

At first I was put into the countryside in the Tagrey District. We lived in a village in the forest. We had to build it—a row of small huts. They were raised up from the ground and were made of bamboo and wood with coconut leaves for the roofs. There was one family to each house.

There was a bigger hut in the center of the small ones where they distributed the food. The old men and women also used this big hut to take care of the small children. Pol Pot's soldiers forced everybody else to work.

There was not enough food to eat. On some days we got only one cob of corn for the whole day. It was very difficult for the people to live and to work with so little food. If anyone was against the Communists, that person must be killed. If someone didn't have enough food, they didn't want them to say, "Oh, that food is not enough for me." but "Enough, enough, enough." Cannot complain. Just stay and eat and do the work.

After that all the people were dying because there was not enough food and also they had no medicine for treatment of their illnesses.

Many people they killed. Some were soldiers, some were teachers and some were from other government agencies. They didn't want to keep the government workers from Lon Nol's time. They didn't like them. They brought them to the jail. And then they took them from the jail to kill them in the forest. They also killed women, their wives. Sometimes the whole family, small babies, the whole family together.

I didn't actually see anyone killed but when I went out to work I saw them dead in the fields. Not by guns—by sticks. They hit them on the head.

I heard that they were using plastic bags to put over people's heads—blue ones. When they put them on they asked questions, the secret story of their family. If they didn't want to tell them then their whole family must be put like that in the plastic and tied by the neck. After that, they opened it and asked again. If they still had nothing to say they did the same again. And after they got all the information they could, they killed them with a stick.

So I was working on the farm, living in the hut with my

family. For one year my wife and I were together but then they said we could not live with each other and they separated us. After that I was in one place and my wife in another place.

I went to the Umpil district. My wife went to work in the village of Takeo. It was in the Tagrey district—maybe three or four kilometers from the village where she lived. She went back every evening. For me, I only went back once or twice a month.

In the Umpil district all of us had to plant rice and then take care of it. Don't let an animal eat it. Don't let it be destroyed until the rice is ready to harvest.

In the day they made me do that work from six thirty in the morning until about twelve o'clock. There was no food until then. After that, at one o'clock, we started again and worked until five o'clock. Then, at six o'clock I would go to do another job digging the ground to make canals—many of them, some very long, some small, to get water for the rice fields. The big canals were from the river to the canal, the small ones from the canal to the rice field. I worked at that job until nine or ten o'clock. After that I came back to sleep.

There were meetings every week. The Communist Khmer leader would talk about improving production. And he would tell if someone had been lazy in that last week. Three times they would be warned. After that they would kill them. In that meeting, if someone said, "No, the food is not enough. Please give me more," that person was already dead—soon—tonight. They didn't want anybody to say that. They liked all of them to just work.

During that time there was so much rice we produced . . . so much, so much. But they didn't let the people eat in full, just a little bit, little bit. I don't know what they did with the rice.

All of them disliked people who had any knowledge. They liked only the stupid people. It was easy for them to use those people. If anyone had big knowledge he had to be careful.

They let us talk to each other in the farm but they didn't want us to talk about their orders or their regime—just about the work. "Help me to do this." "I will help you to do something." If anyone said anything bad about the regime there was no warning. He would be taken at once and killed.

We lived in groups. Some groups had two or three, some ten, eleven, twelve. The leaders were brought in from different parts of the country. They didn't use leaders from the local neighborhood in case people would refuse to cooperate with them. They were also Khmer — Khmer Rouge — but different in mind, different from the White Khmer.

There were three Khmer Rouge people in my group. They had no guns but no one ever tried to attack them. There were soldiers all around. If I had attacked them they would have called the soldiers to kill not only me . . . all my group would have died. If I am against them, my group is against them. They must die.

I was there from 1975 until 1979.

In that time I got sick. I was very sick for two and a half months. My legs swelled up — so big I could not walk. And not just my legs. My privates too — they swelled up bigger than baseballs and fell down. I could not go to the bathroom. I could not eat. I had no strength to do anything. I had a fever. For the first month I didn't know where I was or what I was doing.

After one month I was very hungry but I had no food. I asked for some from the leader. "No," he said. "They can give you food at the hospital."

But the hospital had no food for me. Just a little bit. Just watery rice, twice a day, at midday and in the evening. But only one plate for one person — no more, and mostly water. The hospital treated me. All the medicine they made by themselves. They gave me round, black tablets to eat and to drink they gave me water they had boiled from roots in the forest. I drank and drank until I got better. I think that medicine did some good for me. I got better.

In the hospital there were so many beds, all together one after one after one. Many rows of beds. And so many people died in there. Some nights I slept there and so many people died. Some told me they had diarrhea, some stomachaches, some headaches. So many kinds of people that were not strong. When I saw that I was very frightened. I prayed to God to be alive for a long time. After that I got better. I was very happy.

Then in 1979 the Vietnamese Communist soldiers came

across the border and into Cambodia. They came to the Borvel District close by in Battambang Province and all the Khmer Rouge jumped up and ran away to attack them. There was no one left to guard us so I had a chance. I ran away to Tagrey to find my family and the soldiers didn't see me leave because they were fighting the Vietnamese.

After I had escaped from Umpil I heard that many other people also got up and ran away to look for their families. I saw some of them in Tagrey. I stayed only one night in Tagrey and then all of my family escaped from there and went away to the Thai border. We walked on small paths in the forest. It was about a hundred kilometers and it took two weeks, maybe three. Walking in the forest is not so fast.

We had some food. I had prepared for a long time. I had heard that the Vietnamese might come two or three months before and when I heard it I started to prepare—to cook some rice and dry it in the sun and put it in a bag, little bit by little bit. I did it secretly. I didn't want anybody to see it. And my wife also was doing this so that when we joined together in Tagrey, we decided to use it to escape. We had to decide that. I said to myself, "If I stay here, I will have no face. I will die. Nobody will see me again. I will be covered by the ground." So we had to go.

When we first came to the border we didn't come into Thailand. We stayed in the Chomrontamey camp. It was a Khmer free camp. They were all refugees. So many kind of refugees in that camp. We stayed there for a month and in that camp it was very easy to get food and other things we needed. All the internationals—the UNHCR—knew that the refugees were there and they gave food to them. And I could bring wood from the forest and sell it in the market and get money to buy rice and other things.

After that, on October 24, 1979, they opened the border to receive the refugees to live in the Khao I Dang camp in Thailand. They had a bus like the Philippine bus to take all the people. And after that, they gave us clothing, medicine, pots to cook in, all that we needed. They took care of us very well. We were grateful to the UNHCR.

In Thailand I started teaching backward students. They sent me to the Sakeo 2 camp and I enrolled as a candidate to be a teacher. After I passed as a teacher I volunteered and they gave me an assignment to the special school. Out of a hundred and twenty teachers they assigned the special school to only one—to me—to build and organize it. No one else wanted it because all the students were mute or deaf, mentally retarded or physically handicapped.

I wanted to do it because I had sorrow for them—they had all been destroyed during Pol Pot's time. Some of them had been born that way but some had been punished and become mentally retarded. There were both adults and chidlren. I knew no sign language so I just compared the sound with the action. At first it was very difficult. I encouraged them by rewarding them with biscuits. Several of the deaf mutes started doing well and their parents spread the word. So people started to know about my work.

In 1982 I moved from Sakeo 2 back to Khao I Dang. There I had a new system to organize. I worked with a Thai assistant who went back and forth to Bangkok for me, going to the special school there. We were working on developing a sign language for Khmer people because at that time in Cambodia there was no sign language. There was just me and the Thai helper—two persons. I did not travel to Bangkok because I didn't have the freedom.

We used the Thai and English systems as a model. We had to compare them and get out the sounds to form into Khmer. We compared all the sounds. There were so many—consonants, vowels, punctuations, independent vowels. For the numbers we used the international signs—the same as Thai and English. Some sounds that are in Khmer are not in English or Thai and we had to make them up.

And so we developed a sign language for the Khmer people. After that, in late 1983 and 1984, we also developed a Braille system for the Khmer. We did it the same way as we had done the sign language, modelling it on the English and the Thai systems. My books have been sent to other countries like America, Canada, Australia. They are called *Braille* and *Sign Language*.

I left Khao I Dang in February 1985 and went to the Panat Nikhom transit center in Chunburi Province where I stayed three and a half months.

After that I left Thailand and came to the Philippines on 26 June, 1985. That was five months ago. I have three work credits here in this camp. One is with Community Mental Health and Family Services. The second is Socio-Cultural Chairman for the Khmer at the camp here. And the third is assistant teacher for the International Catholic Migration Commission. It makes me very busy.

My whole family is going to finish classes here on the 14th of December, 1985. I'm not sure when I am going to the United States but it will be soon after that.

My younger brother is a Buddhist monk in Boston. He was a monk in Thailand from sixteen years old. He wears the yellow robes — just like a sarong but very big. He escaped from Cambodia in 1974 before Pol Pot's time because he knew the situation was going to be bad. I am going to join him there. [PRPC, November 7, 1985.]

The Snake Who Became a Refugee

Told by Lucy*

This next story has become part of PRPC folklore. It makes the rounds of coffee klatch and cocktail party in the extended refugee community of United States and Filipino officialdom. This is the first time it has been recorded in print.

There used to be a snake in the camp. It was brought by a refugee family. It was nine feet long and it was a python. Many people came here to see that snake and there's a story about it.

There was a Khmer family who escaped from Cambodia and got to the Khao I Dang refugee camp in Thailand. They stayed there for several years and their children grew. When their son reached fifteen years old he decided he wanted to go back to join the guerrilla fighters in Cambodia and they couldn't stop him.

A few days before he left, the father woke one morning and saw a big snake inside their billet. Then he observed that the snake and the son who planned to go back to Cambodia seemed to have

*A Filipino staffer at the refugee camp.

129

a very special relationship — a kind of affinity. They were very close for the remaining days the son was still there in camp. He and the snake were always together, as though they were talking together or communicating somehow.

Then, when the son decided it was time for him to leave, he told the family, "I am leaving. But I've asked the snake to stay with you as my replacement." So he left. And the snake was left with the family and they started treating it as a child. It lived with them, slept with them, ate with them. They treated it just like the son.

Now the camp authorities knew there was a snake but because it was being like a son, like a person, they let it stay on.

The problem came when they were to come here to the Philippines. How would they transport the snake here? There was an attempt to make an arrangement for it to join them legally but it didn't go through. And so the family just placed the snake in a basket and got it to the Philippines without the authorities knowing it. They arrived in camp with the python in the basket.

They stayed in one of the neighborhoods here and the snake became an attraction. You would see refugee staff members and visitors having pictures taken with the python draped around them . . . everybody except me.

And since the family never heard from the son any more and because they were Buddhists, they believed that the son's spirit was in the snake and they kept on treating him like a member of the family. They took good care of him. They shampooed him. They put baby powder on him. And the snake had his own preferences too. He preferred people who visited him to wear perfume and he liked flowers. So sometimes when people went to visit him, they would bring flowers.

One time he got so tired with all the visitors that he started crawling up the ladder to the hut to take a nap. But the mother said, "I tell you, sit down there. We have visitors. You're not going anywhere until I fetch you a glass of water." And he came down and took the water. And the mother said, "Now you may go up and rest." And he did. So they took good care of the snake and all was well.

Then the problem arose again. Will they allow the snake to

go to the United States? The case was referred to us and we assigned it to one of our caseworkers. The caseworker made a report advocating that for cultural reasons and for religious reasons it would be best for the snake to remain with the family because they really believed that the spirit of the son had gone into the snake. The American government said, "We don't think it can be done."

So the family said, "OK, we will leave but, you know, that snake is our son. And if he really shouldn't go with us, he would have been left behind in Kao I Dang. The fact that we were able to get the snake away from Kao I Dang to the Philippines makes us believe that he is meant for us and therefore by all means that snake will go with us to the United States." Such faith they had.

So administrative matters were being done among the officers here. There was still misgiving. Some of the Americans found it hard to believe that anyone would treat a snake like a person. But some were sympathetic and thought that the family should have the snake.

Finally, about two weeks ago, we heard the good news. The snake had been given a special visa. So they prepared a box for him and put him on the plane. And one week after they departed we got a telex from the Joint Voluntary Agency. It said, "The eighth member of the family arrived without a ripple. He is now in a Buddhist temple." And so their faith was rewarded. [PRPC, October 24, 1985.]

These Vietnamese Are No Better Than Pol Pot

Heng Houn

Heng Houn is a small man, dark and very shy. When I met him in May of 1986 his face was set and clouded. He wriggled nervously in his seat and wrung his hands. Although he had been through the compulsory language lessons, he still spoke no English at all. The trauma of his life was so overwhelming that it was all he could do to make it through each day. This learning problem is very common amongst new refugees.

Heng Houn was wrestling with a Catch-22 of United States immigration law. After arriving in the Philippines two years previously, his wife had lapsed into a state of severe depression. Her husband was convinced that if she could join her mother in the United States she would recover but United States law required that she demonstrate mental stability for a period of three months before she could leave.

Most refugees spend up to a maximum of six months in the Philippine Refugee Processing Center. When I met Heng Houn in May of 1986 the family had been there for two years. When I left the Philippines in August of that year they were still there.

I used to be a farmer in Cambodia. I lived in Talam village in Battambang Province. When I was seven years old I went to school in the temple but I had no mother and after five years I had to stop studying to help the family. There were five children in all — an older brother and sister, me, and a younger brother and sister.

We grew rice on a farm forty kilometers square. We had a farmer's house — not too big. It was raised off the ground on stilts and made of wood with fibro roofing. For working we wore shirts and cotton pants, sometimes long and sometimes short. Work clothes were always a dark color — black or dark blue. After work we would change into lighter colors. The clothes were always the same style. The men wore baggy shirts hanging out over loose pants. The women wore blouses over a sarong.

Rural Cambodia has pleasant weather. We had a rainy season and a windy season but we didn't have big storms like in other countries. It is never cold. Cool but not enough for warm clothes.

It was a pleasant enough life and I lived quietly there until twenty-one years of age when I married a girl from the Pralay Loun Loen area and went on with the business of the farm.

Then the Khmer Rouge came. They would go into the villages and force the people to go with them to the jungle so we became afraid to go too far from our houses in our farm work in case we should be caught and carried off. Two of my cousins were taken like this.

When people were taken away, nobody dared to ask why. The Khmer Rouge said, "You have to go," and they had to go. Some people did manage to escape and come back to their homes but most never came home again. I don't know what happened to them. The people who came back told us that the Khmer Rouge had said, "You have to learn from us. We will train you. Most important, you have to grow rice for us."

"What for?" they asked.

"We will train you to get your country out of the problems brought on by the Lon Nol government. Don't try to escape from us. But if you should go back home don't say anything bad about us. If you do we will follow and kill you." So the people didn't talk about them. They were afraid.

Molina Humphrey, interpreter for this and a number of the other oral histories, with her husband, Ben.

The Khmer Rouge were coming more and more all the time until I felt I could not stay there on the farm any longer so I moved into the city of Battambang, taking my wife and little son with me. My brother and sister left the farm too but they went off another way.

In Battambang I had to find a new occupation so I took work as a tricycle operator, the sort that you pedal. I made a bare living at this. I could have made more money if I had taken passengers for long distances but I was afraid to go out of the city and so only did short trips like taking people from home to market and back. It was not enough but I was afraid to venture into the countryside.

The Khmer Rouge came into the city and fought every day until 1975.

One day in 1975 at six o'clock in the evening I saw with my own eyes many Khmer Rouge soldiers. They were dressed all in black—shirts, pants and hats—and carried guns. They had many big pictures of Sambech Euv Sihanouk* on their cars and they drove around the city showing them to all the people and calling to us, "Here, here, Sambech Euv is here. Come to receive Sambech Euv. He is coming to help save you from the Lon Nol regime. Come to us. Come to us. Sambech Euv, Sambech Euv is here." They knew that the people loved the King Father and they were trying to fool them into thinking, "Sambech Euv is coming. Sambech Euv is coming." I said to myself, "Wow! Sambech Euv is back. Everything is going to be all right." They lied to us.

The next day they made an announcement. "All military men! You must bring your guns to us at the bridge statues."† And the Khmer Rouge stood by the statues at the ends of the bridges and the military brought all their guns and weapons and left them there.

Then the Khmer Rouge called all the military together to a meeting in the assembly. There they told them, "All the officers are to go to the capital, Phnom Penh, to receive Sambech Euv." And they sent them all off. The enlisted men they sent off in another direction—we call it the Road of Mom.

The day after that I saw the wife of one of the officers. She broke down and cried. "They have taken my husband and killed him."

After the Khmer Rouge had taken over the city they went to the big warehouses and stores where bread and rice and so on were stored and sold. They opened the doors and called to all the poor people, "We have come here to help you. Come and get food. Take the rice. Take the bread. Take everything. You don't have to pay for it."

I could not work with my tricycle any more because no one wanted to use me so I went with the others to get free rice and bread. I was very happy. I thought, "The Khmer Rouge really have come to help. At last the fighting is going to be over. There

*We called him Sambech Euv, which means King Father, because we loved him very much. —Interpreter.

†In Cambodia there are statues at each end of every bridge, many of the Buddha; the Khmer make beautiful statues. —Interpreter.

will be no more rockets coming into the city. They really are going to be good to us. They will give us food and we will never be hungry again." But no, it was not like this. The Khmer Rouge had lied to the people to make them think that they were very nice.

I went to get food but I couldn't because there were too many people. And the free food was only for one day. After that they said, "That's enough. If you want food you have to buy it from us—the Khmer Rouge. It will be very cheap. One kilo of pork for only twenty-five riel." So there was one day of selling.

Then they made another announcement. (They had loud hailers and they rode all around the city on tricycles, one pedalling and one shouting through a loud hailer to the people.) "Everybody has to get out of Battambang because we have to fight. We have to clear out our enemies. Anyone who does not leave will be shot. Do not go to another city. Get out from the city and go into the countryside."

Then Khmer Rouge with guns were on the streets, coming to the houses, chasing people away. We found out later that this was happening all over the country.

People panicked. They ran and picked up their things and left. They were terrified of being shot. I had no choice. I snatched up a few possessions and a small bag to carry them in, took my wife and son and fled from the house onto the road. The whole city was out on the road, some running, some walking, all of them in fear.

Before long we came to a place called Thmar Kaul and there, in the ditch that ran alongside the road, I saw the bodies of the military. Pol Pot had killed them, many, many of them. Too many to count. Too many to bury one by one. I heard later that they had used a tractor to get all these bodies into the ditch.

I could not stand there and look. Pol Pot's soldiers were all along the side of the road saying, "Go! Go! Go!" Some had their bayonets fixed. But I was weak from hunger and could not run any more or even walk fast. I crept along little bit by little bit. Maybe thirty minutes it took me to pass these awful sights.

I headed for a village called Mongkol Borey because my mother-in-law lived there and I was hoping that I would be able to find her but when I got there she had run away, I don't know where. So I went off in another direction for about ten kilometers until I came to a part of the jungle where Pol Pot's soldiers were allowing people to stop.

They said, "O.K. You can stay here but you have to build huts for yourselves. You have to cut grass and you have to cut wood and you have to build your houses by yourselves." There were about one hundred of us there.

Then they said, "You have to form working groups." And so we did. Group number one, group number two, group number three. I was in the third group. Each group was given a leader, one of Pol Pot's men from the jungle.

Then they called us all together for a meeting. The man from the jungle who was in charge stood up before us and said, "I am in charge here. I represent Pol Pot. You are the People of March Seventeen. This was the day you were delivered from Lon Nol. It is a great day for you and you will be called by it."

He went on, "I want to know your backgrounds. Tell me your backgrounds. Where are you from?" Tell me who you are so we will help you." One at a time the people told all about themselves. They told the truth — this one was military, this one was a teacher. They didn't know any better.

Then the leader said to the teachers and the military men, "We are going to send you away for training. You need to learn new things. You need some background on what we are planning to do to help your country."

There were ten of them altogether. They were very happy and went off into the jungle willingly. I watched them go and I remembered how the military had been taken out of Battambang. I remembered how they had been deceived into thinking that they were going to Phnom Penh to welcome Sambech Euv. Then I remembered what I had seen along the road from Battambang and my heart became heavy inside me. I said to myself, "They are getting rid of the fighters and the thinkers so that we cannot stand against them." And they never came back. No one ever found out for sure what happened to them but I know in my heart that they were all killed.

Then there was another meeting. This time they said, "Everyone who has gold or jewelry must give it to us. If you want to keep it you are our enemy." They made a rough table, a piece of wood laid over two supports, and we had to line up in front of it and lay down our watches and our rings and our gold one by one. They watched us very carefully to see if we might be holding anything back. A few people, in their fear, forgot that they were wearing gold around their necks and the Khmer Rouge snatched it from them. Others hid it on their bodies and were found out. One man hid a gold chain by putting it around his ankle inside the cuff of his trousers but the Khmer Rouge knew all the hiding places and very few were successful in keeping what they had.

For the first three days they gave us rice to eat. After that they said, "Don't eat rice any more. Eat rice soup." And they gave us one milk can of rice for ten people for a day. (A milk can is about six inches high.) They handed out the food saying, "Here, that's enough for you."

We were called together for another meeting. The leader said, "I want you to listen to me very carefully. We are going to work hard here. We are going to grow rice and we are going to eat rice, OK? It's not going to be like the last government. They grew rice on the backs of the people. They made slaves out of your bodies. We are different. We are all farmers together. Please, try to understand that what we are doing here is important for the recovery of your country." We knew that what they said about the previous government was not true but we dared not say so.

Then they started to work us hard day and night. We tilled the ground and grew rice. We cut wood and carried it back to the camp for firewood. I worked so hard. We all did. I always tried to finish what I was assigned quickly but as soon as it was done I was given more to do. I never relaxed. At night time we had no light. We worked in the fields at night by the light of burning rice husks.

When the Khmer Rouge ordered us to do this we had to do it. When they ordered us to go this way we had to go this way. If we hadn't they would have said, "You are our enemy" and killed us right away. What I am telling you is the truth that I saw with my own eyes and heard with my own ears. What happened in other places I do not know. I could not go away from that place.

When Pol Pot's men wanted to teach the people they would order us to stop work and then they would hold a meeting from six in the morning till five in the afternoon. We had rice soup at twelve, then back to the meeting again. These meetings were not regular. Sometimes we would have one every other day, sometimes there would be three or four days or a week in between. We never knew when to expect them.

Before the meeting started, the soldiers would say, "All of you pay attention. You must listen carefully to everything we tell you. It is very important for your country. If you fall asleep we will know that you are our enemy, that you don't love your country and we will have to kill you."

Then they would start to teach us. They would tell us, "If you want to build your country you must work hard. If you want to eat coconuts, you must grow the coconuts. If you grow coconuts from here to Battambang then, when you are on the road from here to Battambang you can stop anywhere you want and have coconuts to eat. If you work hard you will get the rewards."

They looked down on the Buddhist religion. "Hah," they said. "The monks are very lazy. They are selfish. That is why they want to be monks. If you want a religion to make change in your country, set your will to get water from the river to make your farm grow the best it can. Make a religion out of your work."

"You know," they would say, "in Cambodia we have a lot of rice. In other countries they have tractors and other machines to work their farms. We don't like that. We grow our rice by our own labor. We could easily buy a tractor for just two three-hundred-kilogram sacks of rice. But we choose not to do that. It is best to do it with our own labor."

And so they talked and talked, all the day long. It was propaganda and lies. Much of what they said was pure nonsense. Everybody had to pay attention because they were afraid of being killed. Then they would ask, "Any questions? Would anyone like to say something?" But no one dared.

They would try to look as though they cared about us. They would say, "Here is your food. Is it enough?"

We were very hungry but too afraid to say so. "Yes, yes, that's enough," we would say. We knew that anyone who dared to complain would be killed right away. "You are never satisfied with what we do for you," they would say. "You are our enemy." And that person would be taken away and never seen again.

There was a boy, only ten years old. He didn't know what he was doing. He said, "Before when we were farmers we ate rice. Now when we work so hard as farmers we don't have rice to eat, only rice soup." When Pol Pot's soldiers heard that, they took the boy and killed him.

Pol Pot's men knew perfectly well where the good rice growing country was. But they hadn't chosen to go there. Instead they had chosen a very dry place. The ground was hard and it was difficult to break it up but they forced us to do it. My friends and I tried to improvise a plow to dig the dry land but they said, "If you do that we will kill you."

Rice needs a lot of water and there was no irrigation. We had to carry the water from the canal. We spent a lot of our time hauling water. We worked very hard at it because it was our lives. Sometimes they told me to use my hands to get the people's stools to throw on the farm to fertilize it. In the rainy season the stools had big worms in them. It was my life so I had to do it.

My wife and my son became very skinny — like skeletons. As for me, the rice soup was not enough to keep me alive. The only reason I still have life in me now is because I ate leaves. They kept me from dying.

The first rice harvest was approaching. One day they ordered ten of us to take wagons hooked up to cows and go into the city of Mongkol Borey to carry back a big load of wood. On the way to the city we went by a canal and in it I saw many statues of Buddha, big ones and small ones, some of them broken. They had hauled them all to the canal and thrown them there. I said to myself, "They are trying to do away with our religion," and I was sad.

When we arrived in the city it was very quiet. No one was around except Pol Pot's military. The houses were all closed up and the market was deserted. The soldiers had us load up the wagons with big pieces of lumber and ordered us to carry it back to the area of our camp to build a warehouse for the rice.

When harvest time came we gathered the rice and dried it in the sun and shook out the husks in the wind. There was a lot of it but when it was ready they kept only a little for us and the rest went to the warehouse to be sent away. They told us, "This rice is for the big leaders somewhere else. It is not for you. You eat rice soup."

So after working so hard to grow all that rice we still only got a little as rice soup. They themselves ate a lot of rice. They were fat and very healthy. They ate chickens and fish and vegetables and sometimes they would give us one leg of chicken between all of us.

The people were in a terrible condition. They got sick. Their bodies swelled from lack of food and they got diarrhea and stomach pains from eating strange things — roots, leaves, insects, rats, anything they could lay their hands on. They went to the hospital and there was no medicine. It was no hospital at all. It was just a long building with many small cots for dying. And the people lay down on the cots and died there. This "hospital" was five hundred or so meters from the camp. It was used by a number of similar camps in the area around.

In the daytime there were only three soldiers with us in the camp — the leader, the assistant leader and the secretary. These three did not change over the time I was there. They had their wives and children with them in the camp. But at night we saw many, many soldiers. We never knew how many. They would come and hide and spy on us, listening to hear if they could catch anyone talking. When they did that person would not be in the camp any longer the next morning. The nights were very dark and fearful.

We lived like this for four years. After the first year and a half there were only thirty left of the original hundred. Ten babies were born but they were very skinny and five of them died. My son was one of those who survived.

Then in 1979 the Vietnamese came to Cambodia. They came to our camp and I saw them fighting. I saw Pol Pot's men being chased out by the Vietnamese and I ran away. I could not go back to Talam or to Battambang City so I went to Mongkol Borey which was where my mother-in-law had lived. But Pol Pot's men had taken everything so I got some wood and set about building another place to live.

Just like the Khmer Rouge, the Vietnamese said, "We have come here to help you. Khmer and Vietnamese, we will stick together and work together and share together. We love the Khmer." But it wasn't true. When the Vietnamese saw Khmer chickens they took them and ate them by themselves. When they saw coconuts they took them and ate them by themselves. When they saw cows they shot them and ate the beef themselves.

Then they ordered the Khmer to be farmers just like Pol Pot had done. Immediately I said to myself, "Oh, they will not save us. These Vietnamese are no better than Pol Pot. They will do to us just the same as Pol Pot did."

I remembered my grandfather telling me how the Vietnamese used to take three Khmer heads and set them in a triangle on the ground. Then they would light a fire in the triangle and set a pot on the heads for a stove. I thought about this and I thought about the war that would certainly swallow up our country and I was afraid. I could not stay with the Vietnamese regime. I had to escape. So I decided to try to get to the border with Thailand.

I set off walking through the jungle with my wife and my two sons. It wasn't easy for them. One was only a baby. We took some rice with us and a small pot. When we were hungry we stopped and cooked some of the rice.

We went for three days and three nights and I saw many other people making their way through the jungle—escaping just like us. I didn't know how to get to the border but everyone was going and we asked each other and so we made our way. It is flat countryside in that part of Cambodia, especially close to the border, and the jungle is not dense. Fortunately it was the dry season.

On the fourth day in the morning we came to the border and there we saw a big truck. It was the UNHCR and they asked us, "Who wants to go to Khao I Dang?" I was so happy.

I stayed in Thailand for four years in the Khao I Dang and Surin camps. We had two more babies, one in each camp. We had our last baby here in the Philippines. She is eight months old. All the rest are boys. The oldest is now twelve, then eight, five and four.

After we escaped from Cambodia and all those fearful times were over my wife became sick. She lost two brothers under Pol Pot's regime and doesn't know what happened to them. Also, she was not poor before all this happened. Not too rich but she had a nice house and some jewelry. Pol Pot took all that. Then there was the camp with no food and nothing but hard labor and death for four years.

She started to think too much about the past and it made her sick. Sometimes she would seem quite normal but other times she would go away inside her head and not be able to do anything. I could not leave her alone.

Most people are here in the Philippine camp for only a few months but we have had to stay on because of my wife's illness. We have been here for over two years now. It is too long. The children have finished the school program and there is nothing more for them to do. I have been very worried about them. I even requested that they be allowed to go ahead to the United States so that they could go to school.

I tried very hard to make everything run smoothly so that my wife would get better but I would get so worried about her and what was going to happen to my children that I was upset all the time. I tried to learn English but I could not get anything in my mind. I had to be constantly seeing to this and to that for the children, doing the cooking and taking care of the baby and my wife. And I felt bad because I had no time to find a way to make a little money so that the children could have treats sometimes like the other refugee children—cookies or a small toy. I got overwrought and anxious and sometimes I thought I would die before all of them.

But now my wife is getting better. She understands that the United States immigration laws will not allow her to leave here until she is and she has been trying very hard. She has started growing bean sprouts and selling them in the market place. She combs her hair and tries to look nice. She is taking care of the children and doing the cooking again.

I am much happier now. I am sure that she will be completely well very soon and then we can go and join her parents who are in the United States now. (We met up with them again in Khao I Dang but they were a separate case from us and they went on ahead of us.) They are in Utah waiting for us. They have enough money to help us get started and we also have a brother and a sister there who will help. [PRPC, April 24, 1986; as of August 1986 Heng Houn and his family were still in the Philippine Refugee Processing Center with no indication of when they would be able to leave — J.S.]

The Eyes That Watched Me

Meach Pok

When first interviewing refugees I was very hesitant to probe too deeply for fear of upsetting them. And, indeed, some did weep as they told their stories. Some became angry and others simply recounted the horror of their lives with no show of emotion. As time went on I became braver and found that my questions were welcomed rather than resented. I would come back time after time, demanding dates and place names, asking for locations on maps and insisting that inconsistencies be cleared up. I became immersed in getting as close to the truth as possible and found myself inured to the suffering of the story-tellers.

Not until I set out to drive home through the mountain sunset would the pain of the day bear down in a cloud of exhaustion and I would blow it away in a blast of country music. Dolly Parton's crystal voice will always take me back to that winding drive through the Philippine mountains, the shining red sea glimpsed at intervals to the right, the children in their blue and white uniforms walking home from school in the dust of the roadside and their parents, on crude benches outside their huts, suspended in time at the end of the working day.

It was after one such drive that I bathed and dressed and went off to one of the interminable cocktail parties that diplomats are expected to smile through. I fell into conversation with an Englishman, a representative of his country. He asked me what I was doing to keep myself busy. I told him. He

147

looked amused. "Refugees, eh?" he said. "Well now, don't you think those chappies are laying it on just a bit thick?"

My name is Meach Pok and I left my country because Pol Pot killed my family and I could not stay there.

Before that I was a farmer. We lived in Kompong Speu village close to Phnom Penh. We grew rice and thnot. Thnot is similar to coconut. The tree looks like a small palm. It was our own farm. It belonged to my husband, Miet Pin. I don't know how to measure it. It was not big but enough for our family. We had a small wooden house.

When Pol Pot's troops came to Cambodia, they killed and beat the people. They forced them to work hard but they never gave them enough food to eat. They didn't let anybody stay in their own houses. They said, "You have to get out of your house, your village. You cannot stay here."

I don't really know why they told everybody to get out. They just said, "We have to make a new policy in this country. We don't want you to stay in the same house as before. We want you to learn something new." My family was moved from Kompong Speu. They separated us from each other and sent us to different villages.

I heard later that my fifteen-year-old daughter had been put in prison and made to do hard labor. They were going to kill her but a soldier pitied her and released her. So right now I still have one daughter in Cambodia. Somebody who just escaped from there told me that in 1981 she was staying with her uncle in Battambang City. She was O.K. then but I have heard nothing since. She is twenty-one years old now.

My husband and me they sent to other farms. I never saw him again but four years later I heard that he had died because he was hungry.

They forced me to do heavy work on the farm, to grow rice and to carry great loads on my back. I didn't have enough rice to eat and my knee swelled up bigger than my head. They gave me no medicine except for a small, black pill that looked like a rabbit dropping. I don't know what it was. I took it and . . . nothing. I still had to work.

We lived in a hut. It was maybe twelve or fourteen feet square. At first there were sixteen women in my hut — then eighteen, then twenty, then more than twenty. The hut had only a roof and poles to hold it up. Storms would come and the wind would drive the rain through the hut. We would be cold and wet and the floor would become mud.

They made us stay together like this because Pol Pot wanted to train all the women to work hard.

There were other huts like this around — not very close but we could see them because there were only scattered trees in that area. All the women worked on the farm but we were not allowed to visit each other's huts.

And we were not allowed to talk to the other people in our hut. There were guards. They watched us. If anyone talked they would kill them right away so we just kept quiet and worked and kept quiet and worked and ate and slept — no talking.

At six o'clock in the morning everybody would wake up and go to the farm and work. There was no morning meal. At twelve o'clock they gave us lunch but a very small amount — rice soup, almost water, two big spoons for each person. After we had eaten that we had to go back to work. Then at six o'clock we went back to the hut. Two more spoons of watery soup and they let us rest.

Sometimes they would call a meeting at night. They said we had to learn a new policy. They told us their Communist prop-aganda and we had to listen. Every meeting they would say, "Now there is a new policy here — the Communist policy. You have to work hard. You have to rebuild your country. This is good — to rebuild your country. Before you were so lazy. You didn't want to work. You just relaxed and took your time. You didn't do anything to rebuild your country. So now we don't want you to talk to the other people here because we don't want you to waste your time. When you work, think about the work and don't try to talk. We don't like that and we are very strict about it. If you don't obey the rules here, you will see."

People did talk to each other sometimes. If it was about work then they wouldn't do anything. But if it was about the past or if they criticized the new policy or wanted to know about what was happening in another place, they would catch them and kill them. They killed many people.

I never saw anyone killed with my own eyes but I saw them tied and taken away by the soldiers. I knew that they would be killed then. Many people were taken away like that and none of them came back. I have heard from many people that they killed them with knives or hit them until they were dead. And they would take pieces of sharp bamboo and stab the women in the breasts and in the vagina before they killed them. The women were mostly wives of military officers and government officials. In my hut sometimes four or five would be taken away at once, sometimes nine or ten.

My parents were killed and my uncle and brother and sister. I don't know where they were or how they died. I just heard about it.

The reason they killed all those people was because they didn't want them to talk about the old regime or remind each other what it had been like before. They had spies in amongst us and they would listen. Always they spied upon us.

I was always very careful. I never talked. I didn't dare. The soldiers would tell us, "We have eyes to watch you." I never knew where were the eyes that watched me and there were guards all around so I obeyed everything.

When people got sick they would not give them any food to eat and so they would just die. When they found that people had died in the hut they would take them and bury them in the dirt. There was no coffin.

When I got sick, they said, "O.K. You are sick. You cannot have any rice." And they left me hungry. But my friends took such pity on me that they hid some dog meat and gave it to me. I didn't know it was dog meat. I thought it was beef. I don't know where they got it from.

After the Vietnamese Communists fought with Pol Pot and took over our country, there was great confusion all around and all the people tried to escape through the jungle. They wanted to get away from Cambodia because they were even more afraid of the Vietnamese Communists than of Pol Pot's soldiers.

My children saw the Vietnamese soldiers come. They saw many people killed. They ran away to the farm where they had heard I was and they found me and I ran with them. I didn't know anything. I was afraid. I just ran and ran. And then we came into the jungle and we just kept on going. We saw many people die on the way. They had no food and they died as they went through the forest.

We did not die. We went on and begged for food and went on. We went through the jungle and over the mountains, I don't know for how long, until we came to the Thai border.

I didn't see any Communist soldiers in the jungle — only the Thai military near the border. They didn't know who was Khmer Rouge and who was not so any Khmer they caught they killed. They were protecting the border.

Many people slipped across by themselves but we were found by a group of internationals from UNHCR. They knew there were many refugees coming from Thailand and they were waiting to help them. They had a big truck and they looked like Americans. They put all the people into the truck and took us across the border to the Khao I Dang camp.

That was in 1979. We lived and worked there and my children went to school.

Then, on August 7, 1985, I came here to the Philippines. And now I am forty-seven years old. I don't know when I will go to the United States or where I will go when I get there. [PRPC, November 6, 1985; Meach Pok left for the United States on February 20, 1986. She now lives in Portland, Oregon — J.S.]

Weep for My Children

Told by Nina

This story was told to me by a Filipino social worker in a little cramped office in the Community Mental Health Services building at the refugee camp. The door and the louvred windows were wide open in the hope of catching any passing breeze. A ceiling fan clicked monotonously overhead and the thick tropical air stirred clammily beneath it.

There were four of us — myself and three Filipino staffers. They spoke to me of the emotional trauma that they dealt with day-to-day among refugees who had been abused or raped, had lost loved ones or had seen them killed.

The mental turmoil following rape is an especially hard one to deal with. This story is about a Cambodian but many Vietnamese women who have escaped by boat have been raped not once but many times, and this at a time when they were already in fear for their lives.

A common reaction is guilt. The woman feels guilty because she feels that somehow she attracted the attack. The husband feels guilty because he had to stand by and watch and could do nothing to help. Sometimes this guilt translates into anger and violence later on, sometimes it causes impotence.

They told me of an old man who had been on a boat where all the women were raped while the men were held at gunpoint. None of them were relatives of his but he had nightmares afterwards for many months and would wake in the night crying out and blaming himself.

153

There was a Cambodian lady in camp and I was asked to get in touch with her. She was rather young, maybe in her early thirties. She was well educated and came from a very rich family. She had two daughters with her. One was thirteen years old but she looked only about nine years old...very undernourished. The second was also a girl, about two years old.

This lady was always having headaches but the doctors couldn't find anything wrong with her so they recommended counselling. The first time I went to visit I couldn't find her so I left a message that I would like to see her.

When she came to the office she was very fearful. "Why are you looking for me?" That was always the reaction of Cambodians in the early years of this camp. They were so scared when we went to the village and said, "Good afternoon. Is so-and-so in?"

It was because in Cambodia Pol Pot's soldiers would come and say, "So-and-so, can you come with me to the office?" or "Can you come fishing with me?" And they would never return.

When we were first working here, we wouldn't see any men when we went down to the Cambodian neighborhoods. There were only women in the families. The men had all been killed.

Now the story of the lady was this. Her husband was dead. He had been a navy officer and he was hurt in the war and so he was paralyzed. Then later on, during Pol Pot's time, he was beaten to death...clubbed to death in front of her because they were trying to kill all the government officials and educated people. There was great persecution.

When Pol Pot's soldiers took over, this woman and her family had gone into hiding in a village and lived just like the other villagers but somehow they were traced and hunted down. The soldiers tried to get the husband to come with them but he refused and so they killed him right in front of his wife and child. They had had five children—four sons, but three of them had died of starvation.

So the woman escaped with her one little son and her daughter. They were going through the mountains when she found that the baby son she had in her arms had died of starvation too. So all her family was dead except her and her little daughter.

Then they were captured by Pol Pot's soldiers and put in prison. Somehow the soldiers never harmed the little girl. They liked her. And the woman was clever. She put dirt on her face and made herself ugly. That kept her from being raped. But she was tortured many times. They wanted to know her identity and she would not tell. So they would put her in a plastic sheet and tie it all up around her until she suffocated and fainted and then they would open it up and throw water on her. Then she would have to go and work in the fields and cut down trees.

One day she lost the knife she was using in the forest. She was so frightened that she could not look for it properly. But there was a European in the forest and he had a metal detector and he helped her look for it. He was able to pick up where it was and gave it back to her. She did not know who he was or where he came from but she was seen with him and accused of having contacts with the outside and they put her in isolation in the prison. The daughter pitied the mother and got leftovers from the soldiers and brought them to her. That is how she survived in prison.

Then the Vietnamese soldiers took over Cambodia and all the prisoners were to be executed before they got to the camp where she was. All the other prisoners were massacred but she escaped with her daughter.

She was going to make her way to Thailand but she was caught by some resistance fighters who were hidden in the forest, and raped. By the time she reached Thailand she found she was pregnant. She wanted to get rid of the baby. She said, "If only I could get rid of this baby. I don't want to keep it. But how can I do it? I don't know how." So there was no other way but to keep it. And she gave birth in the Khao I Dang camp in Thailand and the baby was another girl.

All through that time and until she came to the camp here in the Philippines she had no time to resolve all her emotional problems. She was very calm and that was what saved her life.

But when she got here she started having severe headaches and she would come to my office and sit down and cry and cry and shake all over. And she would say, "I don't understand all of this. My husband has been dead a long time now. It's seven years since he was killed but it is now that I am missing him." And there was so much anger and so much pressure on her because she had wanted to get rid of the baby and couldn't.

So I said to her, "For all these years you have been so busy trying to stay alive that you have had no time to grieve. But now there is no danger to your life any more and all the hurting is coming out. This is the time that you are recalling your loss and so you are having all these symptoms—fear, a lot of fear and crying and headaches and hatred for your baby daughter."

At the time she was coming to my office I used to have a collection of dolls on the shelves. One day she said, "Can I have one of those dolls?" So I gave her one. "And could I have another one?" So she got a second one. She told me, "I need these two dolls for my children." But the dolls were not for the girls. They were never played with. They were used by her at night. She would take them into the bed with her and they would help her to remember two of her dead children. She told me this later.

The time went along and one day she came and said she needed money. So I said perhaps I could help her if she would tell me what the money was to be used for but she wouldn't say.

She used to wear a sarong all the time. But one day I saw her in pants and commented on how lovely she looked. Later, she came to me and cried and said, "You know you said how lovely I looked? I used to wear pants but I tell you I am so ashamed and so upset because I have no undergarments and I don't know how to manage."

And that was an important lesson to me in my work with other refugees. I am always conscious that they might be too embarrassed to say, "I need some underwear." Things like that can bother them a great deal.

So we went shopping and she picked out some nice nylon underwear. And when she got home her little girl looked at it and said, "Oh my, I must have some of those." And so we got the little girl some nice underwear too.

Then one day this woman said to me, "You know, I pity my daughter because with me it is so different. I was brought up in a very happy environment. I had all the enjoyment and comfort I could want. And I knew what it was like to wear something expensive. But my child has never experienced that. Every night she opens the underwear that you gave her and she looks at it piece by piece and folds it back. And she says, "It is so pretty. But I will save it and wear it some day when I get to America. Yes, that's the time I will wear it." [PRPC, October 24, 1985.]

Laos—
Land of the Seminar Camps

Not So Wonderful
Was That Time

Khamsamong Somvong

Khamsamong is a gentle man with straight black hair brushed down over one side of his forehead, one discolored front tooth and, these days, a comfortable bulge over the belt. Although he looks sad much of the time, his face lights up and glows when he smiles.

He always met me, beaming, with the standard Lao greeting — hands raised almost to the forehead, templed as if in prayer. After the first few times of putting my hand out to him I found myself using the same greeting. I was in his territory and the Western handshake somehow seemed gauche.

My meetings with Khamsamong were interrupted by the Philippine revolution. During this time American officials living in Manila were asked not to travel out of the city for fear of getting into trouble and tying up valuable security staff. When I finally got to see him after the furor had died down and the streets outside Camp Crame and Camp Aguinaldo were clear of people and debris, allowing me access to the highway to Clark Air Base and on to Bataan, I asked, "Well, what do you think of the revolution here?"

He looked solemn. "Ma'am, I saw it before also in my own country. After the new government all the people were so happy, so happy. But then the Communists tricked us. They said they wanted a coalition government but they tricked us. And then they killed us. Do not trust them, ma'am. Do not ever trust the Communists."

Asking around the camp I found that, even though the refugees were not fully aware of all that had happened in Manila, the knowledge that a revolution was under way had brought terror to many hearts. Some were near panic, thinking that they had escaped, only to fall into the same situation again.

I am a civilian but I used to be in the military. I was a first lieutenant and a graduate from the Military Academy of Laos. I attended a leadership course in Fort Knox, Kentucky, and a Ranger Airborne course in Fort Benning, Georgia, graduating in 1972.

I came back from the United States in 1973 to a very mixed-up situation in Laos. There were three main conflicting political groups — the rightists who were loyal to the royal government, the leftists or Pathet Lao who were supported by the Vietnamese Communists and the neutralists who were a military faction originally headed by General Kong Le. (General Kong Le went to Thailand on official business in 1967. While he was there, Colonel Somphet took the opportunity to prevent him from coming back to his old position. On his return, Kong Le went to the Indonesian Embassy in Vientiane for help and they took him to Indonesia. About two years later he went on to France, where he still is.)

The leftists were headed by Souphanouvong and Kaisone Phomvihane, the rightists by Souvanna Phouma. The power of the leftists became greater than that of the neutralists and loyalists. They spread propaganda among the students and the civil servants and even some of the military in order to make them disobey the orders of Prime Minister Souvanna Phouma.

Then a convention was held in Paris for peace talks. Henry Kissinger was there and Le Duc Tho of Vietnam. Le Duc Tho promised a cease-fire in Laos and, on February 21, 1973, an agreement was reached between the rightists, the leftists and the neutralists that a coalition government would be formed between the three groups.* It was also agreed that Vientiane and Luang

---

*The agreement referred to is the Agreement on Restoring Peace and Achieving National Concord in Laos, also referred to as "The Vientiene Agreement." It was signed in Vientiane by Pheng Phongsavanh for the Vientiane Government and Phoumi Vongvichit for the Laotian Patriotic Forces. —J.S.

Khamsamong Somvong.

Prabang cities were to be neutral territory so that the three groups could come together to work out a plan.

In September of that year a sub-convention was held in Vientiane City and the National Political Coalition Council was formed to implement the Vientiane Agreement. This council was composed of sixteen leftists, sixteen rightists and ten neutralists, forty-two members in all. Five of the neutralists were nominated by the leftists and five by the rightists.

Then, in May of 1974, the National Political Coalition Council met in Vientiane City. Eighteen political resolutions were issued [see page 173]. On paper they looked very good for the future of Laos. But not so wonderful was that time.

The political situation was still very mixed up and very confused. General Vang Pao continued airborne bombing of the leftist area and it was not to be until May of 1975 that the Royal Lao Army would disarm. (The only Hmong general in the Lao Army, General Vang Pao was Commander of the Second Military Region, Xieng Khouang Province. He now lives in California.)

Once they had got themselves into power, the Pathet Lao ignored the eighteen political resolutions. It had all been a ploy to allay the fears of the people and bluff the international community. And the agreement to the neutrality of Vientiane and Luang Prabang was just to enable them to bring Pathet Lao troops into those cities so that they could follow their plan to take over full control of the government.

Then the Pathet Lao set about breaking up the Lao military by separating out the higher ranks — the generals, the senior officers, the junior officers, the noncommissioned officers — to keep us from forming groups to fight against them.

In the Vang Vieng area of Vientiane Province the Pathet Lao gathered approximately four hundred junior officers. I was one of them. We waited there going through a political orientation of the Communists. They taught some very good things like independence, economic development, freedom of speech, respect for the individual and so on.

And we were waiting, waiting, and undergoing this political orientation until the king of Laos fell down. It happened like this:

Most of the Lao people didn't understand what the Communists were up to. They were just anxious to see peace in their time and no more war in their country. They were still loyal to the king, but they were also swayed by the Pathet Lao. They didn't understand. But the Pathet Lao did and on October 11, 1975, they decided to exploit the people's divided loyalties to bring about the downfall of the coalition.

They gathered together a great crowd of people under the pretext of denouncing the rightists and congratulating the National Political Coalition Council.

These people moved through Luang Prabang City and when they came to the Provincial Office, Pathet Lao soldiers gave them posters demonstrating against King Sri Savang Vatthana.

When the people saw the posters, they realized the cunning of the Pathet Lao. They wanted to disperse but they could not. It was too late. The Pathet Lao had set up armed troops everywhere and the people were in a tumult. They cried to the king to resign from his throne and he agreed. They had not intended to do this. They had not understood where their actions would lead.

By December 2, 1975, the Pathet Lao were full of power. They had organized their forces — tanks, anti-aircraft guns, infantry batallions — ready to take over the whole country. Then they commanded Crown Prince Vongsavang to read the King's official resignation from the throne and declared the Lao People's Democratic Republic.

Prince Souphanouvong, who had been the official leader of the leftists before the coalition, became president and speaker of the Supreme People's Council, with the king designated as his advisor. Kaisone Phomvihane, who had plotted with Souphanouvong from the outside, became prime minister. He was the puppet of the Vietnamese Communists. Prince Souvanna Phouma was made a government advisor and Crown Prince Vongsavang a member of the Supreme People's Council.

The seven persons making up the Lao Politburo were now members of the Supreme People's Council. This meant the end of the Kingdom of Laos. The leftists had full power and would rule the people in the ways of Marx and Lenin.

And then they sent us to reeducation ["seminar"] camps. Laos has many, many camps — in the Viengxay area in the north, in Xieng Khouang Province, in Saravanh province and in many other places.

On December 31, 1975, I was moved to Xieng Khouang Province with the rest of the four hundred junior officers who had been taken with me. We were moved by a convoy of trucks and the Pathet Lao held guns on us. We didn't have any way to fight back. No, no, we didn't have any way. We were thinking and thinking about how to escape but we didn't know how. We were surrounded by Vietnamese soldiers and under the gun. And so we came to Xieng Khouang.

When I first arrived in Xieng Khouang I was completely surprised. I didn't see any houses there. I saw only bomb craters. There were so many in that area. Then a meeting was called and a voice came to us in a monotone — it was some officer of the Pathet Lao. He said he wasn't afraid of anybody there and we must respect the regulations of the Pathet Lao. He also told us not to talk to the local people and not to go far away without permission.

Later in the day they gave us some rice. That first time they gave us plenty to feed ourselves well but after that they cut off a little bit, a little bit each time.

We were supposed to be there three or four months while each person wrote a short biography for verification by the Pathet Lao officers. We were afraid to tell the truth. For example, I had just graduated from Fort Benning. If I said so I would be caught and accused of being an American spy.

It was hard to live there. In the morning we were delivered to a job site far away from the camp to chop wood to build houses. And everybody there got sick and sick. There was no medical help and we weren't allowed to talk with the people around the camp. So we were thinking, all the time thinking about trying to escape.

The first group of my friends — maybe eight or ten people — decided to escape from Xieng Khouang by walking and they made it safely. They are still in the resistance in Thailand along the border of the Mekong River, but they are safe.

After this experience the Pathet Lao guarded us even more closely and wouldn't allow us to go anywhere at all alone. When a second group of my friends decided to escape — sixteen of them — they were killed, all but one person. After that they started to get in the results of their checks on the biographies we had written and many were killed and many were put in jail and let die just shortly and shortly.

We had no medical care. We hadn't enough rice to eat. We were just working and working. We had to try to grow vegetables, to raise chickens in order to eat. Only about one meal a month did I manage to get enough to eat. Otherwise no more, no more. And

I kept thinking about finding a way to escape. But I couldn't, I couldn't find a way because although the first group escaped safely, the second group was killed, all but one of them. He was my friend. But he is dead now too. His name was Khamsout. He was a first lieutenant. He was filled with sorrow, deep sorrow, but he escaped in order to fight the Pathet Lao. He joined the resistance and died fighting in the Vang Vieng area.

We wanted to fight too but the area was surrounded by North Vietnamese troops and we couldn't fight them. And the people in the area didn't understand us. The Pathet Lao told them that we were American soldiers so they mustn't talk to us and they mustn't give us food. It was not safe to try to go into the village — we would be killed by the Defense Authority.

So we just worked and worked. I was based in Ban Ngoa seminar camp with the rest of my battalion, Battalion 522, and I worked around Xieng Khouang province. Pathet Lao officers would deliver us to the work site and we would build houses, fix roads and cut wood to make hospitals. We were very unhappy there with no rice and yet working, working hard. The people became weaker and weaker and some people died and some were killed.

One day some UNHCR officials were in the area and I heard them talking. They had come to Xieng Khouang to Pathet Lao headquarters to find out how many people had died in the seminar camps. But they wouldn't allow them to know something like that.

The situation for us became worse and worse and we didn't have a way to talk with anybody or find a way to escape. We thought about escaping all the time but we couldn't find a way. The people in the camp had to keep their eyes closed, keep their ears closed, keep their mouths closed. Otherwise they would be killed. If a Pathet Lao officer delivered a job to you and you said it was hard to do, you would be killed or put in jail. And so the people became stupid, stupid because they kept their eyes closed, their ears closed, their mouths closed. We didn't have any kind of freedom. We didn't have any kind of respect for religion. No religion any more. Just attacks on the old regime — bad words, bad words. And no more religion.

The economic situation was bad everywhere. The people didn't have enough rice to eat. They didn't have medical care in the hospitals. They had fallen into a bad economic crisis.

As things got worse, the Vietnamese soldiers came more and more often into the camp looking for food from us. Even they didn't have enough rice to eat so they came to us to ask for something to eat. And they would kill us if they thought we were wandering too far away or if they found us saying prayers. The life we lived in seminar camp was very dangerous.

The political situation was also very dangerous and the people didn't believe in the Kaisone regime any more. As for the social situation, they just made orders. Obey this order, obey that order. Respect only the Party. And if you don't obey, you will be punished — that means to be killed or put in prison.

In the seminar camp there were a few men who were Communists. They were there to execute the policy of the Politburo. And it was they who decided who should be killed in the camp. We were supposed to respect the Party only. If one of the Communists said, "This is red," we had to say, "Yes, this is red." If we said "No, this is black," we would be killed.

So I lived a very hard life in there. I saw many people killed before me. And I got sick. I went to the hospital but I didn't get any kind of medicine. Just local medicine — some kind of wood to boil and drink the water. There was only a little rice to eat and so I became thinner and thinner. And still I couldn't find a way to fight back or escape.

They wouldn't allow my wife to visit me because they found out that I had graduated from the United States. So I just tried to stay alive there, to keep my mouth shut.

While I was there, there was political trouble in Luang Prabang City. In March of 1977 the Communists accused King Sri Savang Vatthana of opposing their policies and arrested him along with the Queen, Crown Prince Vongsavang, Tchiao Tod, Tchiao Bouavone, Tchiao Khamsouk, Tchiao Souphantharangsy and Tchiao Keua.* They sent them to Viengxay in Sam Neua

---

*Tchiao Keua was the Prince's nickname. I do not know his full name. He

Province in northeastern Laos, close to the Vietnamese border. When they got there they were separated and sent to different places around Viengxay. Later, all of them were killed.

Late in 1983 I finally found a way to contact my wife and escape from seminar camp. It happened like this: In the Xieng Khouang area the situation was becoming very bad because of the economic crisis and the Pathet Lao officers wanted to get money to feed themselves. Many private trucks were carrying goods from Thailand via Vientiane to Xieng Khouang Province and they went by the camp. These trucks belonged to very small private businesses or to collective businesses.

The Pathet Lao officers saw these goods. And when they saw them they wanted them. They wanted food and money for themselves and for their children also. They wanted to get things — bicycles or food — to make it easier, to make it more comfortable for them.

It was because of the economic crisis that I started to think that there were now ways to escape. The first way was to escape directly from the camp but that was very dangerous and fifteen people had been killed trying.

The second way was to write a letter to my family asking them to bribe the officials at headquarters in Vientiane to sign permission papers for travel from Xieng Khouang Province to Vientiane City and have the letter carried by someone in a private truck. It is a long way from Xieng Khouang Province to Vientiane City, approximately six hundred kilometers. If we tried to go without permission papers we would be caught at one of the many checkpoints along the way.

The third way was to make contact with a truck driver going between Vientiane and Xieng Khouang and pay him to add an

---

was Crown Prince Vongsavang's brother. It was the custom for the king to have many wives. I don't know exactly how many he had but it must have been more than ten. Prince Tchiao Bouavone, Prince Tchiao Khamsouk and Prince Tchiao Souphantharangsy were also the king's sons, all by different mothers. Prince Tchiao Souphantharangsy was chief of the Royal Chamber. He was like a royal secretary and controlled all the paperwork going to the king. Tchiao Tod was the king's nephew. — Speaker.

extra name to his passenger list. The truck driver had to have approval for any people travelling with him. He would make a list and have a paper signed in Vientiane and he would show this paper at the checkpoints. Then he could pick up an extra passenger along the way and the name would already be on the list. But it would be hard to get on the truck without being seen by the Pathet Lao.

The fourth way was to give a bribe directly to a Pathet Lao officer. And this is what I did.

I got two bars of gold from my wife. She sent them by one of the private businessmen. With these I bought some cows for the Pathet Lao officers and some other goods for their children. Then I spoke openly to them. "I would like to go to see my family after this long time." And they said, "No. You cannot have permission." So I gave them some money and they gave me permission to go to Vientiane.

From the time I was taken to Xieng Khouang until I found a way to escape in late 1983, it was eight and a half years. I was in seminar camp from May 9, 1975, until December 1983.

When I reached Vientiane my family was very happy but my body was very, very frail. So I fed myself in Vientiane and I thought and thought and decided I would like to escape from Laos. I would try to find a place to go across the River Mekong to the Thai border. But it was not until February 1984 that I found the place. Until then I stayed with my family and I hid myself around Vientiane City. They had given me about fifteen days to be away from the camp—just temporary. So I was hiding around and going from place to place that I thought would be safe.

At that time Vientiane City was not the same as before. Everything had become dirty and there were no goods to be bought. And even if we had money we were not always able to buy rice. So life was very hard in the city and many people starved and little children too.

In February of 1984 I was spotted by a policeman and he filed my name as one to catch and send back to the seminar camp. One of my friends ran and told me, "You should go away right now. Otherwise you will be arrested by the Pathet Lao."

But I didn't know how to do it. I told my wife I would like to go by myself and swim across the river. But my wife said, "You just stay calm," and she went and found out about a bus from Vientiane to Khammouane Province. That was on Saturday evening.

On Sunday morning at four o'clock the bus was to leave Vientiane for Khammouane Province in the middle part of Laos. I was worried about being caught at one of the checkpoints but my wife told me there was only one checkpoint — just at the border of Vientiane City. I would have to pass that before getting on the bus. I must disguise myself as a farmer with the baggy black pants and the big hat.

So, early in the morning — about four o'clock — my brother carried me with my wife and little baby by motorcycle out of Vientiane City about five kilometers into Vientiane Province. There we waited and at about five o'clock the bus came along and we got on. We went along a difficult road for a long time and reached Khammouane Province at about ten o'clock in the evening. I thought, "I am safe now. I have avoided being arrested by the Communists."

We stayed there with my wife's parents for two days while I looked for a way to cross the River Mekong in Khammouane Province. There were soldiers on the river watching but I found a place in the forest where we could cross by boat and pay them some money to guide us. We pretended we were going camping and some of the guards who had a boat for fishing along the River Mekong took me and my wife and my little baby across the River Mekong and safely to Thailand.

I was a refugee in Thailand for a year and a half in the Na Pho camp. It was good there but very crowded, very crowded. And so many types of people were mixed up together — civil servants, military, farmers — they found it hard to get on together.

I arrived here in the Philippines on September 14, 1985. My family needs to study more English, maybe for six months. As for me, I will wait for them but I don't need so much study because I knew English before. I just need some practice because eight and nine years in seminar camp has made me stupid. I have forgotten many words and my intonation is not so good.

I will go to Portland in Oregon to join my old mother and my younger sister. I have no plans yet. I will try to find work as soon as I arrive and I will work hard to earn my living. If it is possible I would like to study at the same time. I think that I would like to be an engineer. And now I have told you my real story.

* * *

Now I want to tell you what I just heard but didn't see for myself. I heard that there were many bad things happening in the Viengxay area. Many generals and senior officers had been taken there and separated into different seminar camps, like Camp 04, Camp 05 and Camp 06. These were very hard camps, harder even than the others and many died.

The supreme Commander-in-Chief of the Royal Lao Army, General Bounpone, was killed there and many other generals also. The king and queen and Crown Prince Vongsavang died in that same area.

But I think that right now the Communist Party in Laos is not very strong and so the Communists are trying to organize an army and to drive people into it to train.

We have 60,000 Vietnamese troops along the Mekong border between Laos and Thailand. If we could get some help to fight only 60,000 Vietnamese troops I think they would not be strong enough and maybe the Communist Party wouldn't remain.

I remember that when I was in Vientiane City I overheard a dispute between some Pathet Lao officers. They were arguing over where they could find rice to feed themselves and their families. They would often fight among themselves because the economic crisis was very bad for them too. Some of them deserted and ran away. Some of them just hid around Vientiane City and some left the country.

They were too young to remember what it was like before Communism. They had been like blind men. They had just followed the Party and the regulations of the Party. But they could see what it was like in Vientiane now. And then some people started going to Thailand and coming back and telling about the comfortable life there, so they wanted to go also.

Right now there are many Pathet Lao soldiers who have become refugees in Na Pho Camp in Thailand. They can't go any farther. They are just being held there. They want to go to the United States but they can't. The United States doesn't like letting Communist soldiers into their country.

There are also some Pathet Lao who joined the resistance and are fighting against the Vietnamese and Red Lao troops.

When I was in Thailand I was thinking and thinking about running back to Laos to join the resistance but I couldn't find a way. I completely don't want the Communists there. And even themselves also, they try to escape but they can't find a way.

And so I think that the Communists are not so strong. If we could just have some help I think that we could take back Laos.

* * *

THE EIGHTEEN POLITICAL RESOLUTIONS OF THE COALITION GOVERNMENT

These are as recalled by Khamsamong Somvong from indoctrination sessions in seminar camp. He wrote them in Lao and together we figured out a translation. They are not word-for-word but the order and essential content parallel May 30, 1974, Vientiane radio reports:

Domestic Policy

(1) All Lao ethnic groups to be united as one country.

(2) Economic and social equality.

(3) Democracy.

(4) Election of the coalition government by democratic polls held at all levels, from the village to the parliament.

(5) Freedom of religion.

(6) Equality of the sexes.

(7) Economic and social development for national self-sufficiency.

(8) Abandonment of the old ways and development of an advanced technological society.

(9) A system of health care at all levels throughout the country.

(10) An increased standard of living through full employment.

(11) Elimination of old ways imposed by foreign cultures and development of a Lao way.

(12) A defense system to be built at the local level.

Foreign Policy

(1) A call for all countries to recognize and respect the agreements made at the 1973 peace talks in Paris and Vientiane between the Lao national government and the Pathet Lao in the spirit of the 1954 Geneva Convention whereby fourteen countries guaranteed the neutrality of Laos.

(2) A commitment to international cooperation with all countries of the world.

(3) Aid to be accepted from any country in the world wanting to help Laos with no political conditions on Laos.

(4) A call to all the countries of the world to respect the neutrality of Laos.

(5) A resolution to spread propaganda to support the coalition government.

(6) A commitment to support other countries wanting independence and democracy.

*   *   *

SIGNIFICANT DOCUMENTS

1962: Geneva Agreement on Laos. February 21, 1973: Vientiane Agreement on Restoring Peace and Achieving National Concord. September 14, 1973: Protocol to Vientiane Agreement. May 24, 1974: Program for Achieving Peace, Independence, Neutrality, Democracy, Unification and Prosperity of the Kingdom of Laos. (Referred to as "The Eighteen Articles" or "The Eighteen Political Resolutions.")

Their Words Hide All That Is Bad

Soukan Vignavong

*Soukan is tall for a Lao, with skin the color of a good summer tan drawn
tight across cheekbones just starting to fill out from years of semistarvation.
His dark eyes have a hurt look and he wears large-sized dark-tinted glasses.
His voice is gentle and he has the deferential, half-bowing manner of many
Laotians.*

*We had our conversations in the communications room of the refugee
camp, a small room with metal storage closets for stationery supplies at one
end and a big, old-fashioned standing two-way system at the other. It had
a fixed window out into the main administrative area stretching down one
wall so everyone could keep an eye on who was talking to whom. There was
a makeshift table with a slogan about loving one's work slipped under a clear
plastic cover. A piece of the plastic stuck out from the edge where two of the
tacks holding the cover in place had been removed to slip the slogan in.*

*There were two chairs, a straight-backed wooden one that wobbled and
an old, three-wheeled office chair on which one wheel-mounting was loose,
putting the sitter in constant danger of sudden collapse. I used the chair with
wheels as I thought it would be less unnerving for the story-teller to wobble
a bit than for him to fall off his chair in mid-sentence. By sitting very carefully
I managed to fall off only twice myself. The attraction of this room was a
wall-unit air conditioner. It was prehistoric and wailed loudly so before a*

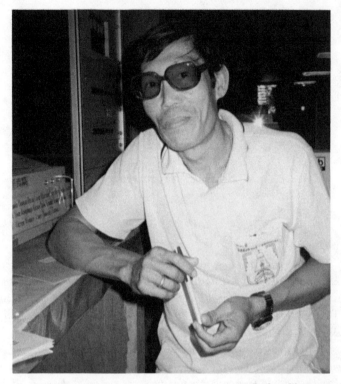

Soukan Vignavong.

taping session I would turn it on high and freeze the room. The coolness would last about an hour. After that we would sweat.

I always got the impression from Soukan that he couldn't really believe what had happened to him, that after all it was just a bad dream. He's in Fort Worth, Texas, now and writes to me. He's doing fine.

Before 1975 I was a government official in the Ministry of Social Welfare at the Department of Labor in Vientiane City.

I began work with the government in January of 1973 after I returned from studying in France. I was a labor inspector and worked in four provinces — Vientiane, Xieng Khouang, Khammouane and Borikhane. I was responsible for the well-being of the laborers in the factories I inspected. I had to make sure that the employees and employers were practicing the labor law.

My wife was in the Ministry of Education teaching in a primary school. My two children — both girls — were at school. The elder was born in 1970 and the younger in 1971. I enjoyed my life. When I returned from France I had my own house. My parents and parents-in-law had built it for me and my wife. It was made of concrete on the bottom and the upper floor was of wood. I also had a car from the government — a jeep — for my work in different areas.

At the beginning of 1975 I was working hard with the factories, especially when the Communists began to organize all kinds of strikes. But I didn't understand that then.

The first thing to happen was a demonstration on the first day of May, which is Labor Day. On this day my office usually organized a celebration. All the factories in the capital would participate. But this year we didn't do it — it was not an opportune time. The demonstration was in protest against the government and the employers. There were no placards. The man at the front carried a small sign. It said only "Le Premier Mai." The demonstrators walked around a route and went to the stadium where they talked about a better life for the workers.

There were no real Communists among the crowd. They were all just regular people, although I did observe that they were not all factory workers — there were also some government clerks and many students. It was not a big demonstration — maybe two hundred people at a guess. But it was the beginning of disaster.

After that there were many, many strikes in the factories and government offices. I had to work day and night trying to solve the problems for the workers. At first I didn't realize that the strikes were being organized from the outside. I was there trying to solve the problems according to the labor law as was my duty. And then I said to myself, "This is not the way, I think." For example, there was a strike in a furniture factory in Vientiane. I was there for a whole week but I could not solve the problems. They asked for higher salaries. I got that from their employers. They asked for better working conditions and they got that. But they stayed on strike. I didn't understand.

Then, towards the end of the week, I started to understand. The man who was the head of the strikers was a student from the Royal Institute of Law in Vientiane where I also had been a student. I heard him talking about property, about ownership of the factory, about the rights of the workers. And then I understood. He was talking about Marxism. I had learned about it when we studied world political systems in Constitutional Law.

Once I realized what was going on, I understood that I could not solve this problem so I returned to my office and told my boss, "This is not a normal strike so I cannot put my hand there."

I do not know what has happened to this factory but I do know that after three days there was no more strike and the employer, who was Japanese, left and was not able to return. The workers took over.

After that there were many, many strikes. There was a big one at the Esso Company but I think the biggest was among the Lao workers at the U.S. Agency for International Development. The whole agency was out on strike. No one was allowed through the fence to work. It lasted a week. They asked for down-time pay and the dissolution of the agency.

They got their down-time pay in accordance with labor rules. The agency was dissolved following the peace agreement in Laos. It would have been anyway. The United States was already thinking about closing the AID program, but the Communists wanted to show to the people their strength against the United States.

The other important strike happened in a saw-mill in Khammouane Province. There I understood more clearly that the strikes were being organized from the outside.

Again I started by trying to solve all the problems. And then one day I found that the head of the strike was the same man—the same very young boy—as at the Japanese furniture factory in Vientiane. This time, because he knew me well by then, he asked me to provide him with some guns. He said, "Can you find me some guns? I want to fight against the military in the Province of Khammouane."

I was taken aback. I didn't understand. I thought it was a joke. But then I realized that he really wanted to do it. He told me that there were many, many Laotian Communist soldiers behind him. They were still in the forest, not in the city, because at that time the Communists were still hiding their forces.

However, I kept on trying to solve the problems by negotiation and finally I got an agreement between the conflicting parties. I returned to Vientiane and reported to my minister.

At the time there were two ministers — one from the Royal Government in Vientiane and one from the Communist Party.* I reported to the minister from Vientiane and he was very happy that I had made a successful arrangement. But two days later I was called to the office of the Communist minister and I was blamed by him. He said that I was only for the employer.

I said, "I don't know. I practice my labor law." And he said, "This labor law protects only the interests of the employer." But I didn't think this was right. Our labor law was based on recommendations made by the International Labor Organization of the United Nations. Then he said to me, "You have to change your mind. But before that, you have to learn."

I didn't understand what he meant. I thought that I had to compare some law books from Socialist countries like the Soviet Union and Vietnam. But it was not like this. Two days later they sent me to a reeducation camp. That was the Communist meaning of "changing my mind."

---

*Minister Pheng Phongsavanh was with the Royal Lao government. He was a very important minister. It was he who signed the Vientiane agreement with the Communists. He later followed me to seminar camp and died there.

The Communist minister was Deuane Sounnarath. He was from Vientiane Province and had been a colonel in the Royal Lao Army in the Second Battalion of parachutists. This battalion had separated from the rest of the army and become an independent neutralist force under General Kong Le, who set up the coup d'état in 1960. These men cooperated with the leftists but were themselves neutral. At that time in Lao politics there was the left, the right and the neutralists in the middle. The political situation pulled at the neutralists until eventually the battalion split. Some went with the Communists and some went with the Royal government. Kong Le joined the government but Deuane Sounnarath joined the Communists. — Speaker.

At first they sent me to the University Pedagogique, a teacher training school at Dong Dok in Vientiane City about ten kilometers east of the River Mekong. But the seminar wasn't at the university. They just used the university as a collection center. They made us think that we were to go there and study so that they could gather us all together easily. They didn't say that we would be taken to a camp.

I arrived on a Monday in July. There were already two hundred or so others before me, all civilians — government clerks and officials. There was one other person there from my ministry — a friend in the Department of Labor who had studied in Czechoslovakia. (He wasn't a Communist. I don't know how he got to study in Czechoslovakia. He was there for six years. People had been going many places to study — even to the Soviet Union — from a long time back.)

The seminar had been under way for about two months when I arrived. People did not yet realize that they had been tricked. The Communists said to us, "You listen!" And they talked about the Eighteen Articles on human rights that the coalition government had prepared.

Everyone was expecting to leave at the end of the seminar and that one day soon — next Monday, next Saturday — there would be a closing ceremony. They spread many, many rumors. They were all saying, "Yes, yes, I hope that I am near the end of my study here and I can go to my office to continue to work as before."

Then, on Friday, August 1, at two o'clock in the afternoon, the Minister of the Interior from the Communist side came and read fifty names from a call list. My name was on the list. They put us on a bus and took us to the Vientiane airport. We were not tied but they locked the door of the bus.

First they flew us to Phonsaven camp in Xieng Khouang Province. I don't know exactly where it is but it's not in Xieng Khouang City — a little outside. There were already about two hundred police there when we arrived. They had been brought in from the police academy at Dong Noune in Vientiane. This academy had been founded by the United States although the teachers were Laotians. I used to teach labor law there.

I talked to the policemen. They said, "Now we understand what is happening and we can't do anything. We are in a very difficult situation."

We were there in Phonsaven for one week, just waiting. The area around was very lush. Flat land with small hills. Very pretty. We stayed here without doing anything — no work, no studying — nothing. They gave us cigarettes and we just smoked and waited. Everybody was asking themselves, "What will happen?" We were all beginning to feel afraid and very anxious for the future.

After a week, we were all put aboard helicopters. They had Soviet helicopters — models Mi-6, Mi-8 and Mi-12. The Mi-12 holds about twelve persons but the Mi-6 and Mi-8 are very big. The Mi-6 is the biggest. It is a troop transport and holds more than a hundred people.

We were driven to a place about thirty minutes from Viengxay airport and when we arrived they separated us. I was with seven other government officials. We were in a compound. In the middle of the compound was a big, concrete building that they told me was a parliament for the Communist Party. Around this, on three sides of a square, there were billets. On one corner of the square was a very nice house where they said the chief of the Communist Party stayed when they held a congress.

On the fourth side of the square there were rocky mountains where they had an electrical generator. We could not hear the noise of the machine — it was deep inside the mountain. I think it ran on gasoline. We used only electricity for lighting at night-time.

You would be able to see this compound if you flew over it in a helicopter although there was dense forest and many mountains around it.

We stayed there for nearly a week without doing anything — just like in Phonsaven. We didn't know why we were there or where our friends were. It was while I was there that I finally faced the fact that I was trapped.

Then they sent us to join the others in another camp nearby. It wasn't really a camp. It was a military post I think. There we were picked up by military cars which took us about a hundred and fifty kilometers to Muong Et in the district of Xieng Kho. The real camp was there — Camp 06. At that time there were more than seven hundred people in the camp. Four hundred or so military, about three hundred police and eighty civil government officials from different ministries.

I was there for many years — from August 1975 to November 1983 and we travelled around Viengxay Province to work. At the beginning it was not so bad. We just had to stay there and for more than two weeks we didn't do anything. We didn't know yet what would happen. We were expecting to have an opening day and then to be told how long — how many months, how many years — we would have to study. Everybody was waiting for them to tell us this date but it never happened.

They had us construct a dormitory-like building, big enough to hold about a thousand people. We made it of bamboo and the roof we made of leaves. It took us two weeks. Then there was a ceremony and it was opened for study. We all went inside and they announced that this was the beginning of the program of study. But they didn't know when the end would be.

And so it started. We studied some documents about Laos' rich natural resources. They talked about the balance of the United States and Soviet Union forces. They compared the power of the United States with that of the Soviet Union and tried to show us which had increased and which had decreased. Of course the Soviet Union had increased. They talked about the political situation in the world. They said there were many strikes and much unemployment in the Capitalist countries and much growth and prosperity in the Communist countries.

We had to learn to say it. We also had to learn that we had been following the wrong way before and now we had to set up a new life and forget everything that we had learned before. "It is all a big error and you have to change," they said.

At the end of the study, we had to write a biography but before we wrote we had to talk in front of everyone. They called it auto-criticism. We were divided into groups and we had to tell everybody everything we had ever done and then write it down. This happened very many, many times. I don't remember how many times from 1975 to 1983.

They asked and they asked. What is your rank? What is your position in the government? Who is your boss? Who are the Americans you worked with? What did you do with the CIA? How many people have you killed? How many kip, how many dollars, have you stolen from others? How many wives have you had? They liked people to tell about the bad things their old boss had done, especially if he was there in the camp. It was to make the boss afraid so that he would confess about himself.

How many . . . what . . . everything, everything. Always the same questions. I told the truth. I had worked with the government two years. I was very new. I told them I had just practiced my duty according to the labor law. I had my director, I had my minister, and I had done everything they told me. I had followed all the labor laws, every regulation, every government rule. I had killed nobody. I had taken no kip from anybody.

But it was very hard for those who had had a long time of service in the government. There were generals, there were colonels, there were first lieutenants, both police and military. They had to talk. If, for example, I was a colonel and I had many soldiers with me in the camp and I didn't talk maybe my colleagues would say that I had done this or that, that I had killed somebody. If I did not say it first then maybe it would be worse for me. Many people became very upset. Some of them were in tears.

Before it started the Communists had collected all our knives — anything that we could use to kill ourselves. They had experience with people committing suicide because it was too hard to say all these things and to write them. Not so for me, but I understand the difficulty of those who had been in important positions, especially those who had been in the secret service.

We were divided into sections of thirty to fifty people and then into groups of ten to twelve. Each section had a designated head and each group had a leader and an assistant. The group leader had to lead the auto-criticism and report to the Pathet Lao. He had to choose a "volunteer" to do an auto-criticism in front of everybody. Whoever was chosen had to do it. He could not refuse.

The Pathet Lao would go from group to group watching what was going on. If we stopped talking when they came up, that meant we were not sincere, we were trying to hide something from them. We were supposed to always be telling the truth. I don't know what they did with the papers we wrote. They never discussed them with us.

Apart from that we had to work. We had to make roads, construct and repair houses for us and for them, cut wood and help the people in the village who needed laborers to repair the roads, to dig irrigation canals — all kinds of manual work.

At first we were not allowed to speak to the people in the village and they wouldn't speak to us. The Communists had taught them to hate us. They had said, "These are your enemies! They are reactionaries. They are against the Communists. They bombed your village. They burned your rice land. They raped your daughters. These are bad people."

But after two years, three years, they became more lax and we would meet with the villagers and talk. After many meetings like this they would allow us to go inside their huts. We talked to them openly and they told us the truth.

They didn't like the Communists. They knew they were living under bad conditions. They knew they were being told lies. They remembered the better times when they were being administered by the French and they knew that the Communists could only administer them by force. But they couldn't do anything about it because the Communists had officials in the village to control them. The Communists were very hard with them. They were very poor. They didn't have enough rice. They had to work hard but they got nothing in return.

The Communists had set up a tax. The official rate was fifteen percent of the rice crop but that was only on paper. It didn't include the many, many things the people had to do. They had to construct a central warehouse in the village to store all the rice that came from the surrounding farms. They had to transport their rice to the district warehouse themselves. They carried it on their backs. They had to come at night to guard the warehouse and in the daytime to process the rice so that the high-ranking officials — Lao, civil and military, and Vietnamese — who came into the village would have white rice to eat.

In each family, all who were sixteen years old and above had to have in their house or in their farm seven kilos of live chickens or pigs. This was reserved for the local administration. When there was a big ceremony, an important visitor or some sort of special occasion, the village chief announced who would give on this round of collections.

The selected people had to take the chickens or pigs they had raised and exchange them for a receipt which they had to keep to prove that they had fulfilled their obligation for this round of collecting. But it was not finished. They had to be ready for the next round.

I saw this happening with my own eyes — people from Ban Nakham, about two kilometers from our camp, carrying many chickens to the Xieng Kho district when many Vietnamese officers came for the opening ceremony of a newly-constructed market there. From Ban Nakham to Xieng Kho is about sixty kilometers. They brought the chickens by walking — they had no transportation.

The villagers had also had to provide the construction materials — wood, concrete, iron — and to feed the workers who built this new market. They were Vietnamese workers. I don't know if they were soldiers — they were not in uniform. Some were from South Vietnam. They told us when we were exchanging cigarettes and soap.

So, although the official tax was only fifteen percent, if you calculate all these extra things in, I think you will find that it actually worked out that they were losing more than fifty percent of their income.

Setting up paper systems is a Communist ruse to make things seem better than they are. If you read only the paper you would say, "Oh, it is good! The tax is only fifteen percent. A little less, a little more — never mind. For your family to pay this is not very hard. You can do it. It is good in your country." But there is nothing good. It's all a deception. You read the paper but you don't see there all the other things that the people are required to do. You don't know how hard they have to work. You don't see what a difficult life they have to live.

And the Communists do this in many, many things. What they write does not show what they mean to do. And what they say is not real. Their words hide all that is bad. And it is easy to believe them because their words are good. For example, they sent us to the seminar and you would think that a seminar is good — a place to learn, to understand more. But in fact it was not like that. It was just a labor camp and very cruel.

For food they gave us rice but very bad rice. Some days there was not even enough for the children. We never knew how much we were going to get. When they gave it to us, they wouldn't say whether it was for two days or three days or one week. They would only say, "I have ten kilos or two kilos for you today and for how many days I don't know. You can eat it as you want — all at one time, in two days, three days. Just do what you like." So we never knew how much we could eat or how much we should save.

We got some salt too and some cans of fish. For ten people one can. We would take a very big bowl of water and put the can into it. We cooked it ourselves over wood fires.

We got sick. Many people had beriberi. I had it. My ankles swelled up very big, and my joints also. At the beginning it was hard but after that many of us looked for forest legumes to eat and that helped us to live. It became a habit to eat these legumes in the forest and after five or six months we become stronger. It helped us to resist disease.

The medical treatment was very poor. One day I was cutting wood outside official work hours. I had gone to the forest with my group — there were ten of us. We were clearing some forest to plant maize and sweet potatoes so that we would have more to eat. I had an accident because I was not very good at chopping wood. My trouser was cut through and my leg was split open. You can still see a big scar on my right leg.

My friends took me to the clinic. But it's not a clinic. They put water on it and sprinkled on a ground-up Ganadin tablet. Ganadin is for diarrhea. Then they put cotton on it and it was finished for me.

I went home and showed it to Doctor Chiampa who shared my hut. He took off the cotton and it was very open so he asked me to look for a needle and thread and he would try to sew me up. I got them from Mr. Samrit Lasaphong — he had been ambassador to many countries but he is dead now. So Doctor Chiampa sewed me up. It hurt a lot but after one week it was much better. Some people had antibiotics with them and they offered to give them to me but I couldn't take them because I am allergic.

If we were very ill we could go to the hospital but there was no medicine. I don't know where the hospital was exactly. I never went there. It wasn't at Muong Et. You had to be escorted into Viengxay. They called it Hospital Number Two. Some people who went came back but many people died there. They did not have proper doctors or medicines.

After three or four years, when they started letting us talk to the villagers, they relaxed the rules about visitors and mail. We started writing to our families and they could write to us although we had to be careful because the Communists read all the letters.

Also they would let our families come to visit. If they said nothing bad about the Communists they would let them go again but some people were kept there.

If they came from Vientiane, for example, and said, "Everything is good in Vientiane now. It's better. The Communists do this, the Communists do that. It's very good, very nice," then they could go back. But if they said, "Things are no good. The Communists come and do this and that. It's very bad," then they made them stay. If they told the truth they stayed. This was not official policy but we saw it happening.

My wife came to visit me one time and stayed for two years. It happened like this: In 1978 I thought, "I am finished. I will die. I will never return to my home." So I wrote a letter to my wife and sent it to the Ministry of Education. My wife didn't have her job any more but one of the men there knew how to find the wives of the seminarists.

All that time they were putting out very strong propaganda to get the wives to join their husbands. This was because the wives of the seminarists were asking and asking about their husbands and they decided to solve the problem by sending them to the seminars too. Then no one would be questioning them all the time.

So my wife came to join me. She left our two children in Vientiane, although some people did bring their children with them. Nobody took care of them there. They just ran around the camp while their parents worked and when they got sick their parents had to look for local medicine.

Two years later, in 1980, my wife's father died and they allowed her to go back to Vientiane. There were no very strong rules for the women, only for the men. I was left there alone.

Then, one day, I became very, very ill with a fever. It was malaria. I wrote to my family and they asked permission for me to be sent to the hospital in Vientiane. I know that they had to pay to get the authorization but I don't know how much. I do know that the officers responsible for the seminar camps were accepting money from the families of seminarists in exchange for their return to Vientiane. I think that many of our friends used this way to "escape" from the camps.

So I was sent back to Vientiane and spent over a month in the hospital before I got better. I was supposed to return to the camp after I became strong. They hadn't said so but I knew that I had not been released. So I asked for permission to make a "basee" or "soukhouan." This is a good luck ceremony for people who have recovered from a very bad condition. It's a Lao custom. You invite your family and friends to eat and you set up a lucky dish with tall flowers and many threads of cotton all round, like a small maypole. Then you all sit around the dish and wrap your wrists to each other with the cotton to wish good luck and success.

So I went to my father's village in Pak Sane. My wife and children had arrived before me. It was Christmas time and the night after Christmas there is always a big celebration in the village because we are Catholics. While this celebration was going on I took my family with me in a boat and crossed the Mekong River. There were guards on the river but we went at seven thirty and it was dark. The river is not too wide at that time of year. It took us about forty-five minutes to get across. My wife and I rowed. My children were too small to help.

I knew there was a Laotian resistance camp on the other side of the river in Thailand. We met some of the resistance fighters and they took us to their camp. We stayed one week and then they sent us to Na Pho refugee camp. We were in Na Pho for about eighteen months and then we came here to the Philippines on the sixteenth of September 1985, so we have been here for about six weeks. My two children are in the American secondary school program here. I have two more in day care.

We will leave for the United States maybe at the end of March. I don't know where we will go. I have no relations. They call me a "free case." I don't know the United States. I have never been there. I think I would like to go to the southeast — to Florida or Louisiana or Tennessee maybe. I think the weather there is good and not very cold. I like warm weather.

*   *   *

There is one thing that I think is very important to tell to all the world: You cannot understand what the situation is like under a Communist regime by reading what the Communists write or by listening to what they say about it. They have tried to deceive the Lao people. For example, the Eighteen Articles of the coalition government: They wrote them. They assured us that they would keep to the agreement. They signed. But in practice they put it all aside, all aside.

And now everybody in Laos knows that you cannot be frank and honest with the regime. The high-ranking Communist officials live a life of hypocrisy and they have made the Lao people act like hypocrites. We have to say yes when we want to say no. We have to say that our enemy is our best friend. We have to say that we agree with the Communist Party when we know that what they say is not true. But we cannot do anything. We have to accept. We have to say yes or they will kill us.

We do not like to be treated like this. It is insupportable. We cannot bear this condition.

For those who were in the former government, it is even harder. We were made to feel such shame because we had been separated from society. If you have been in a seminar camp your friends look at you like a prisoner, an undesirable man in society.

You know they are still friends but they are afraid to talk with you like before. They have to be afraid. They have to be careful about meeting with you. And if something happens in the village you are the first man to be looked for, to be arrested and questioned. It is dangerous all the time. And for your children it will be the same — for your daughter and for your grandson, and the son of your grandson.

I understand that in another country we might be looked at like foreigners, like refugees. It is natural that if you are different from the rest of the country you will be resented. This is understandable. But if you are in your own country and you are discriminated against by society, by your own country, it is much harder.

If I am Lao and my children, my family, are all Lao and you are Lao too and treat me like this then I am many thousand times more hurt. It is as if the country of Laos has passed judgment against me.

We cannot bear this kind of discrimination. It is too hard. I knew when I left my country that I would have nothing but I had no choice. I think it is better than living under such conditions. Now I am far from the Lao Communist administration. I know I will have a lot of problems in my life in the new country but I don't care about this. I don't care about problems when I have the opportunity to solve them but I don't like and I cannot live in a Communist regime overwhelmed with problems and maltreatment that no one can even discuss.

Even in a very successful condition of life in the United States, my eyes will not express a pure happiness. There will always be a big question: "What to do for those who are still suffering in the native country?" This can never be erased from my deep emotion. [PRPC, November 7, 1985; Soukan Vignavong now lives in Fort Worth, Texas. He was sponsored by the International Rescue Committee — J.S.]

For Ten Years He Had Me

Bounsy and Samly Khamphouy

Bounsy and Samly are a complementary couple. Bounsy is vibrant though quiet-spoken, and has an aura of serene self-confidence. She is about forty years old with rich, dark hair and will be beautiful when good eating fills out the hollows in her cheeks and fades the shadows round her eyes.

Samly is gentle and soft-spoken, his outward demeanor only occasionally giving a hint of the toughness and tenacity that lies beneath. He bows frequently and ends every sentence with "ma'am" or "sir." His soft brown eyes are magnified and a little distorted by strong glasses. He is neither small nor large and squarely built. His strong, short fingers clench and unclench with earnestness while he talks.

Samly and Bounsy spent their first year in the United States in fear for the life of Samly's youngest brother, Khamchanh, who, with his wife and three young children, was left behind in the Na Pho refugee camp in Thailand. Rejected by the United States Immigration and Naturalization Service for reasons not altogether apparent, Khamchanh was in danger of repatriation to Laos.

Samly's appeal to the United States government for help was inserted in the Congressional Record *on August 7, 1987, by Congressman Jack Kemp. The good news came just after Christmas of 1987: Khamchanh had been approved.*

Those who helped were Congressman Jack Kemp of New York, Congressman Trent Lott of Mississippi, Congressman William S. Broomfield of Michigan, Senator William L. Armstrong of Colorado, Congressman Henry J. Hyde of Illinois, Senator Gordon Humphrey of New Hampshire, Senator Orrin Hatch of Utah, Congressman Gerald B.H. Solomon of New York and Senator Steve Symms of Idaho.

These the Khamphouy family thanks: "We don't have anything to offer you, just ten fingers to pray to God, blessing you and your family."

Before 1975 I worked as a nurse in an obstetrics hospital in Vientiane City. My husband was in the military and I had two small children. In 1975 the Communists came into Vientiane. They took my husband away to a seminar camp in Viengxay and they blamed me because he was a military officer. So I lost my job at the hospital and had no money.

After eight months or so when I went to pick up my husband's salary the official said, "No more salary. You can join your husband in the seminar camp if you want to. So what will you do?"

I said, "I cannot stay here in Vientiane without my husband. I have no money, no job. So can I go join him in the seminar camp?

They said "OK. It's up to you." So I went to live with him in the seminar camp and took my children with me. I was not the only one. This was happening to many of the seminar wives at that time.

There was no life there but work. Mostly I cut grass in the rice fields and wood for building houses. Sometimes I carried water to my husband and the other men when they were working, digging the ground. Sometimes the children had lessons. Some of the prisoners taught them in their free time. But in the daytime they worked in the fields too.

We ate sticky rice. We got maybe two hundred and fifty to three hundred grams for a day—not much more than a handful. Sometimes they allowed us to grow vegetables and keep chickens for ourselves and sometimes they didn't but there was never enough food. I became very thin. I was so tired all the time because I was not getting enough food.

The medicine was poor. Just roots and bark of trees boiled in

Samly Khamphouy.

water — Lao medicine. We drank it and sometimes it seemed to have some effect but really it didn't work. People died. Some starved. Others, when they got letters from their families, thought too much and died of depression. Some were killed by the Communists.

While we were there we heard that in Camp 05 there were twenty-six seminarists the Pathet Lao had accused of trying to kill them. They said they tried to stage an uprising — a coup — in the camp. So they took all those twenty-six people and put them in the jail in the Sop Hao area [for the names of the twenty-six see page 215. — J.S.].

But it wasn't true. Who could rise up against them? All the seminarists were without weapons—without anything—so who could rebel? The Communists just made up these things so that they could kill the high-ranking people—generals and government officials. They said, "Oh, those people staged an uprising against us so we killed them." Then, "Nobody can talk," they said; "nobody can say anything. Just stay quiet." So we were not allowed to ask questions about it.

We learned later that the wife of one of the twenty-six, General Bounpone, was left behind in the camp. She still had some money and paid the Pathet Lao guards to find out what had happened to her husband in jail. She heard about the killings. There was only one survivor. Her husband was beaten to death with sticks. She didn't find out how the others died. She is still a prisoner.

I was in the camp for eight years. Then one day I asked permission to go to Vientiane to look for some medicine for my husband who was sick. They gave me a pass and I went and took my two children with me.

I did not go back. Instead, I consulted with a friend, "How do I get my husband out?" And she told me, "You must pay money if you want to get your husband back."

I went to see the officer in charge of the seminar people and paid him—two bars of gold—four or five hundred American dollars then. My father gave me the money. He sold his house. For this payment the officer agreed to bring my husband back.

Three months later my husband was sent back to Vientiane to join me. He stayed there two weeks while we looked for a way to cross the Mekong River. We bought a small boat and crossed the river during the night. There were guards but we paid them some money to look away. This was in 1984.

On the other side of the river we met some Thai police. We told them that we had escaped from Laos, that my husband was Lao military so we couldn't stay there. They took us to the Nong Khai police station and then they sent us to the Na Pho refugee camp.

We were there a year and I ate a lot and worked as a midwife in the hospital. Then we went to the Panat Nhikom transit center for two weeks and on to the Philippines. We arrived here on

September 15, 1985. I am working in the World Relief clinic here. I am eating and getting fatter.

We have a friend in the United States who was in the same battalion as my husband. We were also in the seminar camp together. He escaped before us in 1982. He asked my husband to go with him but it was very hard to escape so we decided to let him go first. If we got a letter or heard from somebody that he had made it safely, my husband was going to try to escape too.

We didn't hear from him again until we were in the Na Pho camp. We met a friend there who gave us his address. We wrote to him in the United States and got a letter back from him. We were very happy. He is sponsoring us to come to Connecticut.

I have a nursing certificate from the UNHCR hospital and I will look for a job as a nurse in the United States but I need to study English some more here first. I speak French but no English. I don't know yet what my husband will do to earn his living. I think maybe he would like to join the U.S. Army if they will have him. Or he could take up chicken farming. I know that he will work hard and do the best he can if they will let him.

My oldest son is now eighteen. He will study at high school and improve his English too. He doesn't know what he wants to be. Maybe he will learn about electricity or mechanics. The other son is eleven. I have no girls yet.

I have two brothers and one sister still in Na Pho camp but I have lost contact with them. I have written to them but I haven't got any letters back.

But now my husband would like to say some things.

*   *   *

Yes, I need to say some things against the Communists — to blame them. I was a long time in the Communist camp — more than ten years — and I think I know them. When they first took me there they took me by plane with my hands tied. I was in the first group of high-ranking officers. I was a major. We were all tied with rope. They took us to Camp 06 close to the Vietnamese frontier. It is deep forest and high mountains all around.

Later, after two or three months, a second group came. Altogether there were now one thousand, four hundred and forty-eight people. The new seminarists told us that the king also had been taken by the Communists and was out there somewhere in the Viengxay area too.

But then the guards told us, "Don't talk any more. If you do we kill you tonight." So nobody talked. They watched us all the time — every night. Every day the guards stayed close to us. They would have killed us if we talked.

Every day for ten years we worked in the fields and they watched. If anyone talked against them, the following day they would kill him. Some people they put underground. They had a jail underground. I was not put underground. I kept my eyes looking down. I stayed quiet, quiet, always stayed quiet. I knew that even though I was military I had no weapon so it was best to stay quiet like an ignorant person. I felt stupid from not talking but it did not affect my mind.

There were people around the camp. We could see them but we didn't have any contact with them even though they were only about two kilometers away from us. They didn't allow it.

Once I saw Soviet troops come to the camp. They had come to see the Communist commandant — three of them and a driver. I don't know why they came. We didn't come too close because we were afraid. If we had gone near, maybe that night we would have gone to jail or been killed. So we didn't worry about what they were doing, just worried about ourselves. Don't pay attention to them. Just look down.

The Vietnamese came into the camp a lot. They were the security force around the camp and they would come to see the commandant too. They didn't have contact with the prisoners in the camp. I didn't come too close to them either.

Then they moved everyone to the Sop Pane area close to the frontier with Vietnam. Camps 04, 05 and 06 were all brought to the Camp 03 site at Sop Pane and they combined all four camps. Then they dispersed us all around the Sop Pane area.

They started calling the seminar camps by different names — commune, production camp. But really it was the same. It was a change in name only. It was to hide the truth from the people. To blind the people's eyes. To keep them from knowing about the seminarists. Don't let the people in the province know. Don't let the people in Vientiane know. Even the wives of the seminarists didn't know. The Communists would tell them, "Oh, your husband has gone to the seminar. It is very good. Studying and learning, eating and drinking." And most of the people in Vientiane believed them because they didn't see for themselves. They didn't let any visitors go there.

But it was not like this — nothing at all — not anything. We were dying. Many times I thought, "I have no more life, only dreaming. It is finished for me."

All of us said this to ourselves. "There is no more. No more soldiering, no more home, no more life." And we stayed there without talking, without asking questions, without saying anything. They said to us, "You do something," and we did it.

None of the guards were kind to us. None of them helped us. They were low-level. They didn't know anything. They had no education. They only listened to the Communists. When the Communists said "white" they said "white," when they said "red," they said "red." They didn't know anything.

They would say to us, "You are working for the U.S. Army. Shoot, kill all of you." They didn't know anything. When they said things like this we didn't answer, just stayed quiet. Let them say this. It's better. If they want to kill us, let them kill us. If they tell us to go to jail, we will go to jail.

Sometimes we wanted to die. It would be better than staying there. And some people killed themselves. Lieutenant Colonel Boun Eua did that. He took some poison. "I can't stay any more. Adieu. Goodbye to you. Good luck everybody. I don't want to stay any more." And he took poison and died.

I have my friends still there. Maybe six hundred people around the Sop Pane area. I want to help them. When I arrive in the United States, if I can find a way I will write a letter, send something to them — maybe medicine, maybe some candy. I don't know if they will get it. Maybe I can send it by their wives. Maybe they can ask permission to come visit their husbands — hide it and give it to them. Yes, I miss them very much. We stayed together ten years.

It is very hard for them there. It is very far from Vientiane, in the mountains, in the jungle close to the Vietnamese border. It is very difficult to escape from there. I don't know how to help them, just only miss them.

One man did escape from 06 and I met him in the Na Pho camp in Thailand. It was the day I left and I could only talk to him for about one hour. I asked him, "How about our friends? Still living?"

He told me a lot of the friends were dead. "This year," he said, "Colonel Bounleuth Philavong, Lieutenant Colonel Khamphouang Philavanh, Lieutenant Colonel Vandy Thongprachanh. . . ." He said all their names. About twenty people were dead.

I also met a lot of seminar wives in the Na Pho camp. They had been there a long time. They are still there. I don't know why. They don't know how they can come to America. They said to me, "When you meet American people, ask them to help us."

I said, "OK. I will try my best to ask some American people to help you." Maybe it depends on the U.S. government. I don't know how to help them but I told them I would try my best to ask.

The last thing I want to say is: Don't believe the Communists any more. Don't believe them. I know that what they say is all false, not true. Ten years there in the Communist camp was enough for me.

Most people in the world only know about Communism from reading books and listening to what other people say, maybe radio, maybe newspaper. They don't see for themselves. If they saw like I did, if they lived like I did, they would cry.

When the Communists first came to Vientiane the people had heard about the Communist way. It sounded very good for them so they were happy to support them. But after a few years of having the country occupied by the Communists they were all trying to escape. The Communist way has made the Lao people very poor. Everybody there is starving. Now they really know about the Communists.

I met a man who had escaped from Vientiane. He had not been to the seminar. He said to me, "Sir, how long did you stay in the seminar camp?"

"Ten years," I said to him.

"Oh," he said, "I was in Vientiane about four years, five years. It was very hard, sir. How could you bear to stay in seminar camp for ten years?"

"Just stay there," I said. "Do nothing. Just stay there without freedom."

When I was in the seminar, I thought, "If only I could escape to Vientiane I would be so very lucky." But nobody is there in Vientiane any more. Even if they escape from the seminar — the military, the police, the government workers — they can't stay in Vientiane. Stay there one hour and they will catch you again. They watch you all the time. If they find you saying or doing something wrong, they will catch you and kill you.

I knew two other people who escaped and, when they came to Vientiane, they stayed there two months. Now they're gone. I don't know what happened to them. They killed them, I think. A friend told me in Na Pho, "Mr. Baliane was caught again." I was lucky to escape from there.

So be careful. Do not believe that man in the world who is a Communist. His words are very beautiful. He is very nice when he talks but what he does is very bad. This I want to tell to everybody and I am not afraid to use my name. I am not afraid of him. For ten years he had me. What more can he do to me? [PRPC, November 6, 1985.]

Hidden to the People of the World

Khoun Phavorabouth

The betrayal of the commitments made in the Eighteen Articles of the Lao coalition government was a recurring theme in my conversations with the Lao refugees.

Curiously enough, when I was searching for an official copy of these articles, the Lao Embassy in Washington denied any knowledge of them.

I went to the seminar in 1975. I was there for eight years.

I was forty-two years old when I went. Now I am an old man. I was in the military—a lieutenant colonel. The Pathet Lao told me that everybody must go to seminar camp to study and learn. We must study the Eighteen Articles of the coalition government. They sent me with a big group to a camp at Na Pha, close to Viengxay—maybe five kilometers to the south. We didn't know how we should dress so we wore our uniforms.

When we first arrived only thirty people were there before us—all high-level military. Our arrival brought the number up to three hundred and eighty-six people. After that another group of fourteen joined us. There were a few bureaucrats among this last group. We were all men.

Then the Pathet Lao told us, "All of you are prisoners of war." They had checked our records to find out who was strongly anti–Pathet Lao and now they had us. I spent three months there. We built the camp and we studied Pathet Lao policy.

They would say to us, "Why have you come here? Because you made a mistake. You have done everything bad to the Lao people. Your own military is serving the U.S. Army. So all of you have come to this camp."

Then the Pathet Lao separated us. Officers who had worked closely with the U.S. Central Intelligence Agency were sent to Camp 05 in the Sam Teu area, about one hundred and fifty kilometers east and south of Viengxay — a whole day by truck.

I was sent to Camp 04. Major to lieutenant colonel and some mid-level bureaucrats went there. Camp 04 is near to Muong Et, also a whole day by truck from Viengxay. From Muong Et to 04 is one hour by walking along the Nam Et River. High mountains are on both sides of the river.

We were the first group to go to Camp 04. No one was there when we arrived. There was nothing there except jungle. Not high — fourteen to fifteen meters — but very dense. We were at the bottom of a valley.

We slept under the trees at night and in the day we worked clearing the land and building the camp. We cut down trees, cleared rice fields, planted bananas, made a lake for fishing and more lakes for breeding fish.

Each morning the Pathet Lao would separate the prisoners into groups of ten to twenty people and send them to cut wood, build the barracks or construct the road. There was no breakfast before we started work unless we had saved something from the night before.

At six-thirty we started work. We would go ten or twenty kilometers into the mountains to cut wood. We carried it to the camp on our backs. If the trees were small we would carry maybe three or four at one time. If they were big, only one — as much as we could carry.

Two or three guards went with each group. While we worked they would walk around and watch us from three or four meters

Khoun Phavorabouth.

away. They did not beat us, just watched. Sometimes they would tell us to work harder. They would tell us which trees to cut, what time to go back to the camp. We did not say anything to them. We were not allowed to talk to the guards. We just worked.

When the camp was finished it looked like a military camp. There were twenty long wooden barracks about five meters by fifty. Each one would house up to fifty people. They were built on the ground. The floors were of dirt and turned to mud with the rains.

During the rainy season they forced us to work in the rice fields pulling plows like buffaloes.

In the evenings we had meetings about the day's work—who did right, who did wrong. Then they planned the work to do next. No one ever dared to question these plans. After that was done they talked about policy. They told us not to talk about American policy, only Soviet policy. "It is good, Soviet policy," they said. "And American policy, we don't like it," they said.

We could only talk when we were told to. We had to say that the Soviet way is good, the American way is not good. If we had not said that, they would have been angry at us. They did not get angry at me because what they told me to say I said—everything.

We ate at midday and in the evening. There was a little rice but not enough. Maybe three hundred grams for one day. Most of the time this was all we had. Then, from time to time, they would slaughter a pig or a buffalo. Maybe once a month, maybe twice, depending on the Pathet Lao. This one pig or buffalo would be for the whole camp—by then over a thousand people. We got none of the fish we bred for them. All the fish went to the Pathet Lao. The prisoners were not allowed any. They announced that any prisoner caught stealing fish would be sent to jail.

The jail was back down the road towards Viengxay, across the river from Sop Hao village where there used to be an old military camp. I think there had been seminarists there at one stage but they were moved to Camp 05 at Sam Teu because the old Sop Hao camp was on low land—a flood-plain.

The road from Viengxay winds east and north through the mountains. For a while it follows the Nam Ma River, almost at the border with Vietnam. There are rice fields in the hundred or so meters of land between the road and the river. Forty or fifty kilometers from Viengxay, is the village of Sop Hao, on the west side of the road.

Across the river from Sop Hao, toward Vietnam, is the jail. We would go by it as we went out to cut wood. It is underground. We could not see it but we knew it was there. Nobody was supposed to talk about it but we heard things from the village people. Some of these people were sympathetic towards the seminarists and they would talk to us and tell us about a big underground jail. They told us of twenty-six high-ranking officials from 05 who were held there. There was also one prisoner from 06, Major Khene Tuy, who had been a military policeman.

No one from Camp 04 went to this jail. But no one expected to see Vientiane again either. They made plans to escape but couldn't do it. No one escaped. It is very far away over there. The jungle is too dense, the mountains too high. They just stayed there waiting for the day of their dying.

Thirty people died in the time that I was there. When they got sick they would die. The only medicines were penicillin and streptomycin but they were old. Twice I got sick with a fever. I was too sick to work. I went to the camp dispensary. They gave me only aspirin. I did not get better so they tried Lao medicine — root water. My friends gave me food.

In 1984 they pulled together Camps 04, 05 and 06 and brought everyone to Camp 03, in the Sop Pane area farther still back down the road to Viengxay than the Sop Hao jail. This is their headquarters. Then they announced on the radio, "No more seminars in Laos."

They wanted to bluff all the people, to hide the truth from them — from all the world. And everybody believed them. Everyone in the world said: "Now the seminars are no more." But they had been blinded. The real truth is the seminar is still up there now. They do not call the prisoners "seminarists" any more. Now they are called "pholamouangdy" — "good people."

"No more seminars. The seminarists are very good people now," they said. But they are still there working. They are still prisoners. Six hundred people. The world does not know about them.

Those people still living and still in condition to work have been dispersed throughout the Sop Pane area, one hundred here, one hundred there, to cut wood, to build new camps, to work on the roads. The new camps have no names. Just the camp at Sam Teu, at Tham Ting, at Muong Soy, at Pa Hang, at Lao Houng.

Lao Houng was the first of these camps. Lao Houng was the village that had been used by Prime Minister Kaisone of the Lao Communist Party as headquarters for attacking the country of Laos. He lived there before 1975 and was against the Royal

Government of the Kingdom of Laos. The seminar people were contracted out to work at Lao Houng. My friend Samly Khamphouy [see page 191] was there. The old camp sites are not used for seminars any more. The Pathet Lao still use 03 as their headquarters and the prisoners who are sick go there. That is all.

I was more fortunate than the six hundred who remain. When we were collected together in Camp 03, they called a list of names. These people were to go back to Vientiane—free. There were twenty-five of us. Our families had bought our freedom. My wife had paid three bars of gold to get me out—about seven or eight hundred dollars. It was money we had saved when we were still working. She sold her jewelry too. Some paid more than this.

When I reached Vientiane I took my wife and my five children and fled across the Mekong River. And now I am safe. But always I remember the six hundred I left behind, hidden to the people of the world. [PRPC, December 4, 1985.]

Keep Them Until They Die

Boukeo Bounnam

*This story and the three preceding it are of seminarists from camps in
the Viengxay area. While they were not all in the same camp, it seems that
ex-seminarists from these camps — 03, 04, 05 and 06 — have a special feeling
of unity.*

*Viengxay, which is very close to the Vietnamese border in the northeast
of Laos, was the headquarters of the Pathet Lao for some years before the
takeover of the country. The area is very mountainous and wild, the chance
to escape slim and, even after a successful escape, the chances of making it
back to Vientiane undetected almost nonexistent.*

*Those incarcerated in camps in this area felt that they had been sent to
the end of the earth and seemed to feel a depression of hopelessness more severe
than I sensed in seminarists from other regions.*

I was in the Royal Lao Air Force — a full colonel. I was posi-
tioned at Savannakhet in the southern part of Laos. I moved there
from Vientiane headquarters at the end of 1974 and in 1975 I took
up a new job as wing commander at the Savannakhet Air Force
Base. I had five hundred airmen under me.

I had been there seven months when the situation in Laos became very bad. I think it began in May of 1975. The Communists

moved soldiers in. They were all over the province and Savannakhet City too. They wanted to take over the country. Then they
came and took the base. This was in August of 1975. They called
together the officers and told them it would be altogether better for
them to stay there. If anyone were to try to escape he would be sent
away somewhere — we didn't know where.

I stayed on the base with all my officers and airmen. Nobody
moved out. Then, on November twenty-eight 1975, we were all
sent to Phonsaven at Xieng Khouang on the Plain of Jars. That
was my first camp. It was an old Pathet Lao camp and I was there
with my five hundred airmen. Fourteen of us were officers. I was
the only full colonel. The rest were majors and lieutenant colonels.
I stayed there with my airmen about two weeks. There was
nothing to do there only working with wood — cutting firewood,
repairing, building. It was an old camp, you see.

Then, on orders from the Communist government in Vientiane, we fourteen officers were sent to Viengxay far to the east of
Laos, near to Sam Neua. They took us by chopper — Soviet chopper. Every day Soviet choppers brought prisoners to Viengxay to
the Vietnamese seminar camps in that area. Every day.

Viengxay is new. It is a military town. Sam Neua is the city
of the province, the old city. It is bigger than Viengxay. They are
close — about twenty-five kilometers.

From Viengxay we went by truck eight kilometers south to
the old Communist camp at Na Pha. This was on December 17,
1975. It looked like a military camp. It was built of wood and the
roofing was grass. There were four to five hundred prisoners there,
all high-ranking — generals, police and military colonels,
ministers, ambassadors, directors and other civilians. We were all
mixed up together.

We had to stay there about two months and then, in January
of 1976, they moved us east to another old Communist camp. It
was about a hundred and fifty kilometers from Viengxay at the
Nam Ma River right on the Communist frontier.

I think it was an old prison camp because I saw Thai
characters on the rocks in the caves. Before 1970 there were Thai
volunteers fighting in our military. They had been living and

working in Laos. All Lao prisoners, military and civilian, were sent over there to the frontier at Nam Ma. So when I saw the characters I knew that some Thai prisoners had been there.

I stayed there about one year until February 1977 when they moved us again to join another camp. Some of the prisoners came from 06 and 04 at Muong Et. It was again only for high ranks, both military and civilian. This one was a new camp. It was located three kilometers north of Sam Teu City. There were about five hundred prisoners there altogether. They called it Camp 05.

There were also a few families — six or so. One of these was the Bounpone family — General Marthepharack Bounpone, the Armed Forces Commander-in-Chief.

In August and September of 1977, an incident occurred in the camp. First one person, a colonel, and then twenty-six people together were arrested and sent away. I have their names [see page 215]. I know them because I lived and worked and slept with them. They were my friends. There were four ministers, thirteen generals, five police and military colonels, an ambassador, one captain, and two other high ranking civilians — altogether twenty-six people.

The Communist government said they were reactionaries, that they had attempted a coup in the camp. They were arrested, tried before a court and sent away somewhere. I don't know where. And now they are gone. Surely all dead — killed. They are all killed. But they didn't do anything. They didn't say anything. I was there and I say no, no, nothing happened.

That is the way of the Communists. When they want to kill people they make up something so that they can arrest them, kill them. That is the way of the Communists.

After that, in November of 1977, the camp was moved eastward to another site at the Vietnamese frontier. It was at Sop Feua, about fifty kilometers east of Sam Teu City. There we again built a new camp. Its name was still 05. We didn't know why we were being moved. It was the order of the Communist government. It took us about a year to build the new camp there.

Camp 05 at Sam Teu had been on low land, a plain. We could see far, far away. We saw airplanes pass overhead many times. But at Sop Feua there were very high mountains and valleys, jungle and rocks, and very thick, dense forest. The camp was right at the bottom of a deep valley. We didn't see anything flying overhead there but you would be able to see the camp if you flew down the valley in a helicopter.

Every day we were at Camp 05 we worked hard. We had to get up early — four o'clock in the morning, when it was still dark. We worked until six-thirty and came back to the camp to eat breakfast. They gave us only rice, old rice. Sometimes they would reduce the rice allowance and later on increase it again. We didn't know why. That is their way. They didn't give us anything to eat beside that. Vegetables we had to grow ourselves. We didn't have anywhere to buy anything.

There was no medicine. If we were sick we stayed sick or we had to get medicine from our family. We would write to them and they would send it. But it was difficult because the Communists took most of it before it got to us.

At seven-thirty we went back to work until eleven-thirty or twelve. Then rice and a few vegetables for lunch and back to work from one-thirty or so to four-thirty. The times were not rigid but generally we had one and a half to two hours to eat lunch and relax in the middle of the day before going back to work. Most of the time we were building the camp — cutting wood in the forest and building houses and roads.

In the evening after eating dinner we had to study. We had to solve the problems of work for the next day and after that we had to study the Communist system. We studied everything to do with the Communist regime — economics, politics — until eight or eight-thirty. They liked to give us problems to solve. They were about politics, about the way of the Communists.

And every week, every Friday, we had to solve the problems that had arisen for the whole week. Sometimes they gave lectures about Communist policies to solve the problems. The seminarists had to discuss the problems among themselves. Sometimes the Communists would come and listen to what we were saying and then they would explain the right way to solve the problem. We had to agree with them.

They supported the Marxist/Leninist regime in everything. Communism is better than capitalism. They made comparisons between the free world and the Communist world. They said that the United States is the head of the free world. And they said that the United States had fallen. No victory.

They said that when the Communists came into Laos it was very good. Better than before. Better than if America had stayed. They said that they do justice. Communism is justice above everything. They told us that America came into Laos, into Indochina, and didn't do anything. I didn't believe this stuff but we had to talk sitting there with them. You cannot tell them that the Communist way is bad. That would be the end of you.

If you said something wrong, they would send you away somewhere. We didn't know where. People just vanished. They never came back. For instance, there were two students who were the sons of seminarists in the camp. They said many bad things about Communism and they arrested these two men and sent them to prison somewhere outside the camp. We didn't know where. They didn't come back.

In August of 1978, almost one year from when we had moved there, four military colonels tried to escape. They knew the area quite well. It was their home region. They contacted their relatives and then they went on foot through the forest. But they failed. After about a week they were arrested, all four arrested and then killed at the same time. They shot them. There was no trial. They were just shot. Arrested and then shot.

In January 1980, came the time of the beginning of a release of seminarists. They could go back to their families. They sent Communist officers to take them and bring them to Vientiane. I don't know why that was the time for releases. Maybe they wanted to let some seminarists free to make people in Vientiane believe in their system. They released about eighty people during 1980. By mid-1981 they had stopped. I don't know why they stopped either but at least the released men never came back to the camp again.

After the releases they planned to move the camp again and in June of 1981 it was moved north to Sop Ting about forty kilometers north of Sam Teu City. This time it was along the road between Viengxay and Sam Teu. We stayed there until 1983. Then, in April of 1983 the camp was burned, all burned, by a fire from outside I think. From the rice fields maybe. And so we had to move to the north again, this time to Houei Tagua, which means "the eye of the dragon."

It was a road construction camp, also along the road between Viengxay and Sam Teu. Here the Vietnamese divided the camp into three parts and dispersed the prisoners. We built the road. Each group had responsibility for a section. And we built houses and did other construction. We worked hard. We were there about one year.

And then early in 1984 I was released to my family. My wife was still in Vientiane. I had sent messages to her many times to tell her that if she could find any way to escape from Laos to the free world she should do so. But she stayed there to try to get me back.

During those years she worked on building good relations with some of the members of the Communist committee in the Ministry of Interior. She paid them bribes many times: 12,000 baht — about 500 dollars. She managed to make them believe she was sympathetic to them and became friendly with them. And then, when they believed her, they put my name on the list of seminarists to be brought back and submitted it to the Communist committee.

There were about sixty prisoners released between January and April of 1984. I was one of them. I left the construction camp in February and went by truck to Sop Pane, which is the headquarters for Vietnamese road construction. It is the central detention camp. Then, in April, they sent me from there about thirty kilometers west to the old air field at Sam Neua where they put me on a chopper. A Soviet chopper. A Mi-8, I think. It held twenty-four people.

I came back to Vientiane in April and stayed there about five months. First of all I had to enter a Buddhist monastery and be a monk for a few months. That is the custom of Laos. If you fall into something bad, when you come back you have to be a monk for a while. When I came out of the monastery I spent the next two or three months trying to work out a way to get out of Laos.

I finally escaped with the help of my son-in-law. He was married to my first daughter. She had also been in a Vietnamese detention camp at the Plain of Jars and when she got back to Vientiane they had fled together to Thailand. They had been there a long time when I came back to Vientiane.

One day a letter came from them by secret mail telling me the way to escape. They sent a picture of my niece, a very old picture. They had written on it, "Ready to take you." When I saw the picture I decided it was okay to go with the men who brought it. I asked them what day and what time they could take me across the Mekong and I asked them where we would cross.

These people were making their living getting people out of Vientiane across the Mekong River. They charged for everything. I had seven people altogether in my family and I had to pay about seventeen thousand baht — about seven hundred U.S. dollars.

So I prepared to go. But I stayed quiet. I told nobody, not even the United States embassy. I took only a few clothes. Everything else I left behind — my house and all my possessions. I gathered the family together and left my house in the daytime. The men had a truck to get outside the city. We came to the bank of the Mekong River and stayed in the forest. At midnight we crossed by boat. It was October and the river was small.

In Thailand I joined my son-in-law's house at Nong Khai and stayed there about two weeks. Then they sent me to the Na Pho camp where I stayed for about ten months.

At the Na Pho camp I found one of the students who had been sent to prison for saying bad things about Communism while we had lived together in Camp 05. He and his brother had been in the Phadaeng jail near Viengxay for two years. Then he had escaped, alone, and crossed the Mekong River to Thailand. That was in 1984. He is still in Na Pho. If you go there you will find him. His name is Khoun Praseut. His brother, Than, is in Na Pho too. He somehow got authorization to come from Viengxay and when he arrived in Vientiane, he fled to Thailand. His father and mother are still in the seminar camp.

The Lao monument at the Philippine Refugee Processing Center.

Three months ago I came here to the Philippines. I don't know exactly when I will leave but I will join my sons in the United States. I have three sons there in Oregon. The first one went in 1980 and the other two in 1981. They are studying at Portland University.

*   *   *

When I left Laos there were about two hundred seminarists from Camp 05 dispersed along the road at Houei Tagua in three different places. They are still there. In 1984 there would have been altogether about eight hundred seminarists from Camps 03, 04, 05 and 06 in that area. That doesn't count the prisoners in the Pha-daeng jail near Viengxay. Khoun Praseut, who was there, tells me that there are Communists who have had political problems as well as seminarists in this jail.

They are not sending new people out to the seminar camps. Gradually they will close down. They will keep the prisoners there

The Twenty-Six Accused of Rebellion in Camp 05, September 1977

State Ministers

Pheng Phongsavanh (Minister of Defense)
Toubi Lifoung (Head Buddhist monk, a government position)
Sukan Vilaysane (Minister)
Lian Phavongviengkham (Ambassador to People's Republic of China)

Military Generals

Ouane Ratikoun (retired)
Bounpone Marthepharack (Armed Forces Commander-in-Chief)
Phasouk S. Rajsaphack (Chief of Staff)
Bounleuth Sanichanh (Inspector General)
Bounthieng Venevongsoth (International Control Committee)
Kane Insixiengmay (Logistics—Armed Forces Headquarters)
Atsaphangthong Pathammavong (Asst. to Commander, Region 5—Vientiane Sector)
Thao Ly Lithiluxa (Intelligence—Armed Forced Headquarters)
Nouphet Daoheuang (Commander of Region 3—Savannakhet)
Rattanabanhleung Chounlamountri (General Security Commander)
Tiao Sinh Saysana (Operations—Armed Forces Headquarters)
Thongpanh Knocksi (Information Officer)
Bounchanh Savatphayphane (Operations—Armed Forces headquarters)

Military, Police and Civilians

Kamphanh Thammakhanti (Colonel. See note, page 288, #99)
Amkha Khanthamixay (Colonel—the only one still living. See note, page 286, #1)
Kavin Keonakhone (Police Colonel)
Issara D. Sasorith (Director)
Sery Sayakham (Captain)
Sivilay Phichith (Police Colonel)
Khamchanh Pradith (Ambassador)
Heng Saythavy (Political coalition member)
Khammouk Phengsiaroun (Police Colonel)

Note: Phom Phanthavong (Colonel—Battalion Commander, Ban Keun area, north of Vientiane) was arrested in August 1977, one month before the other twenty-six. See page 291, #214.

---

maybe twenty, thirty years. Keep them until they die. That is the Communist way.

Vientiane City looks very sad these days. Not many people are in the streets. The shops are closed. The people have escaped to Thailand.

A new generation is coming up now to run the Lao government. These people are mostly Communists although there are
some from the former government still. I don't know why they are
still there. Maybe they like the Communists. If they have not
escaped that means they are helping the Communist government.
Many were my friends. One is the Lao ambassador at Bangkok
now. He was my friend, my schoolfellow in high school. His name
is Khamphanh Simalavong. Being the ambassador at Bangkok
means he helps the Communists. And there are many, many
others in Vientiane. They work with the Communist government.

I still hope that one day it will be possible to go back to Laos.
Meanwhile I must tell the children about what happened to their
country. I must tell them about the Communist regime. [PRPC,
December 4, 1985.]

The News Collector

Name Withheld

For this story I had the best interview conditions available in the camp — the office of the liaison officer from the United States Embassy in Manila. We had privacy, a big conference table to spread things out on and air conditioning. Even so, the outside noise from traffic and people reverberated in my sensitive little tape recorder. We worked late into the night with the help of a long-suffering interpreter who filled in the gaps where the storyteller's English failed him.

Even though he was very anxious to tell his story, the teller was more afraid than most of reprisals so his name has been withheld.

He is in the United States now and writes me: "As of now, I have to study eight hours a day. Morning attend ESL course, afternoon is Electronic Assembly course. My two sons are over 18 years so they have to go to vocational course right now at Vietnam youth community. It's hard to them because their English speaking not so good. I'm sorry that I was long time in Thailand camp almost four years. They just have studied English in Philippines three months."

My memory is difficult. I cannot recall everything that happened when I lived in Laos. I want to make a record of my story but I am afraid of the Communists' finding out.

I was a teacher in Laos. I worked for the old government. At first I was at a rural primary school in Khock village near Pak-Ou in Luang Prabang Province where the River Ou crosses the Mekong. I taught all subjects. Then in 1972 I was promoted to be head administrator at Fangum School Number 4 in Luang Prabang City. It was an American vocational school. My supervisor, Mr. Sozum Yamauchi, was Hawaiian. I liked him. The directors of the school were Lao: from 1971 through 1972 Mr. Wat Simoun, who is now in the United States, and from 1974 through 1975 Mr. Chanphet Siboupha, who is now in Thailand.

We taught science, business management, home economics, small industry and agriculture. We had good equipment. There was a tractor for practical agriculture, a metal shop for small industry and many calculators and typewriters for business management. The students were all Lao and ranged from twelve to fifteen years old, both girls and boys.

In 1973 the Pathet Lao became part of the coalition government. When Mr. Sozum Yamauchi heard that he went home to Hawaii. Director Chanpeth organized a small protest against the Communists before going to Malaysia to study and I took over as director of the school.

Then in 1975 — it was in October — the Communists took over my country, my freedom. I was afraid. I hid myself away at home but they found me. They said, "You! Go to seminar! Nobody works here! You are the old government! You worked with Americans! You go to seminar!"

And so, on February 15, 1976, I was sent to a seminar camp. The Communists called them seminar camps because that sounded good and they said it was good to go there to have a new experience. But they were really reeducation camps and that is nothing but a hard labor camp. It was the Na Dou camp in Luang Prabang Province that I was sent to, and I worked there like a laborer. I had to cut wood and carry it long distances. It was used to construct buildings that they were making to hide tanks. The people from the camp did the labor.

After about eighteen months they let me go and I went home to Luang Prabang City. Then the Communists said to me, "Will you work with us?" I said, "I cannot work with you because I am not strong enough and there are many children to take care of. I cannot expect my wife to take care of all my students.

So they said, "If you don't want to work with us in charge of the school, you can be under someone else."

I said, "Yes, O.K." But I wanted to stay home with my family so I did not work at the school. I stayed at home for about six months and went to the fields, fishing for a livelihood.

During this time they would not let us have any freedom of activity. We could not go visiting outside Luang Prabang Province. We could not go to Vientiane. We could not go to Viengxay. They would not give permission to go anywhere. We had to stay where we were. My wife became pregnant during this time.

Then, in January 1978, they caught me and sent me to seminar camp for the second time, along with many people who had not already been. This time they didn't take only the leaders, like the police and the government functionaries, but also the people who worked with the Communists but didn't believe. They were all sent to camps.

There were ninety-four people in my camp this time — fourteen women and eighty men, all soldiers or teachers or government officials and leaders of subdistricts. (In Laos we have districts and subdistricts. A subdistrict is about ten villages.)

This time the camp was at Houi Phay which is between two mountains about eight kilometers south of Luang Prabang City. We worked in the fields and raised goats and cattle for the Communist government there. They used the men and women like machines and when the machines were broken they were put away and not repaired. The sick and dying were made to work.

The guards would say, "You! You are sick? But you still eat so you can work! If you are sick you cannot eat and you lie down." It was really hard — not relaxing.

Some people starved and some people got very ill but the guards didn't give any medicine to them. Sometimes someone in the family, usually the wife, would hear about her husband being sick and would send medicine with the people who worked with the Communists in the camp. They did not have to pay them. They were not Communists themselves but just Lao who worked with the Communists. They were allowed to travel although sometimes they had to pay bribes to the officials in the camp. If they had really been Communists the families could not have sent medicine with them.

The Communists said that if somebody was sick he could go to the hospital and many people went but none ever came back. I don't know what happened to them. Nobody in the camp knew what happened to them. Whether dead or still alive, nobody knew. And then finally their families would be told that they had died but they would not send the body to the family. They would never see them again. After nearly twenty-one months of this, I finally said to myself, "Oh, if I don't escape from here I will wind up dead like the rest." So I decided to escape and every day I waited for the chance.

Then one day, it was October 28, 1979, I was a little sick and I couldn't go out to work hard so they made me go and take care of the goats and cattle.

There were two of us and two soldiers went with us to control us. The guards wanted to go down by the river under the trees and at about eleven o'clock they fell asleep because the weather was nice. I looked up and saw them asleep under the tree. This was my chance!

Now, the cows would eat some grass and go a little way and eat some grass and go a little way. And if they were left to themselves they would keep going on and on. So I followed the cows and before long we came to a big rock. I looked back and the guards were far away and they were still sleeping. I quickly hid behind the rock and ran down to the river. There I saw some friends and I said, "May I go with you? I am afraid of the Communists. I escaped from camp."

And they said, "OK! OK!" And I escaped with them in their boat. I had known that my friends used to fish in the Mekong but I did not know that they would be there when I came to the river bank that day. They took me in their boat to Khok Ya which is up the river in Luang Prabang Province.

There is a liberation organization in Khok Ya so I joined.

There were many members. My job was to collect news.
Sometimes I would get the news from my friends and sometimes
I would get it myself. Then I would send it back to the base
organization in Khok Ya.

*   *   *

One day in 1981 I went up the Ou River to Mouang Khoua
in Phong Saly Province. This area had been ruled by China but
when the Chinese troops withdrew the Vietnamese occupied it. So
I went to see what was happening and to send back news. I asked
the people about the Vietnamese soldiers and troops. They said
they didn't know where they were but they could appear within
about twenty-four hours when there was fighting between the left
and the right in the region. That meant that their troops were
hiding in the big forests.

I went around the area to see what I could see. There had been
a seminar camp at Mouang Khoua for subofficials. It had operated
from 1975 through 1980. It was near the Ou River. A little to the
north there is a road running up to the river from each side. East
of the river the road was built by the Vietnamese and west of the
river, by the Chinese. There is no bridge. A boat is used for crossing back and forth. At night I slept upriver from the crossing in
a friend's boat and watched. There was a troop of Vietnamese
marines in the area. They ferried gasoline across the river. For one
day they used four or five drums.

Then I went east and south toward the border of Luang
Prabang and Sam Neua provinces but I didn't get to the border.
I came instead to a village just to the west of the border and there
I met friends who gave me news. They said, "You shouldn't go on
any farther. It's dangerous for you."

There were many camps on the border. They were bases of
Vietnamese and Soviet troops. One base would be Vietnamese
and the next Soviet and the next Vietnamese and so on down the
border. There was no fighting in this area but there were many
people in these camps, especially chemists and miners because
there were gold and silver mines there. The Soviets and

Vietnamese had taken over the mines in 1980 or 1981. They had come to take the riches of Laos.

The Vietnamese came first. I don't know if they agreed to have the Soviets come or whether they just came. They didn't work together and I don't know if there was any kind of cooperation between them.

They were putting the gold and silver into boxes and labelling the boxes and sending them out of the country. They were taking it in lots about as much as two people can carry. It was going for analysis. They planned to take it all in the next five years, once they had found the richest areas.

They didn't like to use their own people to carry the materials from the mines so they used the people from the nearest villages. They didn't use people from any seminar camp, just from the villages. It was the local people who had been working in the mines who told me what was happening there.

I also learned about how the seminar camps were organized in that area. All the officers — governors and other high-level people — were taken to seminar camps in 1975. In Luang Prabang Province they were put in the Hat Chanh camp which is on the bank of the Ou River in the north of Laos near Muong Ngoi. Then the officers from major up were sent to Boum Yo camp in the north of Phong Saly Province near the border of China. The lower ranks were sent to Oudon Say camp in Luang Prabang Province. From master-sergeant down they were sent to Mouang Khoua camp in Phong Saly.

After China and Vietnam quarrelled with each other — it was 1979 or 1980 — the Vietnamese moved the Boum Yo camp. They split it. Some of the people went to Mouang Kham camp in the north of Xieng Khouang Province near the border of Luang Prabang and some went to a camp down south in Attopeu. I don't know the name of the camp in Attopeu.

Before the Communists occupied Laos there were three Communist factions fighting the former government. These were the Pathet Lao, the Vietnamese and the Chinese. But after Laos fell the new Lao Communist government regarded all the customs of the Leninists. They were like the Vietnamese. The Chinese were worried about this. They didn't like it. And then they left because China is Maoist. So after 1980, China did not help the Lao Communist government anymore.

The Soviets helped them though. They gave them military supplies and there were Soviet representatives cooperating with the Vietnamese. There were many Soviet soldiers inside Laos. Everywhere there was an important base, an important camp, it was controlled by Soviet troops. And there are many Soviet experts in Laos right now.

I also learned about two other camps — 04 and 05. I don't know exactly where they are but somewhere in Sam Neua Province. I think they may be near the border of Vietnam, between Sam Neua and Vietnam.

These camps were only for the high ranks of the military and they were very hard. The people were sent there on a plane with their hands attached at the wrists with rope. And when they arrived in 04 and 05 they were taken into tunnels in the ground. Nobody could see these camps because they were completely under the ground.*

I heard about what had happened to the king and queen when they were taken as prisoners to that same area and how they had died there. In November of 1975 they had denounced the king. There had been demonstrations. Many, many people had come. Communist Party members had got students from the schools and people from everywhere and brought them to Luang Prabang City to join the demonstration. Many people hadn't wanted to be there but the Communists had forced them. Some people had cried because they hadn't wanted to join the demonstrations. But finally the Communists had said that this was the action of the people.

Then in March of 1977 the king, the queen, two princes and some of their high-ranking staff like the first secretary, the second secretary and the head of protocol were taken prisoner. They took them with their hands tied on an airplane to Viengxay. When they got there the king and queen were separated from the others and

---

*Ex-seminarists from 04 and 05 say that it was not the camps themselves that were underground but the jail across the Nam Ma River from Sop Hao. — J.S.

sent to live.in the countryside. They put up a small hut for them and there they lived under Vietnamese control. They could not move around and there were always guards.

Being in that place was very hard for the queen. It was very different from the way she used to live. Here she had to work on a loom. She worked hard just like all the people. Then she caught a disease because she was weak and it overcame her and she died. This was, I think, about a year after they took her prisoner.

The king went on living in that place for about one more year. Then came a Vietnamese expert in psychology and told the people that the king was a bad man. He said he would eat only meat, pure meat with no bones and would walk only on a rug. So Laos should not have a king any more because he was a bad man. The people liked the king but the Vietnamese expert aroused them. They killed him, the Vietnamese. I don't know how they killed him because they took him to another place and he disappeared.*

One of the prisoners, General Houmphanh, went back to Vientiane. The people came from all around and asked for news. He told them the truth about who had died and what was happening. He told the people the king was dead. So the Communists sent him back to the camp and the people throughout all of Laos were very sad and they became very afraid of the Communists, especially the people who had escaped from the camps.

Not long after that, the people got the news that the princes also had died and that twenty-six high officials had been arrested and killed because they had tried to organize demonstrations against the Communists in Camp 05 near Viengxay.

I was told that what they did was complain about human rights violations, referring to the Eighteen Articles agreement between the Vientiane government and the Lao Communist Party. They were officially invited by members of the old government to attend a meeting at Viengxay. When the airplane landed, there were protesters there — people sent there by the Communists.

---

*Accounts of the fate of the king and queen vary somewhat although there is general agreement that they were arrested in March of 1977 and died or were killed in the Viengxay area. See index. — J.S.

And then they were taken to the jail. I was told this by my uncle, Mr. Bounthan Thiraphong, and also some other friends when they came from Viengxay.*

In August 1979, the Communists took the Buddha that is called "Prabang." This Buddha is our most ancient and holy Buddha. It is about four feet high and made of solid gold. The Khmer brought it from Ceylon about 2,000 years ago and then the first king of Laos brought it with him when he came from Cambodia to establish the new kingdom. The Prabang was kept in Luang Prabang City and the Communists took it away to Vientiane and then to Vietnam and then sent it to the Soviet Union. The people asked why they had taken it and they said they had put the Prabang in a safe place. We didn't see it again.

I think that maybe the Vietnamese sent it to the Soviets to pay their debts because the Prabang was the most valuable of all the Buddhas in Laos. One time the World Bank wanted to buy this Prabang and the Lao government, our former government, refused. But the Communists took it for free.

There is another thing the people of Laos don't like very much. This is the plan for taxes, especially the tax on rice. At first the crops were divided into four parts. One part was for the government for tax. The second part was to sell to the government at a low price. The third part was to give to the government for the public stock. And the last part was for the owner.

Now they have a second plan. Under this plan they measure the area of the fields and divide them up into A, B and so on. In A the rice is very good and in B not quite so good. . .on down to the poorest rice. Then they take the most tax from A because it is the best. The people who grow the best rice pay more tax.

Rice is the only thing the people have to eat. There are some work animals that the Communists divide out to the cooperative farm groups. But as for small animals like chickens or pigs, the troops come to the villages and take them away from the people. They don't pay.

---

*The incident involving the twenty-six high officials happened in September of 1977 according to eyewitness Boukeo Bounnam. — J.S.

So many people are very poor because although they work very hard and grow a lot of rice they have to sell it to the government and then they don't have enough left to feed themselves. And the government will not sell them rice again from the public stock. The rice that the government takes is for the Communist Party members only. They store all the rice in sheds and then the Party members come and take it from the stock. But when the people have no rice to eat they cannot ask the government for some of the rice that they sold them in the first place.

There are many other taxes too. From 1975 to 1980 the Communist government allowed the people to sell things without taking sales tax from them. Then in 1980 they made them pay taxes back to 1975. There were many other sorts of taxes — on houses, factories, small businesses — all at the same time. But the people could not pay five years of tax at one time so they started to escape from Laos.

At first the Lao people hadn't thought of going to settle in another country. They wanted only to keep away from the Communists because they were so cruel, so cruel. Some people became refugees many times. At first they escaped inside Laos. For instance, people who lived in Dien Bien Phu when it was still part of Laos fled to Vientiane in 1954 and 1955 during the Indochina war. These were the first Lao refugees. Then, in 1958, when the Communists took Sam Neua Province, the people from there also fled to Vientiane. And at last there was nowhere left to go so they escaped to Thailand.

The last group of refugees that came here to the Philippine camp said that now when the prisoners escape from the seminar camps they go to their families and wait only a few hours or a few days before escaping to Thailand. They also say that the Communist government is now taking annual taxes from the vendors who worked with them from 1975 to 1985. This is especially a problem for Chinese and Vietnamese vendors living in Laos. These people had not had to pay taxes before but now they have to so they cannot live there anymore and are escaping from the country.

But the real refugees should be people like soldiers and

government officials who escaped from the seminar camps — only people who have been persecuted by the Communist government. The Chinese and Vietnamese vendors should not be allowed refugee status.

* * *

When I escaped from Laos to Thailand I took a boat around to Vientiane then another boat across the Mekong River. I had to go this way because I took my old mother and she cannot walk far. There are many, many boats on the Mekong at Vientiane. Big boats too.

I had decided to escape in 1979 to look for freedom but I did not have enough money to pay for the trip so I waited and saved my money. Then, one day, I heard Voice of America announcing the escape of Tchiao Soulivong, the king's nephew. I said to myself, "If I try to leave, the Communists might know about it and track me down and send me away to a further camp or kill me outright." So I planned very carefully. I decided to escape on the first day of January 1982.

I crossed the river in a boat with my family — six children and a very old mother. She is in the United States now, in Santa Ana, California. My sister is there too. She is going to sponsor me. I finish my language classes on January twenty-fifth, 1986, and will leave shortly after that. [PRPC, October 23, 1985; the storyteller is now resettled and living with his family in Santa Ana. — J.S.]

Nobody Can Speak Against Them

Saeng Praseuth and Sisouphanh Ravisong

Saeng Praseuth was introduced to me by the teller of the last story. He had heard I was looking for women to talk to and brought her to me with her husband as interpreter. She was a shy woman, small and nervous. Her English was limited and she was hesitant to practice it on me, so she spoke through her husband.

This story starts as Saeng Praseuth's story, told by herself through her husband, who gave it to me in the third person. Shortly, the story switches to him as the story-teller in consultation with his wife.

After the second meeting Saeng Praseuth didn't come back. Her husband spoke for both of them.

She [Saeng] was a government clerk in Savannakhet City and worked at the Public Works Department as a typist. She was there from 1960 to 1965. Then she married me and after 1967 she didn't work any more. She was a housewife and took care of the children. We had enough food for the family because I had a job in the military. I was a major.

Before 1975 we had a good life. We had a house. We had a

229

car. Our children could go to school. But late in 1975 I was taken to seminar camp—the Sepone camp in Savannakhet Province.

When I had been there for six months, the Communists told my family that they could visit me so my wife came to see me. The first time she came the Communists let her go back to the family in Savannakhet and so she came again and brought three of my children with her. But this time they wouldn't let her go back.

They arrested her in the camp and said, "You visit your husband. You talk to your husband and to other people here. You hear something, some bad news from here, and you go back to Savannakhet and tell people there. You'd better stay here with your husband."

So at that time our family was separated. My wife had left two children in Savannakhet with their old grandmother. The other children, three sons, stayed in Sepone with us. They were about eight, five and two years old then.

She was pregnant but even so she had to do the same work as a man—just as hard. She had to cut down trees and bamboo and burn the land to prepare it for rice planting. The men did the same but we had to do more.

The small children stayed at the camp and they let some of the women take care of them. But children like my eight-year-old son had to help with the work. We were assigned to get things done in a certain time. Like, "Today you must cut down three trees." But the work was always too much. We could not cut it all and carry it in one day. So the children had to help their parents, going to the forest to cut lumber to build houses for the Communists and for ourselves. When we had cut it we had to carry it back to the camp on our backs.

If we couldn't do it all in one day, the Communists would call a meeting and blame us. "Why cannot you do that?" All the officers would be there and the Communist leaders and they would all blame us. They would tell all our fellow prisoners to blame me and my wife and they had to do it: "Why didn't you finish your work like we did?"

And the Communists would say, "They have all finished their work. It is done. Very good. But how about your work? It is not

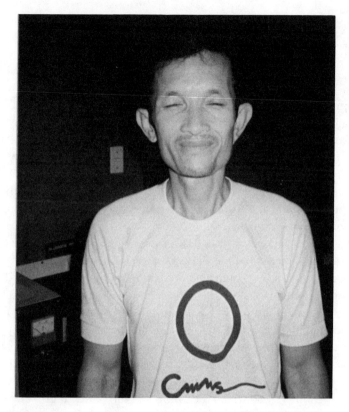

Sisouphanh Ravisong.

finished like all the rest. From now on you must finish your work too."

They didn't beat us for that. They just talked—talking, talking with bad words. And they would do this to anyone who could not finish. So we all tried to work hard. We all tried hard.

Nobody can speak against them. When we were in Sepone, if anyone tried to speak against them they separated them from the seminar camp and sent them to jail. About nineteen people were put in jail like this when I was there. The jails were very, very terrible and no judgment. No one knew how long he would stay there.

They did not put me in jail but I heard what it was like from my friend who was there and escaped. It was far from Sepone, about thirty kilometers west-northwest near a small river. I don't know the name of the district but the jail was called Keng Khanh [see the following chapter].

They had dug it under the ground and they took my friend and put him down there. It was completely underground. He could not see the light and the air was very bad to breathe. They had a bed made of bamboo slats, wide apart. On the end they had two half-circles of wood — like two handcuffs fixed to the bed. And in here they put one leg and then the other so that he could not move. Under the bed was a bamboo pail. If he wanted to go to the bathroom he did it through the bamboo slats as he lay on the bed. The stools and the urine fell down into the pail and in the early morning it was thrown out.

It was dark, very dark down there and the people died in this basement because some stayed there for three months or six months. So many people died there. Two of our good friends died while he was there.

I was not put in jail but I think I would have been if my wife hadn't joined me in the camp. Either that or I would have escaped. I had been talking with a friend of mine, planning an escape, but my wife joined me first and I was not able to do it because now I had to take care of my family.

Another good friend died from a bomb blast. In growing rice we used only manpower — shovels and sticks. The Communists had buffaloes but they wouldn't allow us to use them. While my friend was digging in the ground his shovel hit a bomb and it exploded and killed him. The area had been a battlefield and there were many unexploded bombs there.

Some of our friends tried to escape from the Sepone camp. The first time was in 1976. Two men escaped. And the second time eight. But the eight were killed. They could not escape. Two of them were brought before the whole camp to be killed. They were shot down in front of us all. It was a warning. After that we had another two men escape and then a fourth time two men tried but they couldn't. They were killed too.

So after these four times, the Communists moved the camp from Sepone to Senekheung [also known as Tong Luang]. This was in 1978. I had been in the Sepone camp for more than two years.

They took us to Senekheung by helicopter. It took fifteen or twenty minutes from Sepone. They don't have a good road, only a small trail from Route 9.

We were there one year and in this year two groups escaped from Senekheung. They were killed. And so they moved the camp again, this time to Rako. [Some Lao say "Lako" because they cannot pronounce the "r".] It is two days' walking from Route 9 to Rako. You leave Route 9 and go north near where the Ho Chi Minh Trail crosses Route 9 — where the Americans had a big operation called Operation Lansin because the North Vietnamese were using the Ho Chi Minh Trail in Laos to get to South Vietnam and Cambodia.

Only the men were moved at first. My wife and family were left behind in Senekheung with the other women. She was pregnant again but she had to wait there for the rice to ripen. When it was time for her to have the baby they had only local medicine. The other wives helped with the birth. It was another boy. He was not healthy — very thin and weak. The boy is with me now but he is still very thin and he gets a lot of coughs and small illnesses. He is getting better now but he is still thin.

(The other children were not very healthy either. The Communists had very little medicine — just aspirin and penicillin but it was old. The penicillin they were using in 1975 was from 1967 and 1968 so it was not effective. We still used it. We didn't have any better, although sometimes their grandmother in Savannakhet managed to send us some medicine that she had got from Thailand on the black market. The guards in the camps would go back and forth to Savannakhet so my grandmother made an arrangement with them to take us this medicine. The guards would go to my house to eat and sleep and grandmother would ask them for favors in exchange. It helped us to take care of the children and ourselves.)

When the rice was ready in Senekheung, the women and children harvested it. It was good rice. We had planted it ourselves and taken care of it. But it was all sent away somewhere, I don't know where — to the Communists. To us they just gave old rice, many years old.

When the women and children had finished harvesting they joined us in Rako. Life there was very hard but my wife had to work and also care for the children. She became pregnant again. This one was to be her last.

When it was time for her to have the baby, it was not safe to deliver it in Rako so they sent her to Sethamoua. This is about one hundred and fifty kilometers from Savannakhet on Route 9. There was a clinic there. It was small. There was no doctor, just a nurse, although the Communists called her a doctor. They could not take care of my wife there either so they sent her to Savannakhet and my last son was delivered there. This was the eighth child — five boys and three girls.

After the child was born, the Communists told her to go back to the camp but she refused to go. She stayed there in Savannakhet with her mother. The Communists told her many times to go back but her doctor, who was an ex-director of the old government, wrote her a certificate to say that she was not well enough. She never went back again.

Almost two years later I escaped. It happened that I had the opportunity to go to the Ban Dong camp. This is a reeducation camp for officers south of Rako on Route 9, on the frontier between Vietnam and Laos. We went to get supplies for Rako. They would send guards with prisoners to carry the supplies. We would walk and carry the supplies on our backs. One person would carry ten kilos of rice.

While we were on the trail the guards watched us carefully but when we reached Ban Dong and went inside the camp they stopped watching so we were free inside the camp. We could walk around and we could go outside fifty meters and a hundred meters around the camp. They were not careful with us.

Now, on Route 9 there were convoys to and from Vietnam carrying supplies from Vietnam to Laos. These trucks passed right by the camp. My brother-in-law was a driver in one of these trucks. He was going by and saw me near the road. So he called to me and I thought quickly and went with him to Savannakhet, hiding in the back of the truck. It was not planned. I met him by accident.

I didn't stay in Savannakhet. I let my wife know I had escaped and then I went looking for a way across the Mekong River. I was afraid to stay or I would be caught and sent back.

On that part of the Mekong River there is a lot of traffic, trade with Thailand, so there are boats going back and forth. There is government-to-government trade and there is also the black market trade. People on each side of the Mekong are relatives so they trade with each other behind the backs of the Communists. If they are caught they are sent to jail and their goods confiscated.

I stole one of these boats and crossed the river at night. There were no other boats on the river but the guards did not stop me.

Now, my nephew lived in Sebang Fai, about fifty kilometers north of Savannakhet. He had worked with the Americans but after the Communists took over he was appointed to be chief of the village. I don't really know how he came to be chief. I had taken care of him when he was younger and we had talked many times about the Communists. He didn't like them. In a letter he sent recently he said that he has quit the post now. He did not get along with the Communists.

Anyway, I contacted him and asked him to bring my family to join me in Thailand. So he took care of them and helped them get safely across the river. They came in the daytime because he was chief of the village and the guards knew him. He also knew many people who traded between Laos and Thailand so he asked some of them to help my wife.

We went to the Na Pho camp in Thailand and we were there for almost two years then two weeks in Panat Nikhom transit center and on here to the Philippines. The children are all here. My wife is in much better health. When she was with me in the seminar camp she was very sickly. She got a lot of headaches and backaches. When she was with her parents she didn't lift anything heavy but when she went to the camp she worked very hard carrying water from the river, carrying wood to make fire, and taking care of the children by herself. I couldn't help her very much because I had too much work.

It is very hard in the seminar camps but it is also hard for the people who live in the cities of Laos. People who have escaped tell me that for civilians living in the city there is very little freedom to move from one place to another. If someone lives in Savannakhet and they want to go to Vientiane it is very difficult to arrange it. They have to ask the authorities for a permit but it takes more than a week to get it. And there is a limit on the number of people that can travel together. If in your family you have five people you cannot go all at the same time. Two or three can go and the rest must stay in Savannakhet. They won't allow the whole family to travel together.

It is also very hard to do any trade in the market. My wife's mother used to be a seller in the market but now she cannot do that. They don't have free markets any more. Before 1975 everybody could go to the market and sell anything they liked but now they cannot do that. There are no private traders. It is all run by the government. The import tax is very high so the prices are very high. The Communists do have a low-cost government store but it is for Communist officials. Black market prices are also high because the risk is so high for the traders.

Although government clerks get a house and other benefits, their salary is very low — for one month not enough to buy a sack of rice — so the people are poor. There's not enough to feed their families. They stay because they have a house and a few good things. But they are selling all their goods for money to buy rice and meat so they are getting poorer and more are leaving.

The laborers are worse off. They get a low salary but no other benefits. So they go to work late and come home early to go fishing or to go to the countryside to get rice for their families. Or they steal gasoline and sell it on the black market. The Communist way is not a good way. It is the way to get people to cheat.

The education system is bad now too. If my children were still at school there they wouldn't be able to select the things they wanted to study. The Communists would limit their study because they are the sons of ex-government officials. They would be allowed to finish secondary school but after that they wouldn't be allowed to continue their education.

They do have tertiary education in Laos still. They have created a new Communist university but it's not good. There are many, many graduates from the university, many engineers and doctors, but they cannot get jobs so they take whatever work they can find, jobs for which they are not trained. Actually, that is good because they don't know their jobs very well. They are not trained properly and they have no skill. A nurse in 1975 was better than a doctor is now in 1985.

*   *   *

I wanted to keep a record in the seminar camps but I couldn't because the Communists would find it so I wrote things like dates when I was moved from camp to camp on little pieces of paper and hid them inside my clothing. And then, when I got into Na Pho camp, I got a notebook and wrote it all down.

I want the world to know about the life of the ex-officer and the ex-government clerk, how they went away with their children and how hard life was with them under the Communists. [PRPC, November 6, 1985.]

The Jail of Keng Kanh

Vanhthong Mountry

I first learned of Vanhthong Mountry from his friend, Sisouphanh Ravisong, and went looking for him in the hot, dusty Lao section of the camp, where a few scraggly trees struggle out of hard, red clay, eroded in ridges from the rain.

Refugee quarters are long, makeshift huts with corrugated iron roofs overhanging at the front to form a sort of narrow verandah. Each hut is divided into ten or so one-room sections, each maybe ten feet wide and twenty feet deep. Each section houses one family with a small table, a broad, low slat bed and, at the back, a rudimentary kitchen, although most cooking is done outside over charcoal fires. At one side is a ladder that goes up to a low sleeping area.

The huts are arranged in groups around a more-or-less square open area. Some of these squares have struggling vegetation around the edges but for the most part they are naked—hard as brick under the baking sun and sucking quagmires under the hot tropical rains.

I found Vanhthong with his wife and children outside their quarters. He called his friend from next door to bring his dictionary and we sat and talked. He spoke calmly, showing me his bullet wounds and the scars torn around his ankles by the stocks. I asked him, "With such a life for so long, how did you keep from going crazy?"

He shrugged, "We were soldiers and trained to go through adversity."

Keng Kanh is the name of a small village on the Sekok River to the northwest of Sepone, about fifteen kilometers along Route 9 in Savannakhet Province. The jail there is named after the village. It is only one of the Communist jails in the central part of Laos. It was previously at Ang Kham, in the same area, and was used for prisoners of war. Then the Communists moved it to Keng Kanh and used it for political prisoners, the old Royal Lao military and those in the general population who were antigovernment. Some of the original prisoners were released and some were moved along with the jail.

The jail stands on top of a low hill, with the land falling away on all sides. It is surrounded by a solid wooden beam fence about three meters high. On each corner is a tall guard post with floodlights at night. Outside the fence half a kilometer of land has been cleared of trees all around and beyond that is light forest, the trees no more than fifteen feet high.

I was sent to this jail in March of 1976 after I had tried to escape from the Thak Hong seminar camp at the intersection of Route 9 and the Se Bang Hieng River. Six of us had tried to escape. One had been killed, the other five of us arrested. I had been shot in the left arm and sent to the hospital at the Thak Hong camp and then to the Savannakhet hospital before being sent to the jail at Keng Kanh.

I was there for four years — until December of 1979, when I was sent back to the seminar camp. Over this time the number of prisoners ranged from five hundred to a thousand. When I left there were about six hundred. This jail is still there now, in 1986. I have heard this from other people escaping from Laos.

The jail is classified into three categories. The first is for new prisoners awaiting investigation, the second is for those who have been investigated already, and the third is for selected prisoners from the second category.

The first category is a series of cellars about two meters underground. Each is about one and a half meters high, too low to stand upright, about five and a half meters long and four meters wide. The ceiling is of heavy wooden beams covered with dirt, like a bunker. The floor is bamboo.

Vanhthong Mountry.

There are ten such cellars in all. Each one can hold twenty persons, ten on each side. Running along each wall, about seven tenths of a meter off the ground, is a wooden frame supporting horizontal bamboo slats. These platforms are just wide enough for a man to lie with his head to the wall and his legs sticking out into the center aisle where the guards walk in the daytime.

On the end of these platforms, facing into the middle of the cellar, the wooden frames are in two pieces, one on top of the other, the top and the bottom having matching halves of a circle cut out of them smaller around than a man's ankle. The result is what amounts to a row of legcuffs or stocks fixed tightly into the frame. In here they put the prisoners' legs so that they cannot move.

I was down there for six months and the cuffs were locked day and night. The only exercise was sit-ups and my ankles were bleeding most of the time. I still have the scars.

Under each person was a bamboo pail. If we wanted to go to the bathroom we did it through the bamboo slats as we lay there. Stools and urine fell down into the pail and in the early morning it was thrown away by second category prisoners.

It was very dark down there and smelled bad. Some people died — ten while I was there. When someone died in the night the rats would attack the body. There were many mosquitos and cockroaches all around. They came to the pails under the bed and ran all over us.

We were allowed to talk if we avoided politics but no one wanted to talk except when necessary. We were too afraid of the guards. We got two meals a day, at ten in the morning and four in the afternoon, and once a week we had to report to the leader of the cellar what we had done in the past against the Communists.

Most of us were soldiers, trained to pass through difficulties and dangers, and this helped us not to go crazy. But even so, I would think to myself, "I am dead now. I have died down here." And then I would be surprised that I was still breathing.

Once the first category prisoners had spent six months or so underground and had been investigated, we had to work at husking rice. We were under the control of guards with our legs chained. Work hours were from eight to ten in the morning, with the midday meal at eleven, and two to three-thirty in the afternoon, with the evening meal at four-thirty.

Food was sticky rice and ordinary rice, two hundred and fifty grams uncooked for each person each day. This was about a handful of cooked rice twice a day. Any other food depended on what the third category prisoners could find. Some days there was nothing to eat but rice and salt. We would mix the salt with a little water and put it on the rice.

Sometimes we had soup, one bowl between four or five

persons. It was usually made with bamboo, vegetables or potatoes and occasionally meat or fish. We were also allowed out for exercise, fresh air and a bath for one hour once a week but both our legs were still locked with chains.

After I was allowed above ground, I couldn't see. It was two years before my eyesight was back to normal. I also became partially paralyzed while I was down there. I couldn't walk when I came out. It was because of lack of food and no exercise.

I was in the second category of the jail for two years. It was a series of huts with wooden uprights, bamboo walls and hay for roofing. Each one was twelve meters long and four wide. Inside they were the same design as the first category underground cells, including the leg-cuffs, although these were only locked at night. There were more than twenty of these huts, each holding twenty persons.

Here they kept prisoners who had already been investigated and they could be there for as long as two years before being transferred into the third category.

These prisoners worked inside the camp too. They did the same sort of work as first category prisoners, husking rice and also doing maintenance jobs. Again like first category prisoners, their legs were chained while they worked and they were under the close control of the guards. Their work hours were slightly different from the first category — from seven-thirty to eleven-thirty in the morning and from one to four o'clock in the afternoon.

They got to take a bath once a week and were fed the same food as the first category prisoners. Meals were also at the same time as they were prepared for both first and second categories by the third category prisoners.

I was in the third category for eighteen months. It was another series of huts the same as the second category. Again there were more than twenty huts. It was a place for prisoners selected out of the second category after one or two years. We were prisoners who had followed the prison rules well. We were allowed to work outside the jail — up to about three kilometers away. We looked for food, farmed rice and vegetables, raised poultry, sawed lumber, cut fire-wood, made knives and acted as general craftsmen.

Hours were slightly different from both first and second categories — from seven to eleven in the morning and one to four-thirty in the afternoon.

Third category prisoners ate slightly later than prisoners in the other two categories — about eleven-thirty in the morning and five in the afternoon — as they served as cooks for the others and had to wait until they were done. They got the same amount of rice but could eat alone or in groups as they pleased. They were also in a position to buy food from the local population whenever they got the chance.

Prisoners in both the second and third categories could be sent back to the first category if they did not follow prison rules strictly: do not talk politics against the Communists; do not have anything to do with the local population; do not be late or absent from work more than three times; do not drink liquor; no dating (there were some women in the second and third categories); do not listen to the radio; do not form groups of more than five persons to write or to read certain books (for instance, Western books or the works of Mao Tse-tung); any instruments that could be used for military operations, such as maps, compasses or weapons, are prohibited; do not take photographs or make drawings; do not go outside the limited zone; do not break the eight o'clock evening curfew; there will be no prisoners of war.

This last one meant that anyone who tried to escape would be killed rather than having his sentence extended. There were many who tried to escape but none succeeded. Most were shot as they ran or tried to climb the fence. Some were brought back to camp where all the other prisoners were called out into the yard to watch them be accused and blamed and finally stabbed with knives until they died in front of all their friends.

Most people became handicapped in some way and all were in very bad condition. The most common illnesses were malaria, influenza, diabetes, diarrhea, pneumonia, ulcers, rheumatism, dysentery, bruises, paralysis due to poor nutrition and various allergies. However, health care was limited to a small dispensary with three nurses and a traditional healer. They had little skill and almost no medicine; penicillin labelled good until 1968, aspirin, sulphate, malaria pills, vitamins B1 and B2, and various assorted tablets and injections.

There was one aspect of this jail that made it very different from the re-education or seminar camps — imprisonment there was a term sentence. Military officers, police officers and high-ranking government officials got fifteen to twenty years. General officers got life. Enlisted men and the general population got from five to seven years.

From time to time people would be called out and we would never see them again. We didn't know if they had been released or sent to seminar camp or killed. General Kot Venevongsoth was there for one night and then taken away again.* I heard that he had been sent to the Ban Phadaeng seminar camp about three kilometers from the Vietnamese border.† As far as anyone knows, he is still there.

I met seven or eight fellow-prisoners later on in the Na Pho refugee camp in Thailand. They had been released from jail and fled for their lives across the Mekong. [PRPC, March 25, 1986; the storyteller left the Philippines April 23, 1986, and now lives with his wife and children in Akron, Ohio. — J.S.]

---

*General Kot Venevongsoth's brother was one of the twenty-six high-level officials accused of rebellion in Camp 05, September 1977. — Speaker.

†Not to be confused with the Phadaeng prison camp near Viengxay. — J.S.

The Hell of Kaisone

Name Withheld

The teller of this next story was perhaps the most intensely emotional of all the refugees I talked with. He was a head shorter than me and stocky, with a grin that revealed a mouthful of worn brown stumps. His manner was direct.

He was angry over the fate of his homeland and, free now to speak, he deluged me with details over an intense work session lasting all one Tuesday into the evening, and most of Wednesday.

What with the heat and the concentration of trying to follow details shot at me in rapid but not always comprehensible English, my brain was addled by the end of the second day.

I called a time out and drove back to Manila, the best of noisy country music surprising the little villages all along the way, and spent the next week in front of my computer, tape recorder on the desk beside me, struggling to transform the metallic words into readable form.

Deprived of his audience, my story-teller fell to writing. When I arrived at the camp the next week, he was lying in wait, cheerfully aggressive, papers in hand.

He still writes to me from Los Angeles in passionate, intricately inventive English and seems just as angry with Kaisone as he did the day I met him.

The king and queen of Laos in seminar camp (ca. 1978).

The Communists killed the people of Indochina in different ways. In each country it was a different way. In Vietnam they drove them out onto the sea and they died there. In Cambodia it was the killing fields. And in Laos they kept them confined in small areas with no food and hard labor in order to let them die little by little. They worked people to death in order to escape being directly labelled killers.

The goal of the Communists was to destroy the people and make them become very poor so that they would have no option but to obey orders—to follow the government—so they would be easy to command. They made the rich poor and the poor even poorer. In a Communist country there is no kind of freedom and the people are very sad—just working, working all day.

In 1975 when the Communists took over Laos, they collected together all the military officers and sent them to reeducation camps which they called "seminar camps." They were like concentration camps.

I was sent to the Sepone camp in Savannakhet Province with

a hundred and eighty senior officers. I was a major. In this camp we were fed only a little rice and salt for three months. We had to work very hard every day. I had to dig the ground, chop wood and build the camp. I had to get wood from the forest about sixteen kilometers away and carry it on my back to the camp. I also had to carry the rice supplies to the camp from about thirty kilometers away on my back.

Then we were told we had to be self-sufficient. There was to be no more rice. We had to grow vegetables in order to feed ourselves. Soon everybody seemed like a living skeleton — not like I am now. Many people died.

There were many of these camps all over Laos. The Pathet Lao officers in charge of them were illiterate and ignorant. They could only see one way, not to the right side nor to the left, as though they wore blinkers like a horse. They were commanded by the Vietnamese, who were their "advisors." Vietnamese troops surrounded the camps to protect them. They did not serve as guards inside the camps but if something happened in the camp the Vietnamese troops would help the Pathet Lao. They would arrest and kill the people.

Then people in the outside world started hearing bad things about the seminar camps. The resistance was very powerful then and Amnesty International in London was making demands that they release the people but the Communists didn't want to so they came up with an idea. "Seminar" sounds like a jail but "commune" sounds like something good so they changed the name from "seminar camp" to "commune." They even transferred officers from "seminar camps" to "communes."

Undersecretary of State for Foreign Affairs Khamphay Boupha said in the United Nations that Laos didn't have seminars any more. And it sounded good, pretty good to them. So they believed it.

But the communes were really seminar camps. Only the words were different. The system of working, the system of living was the same — no medical care, inhumanity, no kind of freedom. It was all a bluff to placate the internationals.

The resistance fighters didn't believe. They knew that the

Communists were bluffing but there was nothing more they could do about it. The strength of the dictatorship was too much for them.

The weapon the Communists use to destroy the people is dictatorship/proletariat. They allow them no freedom. No freedom of speech. No freedom of worship. No freedom of the press. Even in the seminar camps if people said anything against the Communists they were arrested and put in jail. That is worse even than the seminar camp.

There are three types of jail. The first is under the ground. The prisoners are there with shackles on their ankles. They cannot see the sun, cannot even breathe fresh air. They stay under the ground all the time.

The second type is above the ground but locked inside. They don't see the sky or the sun or the moon. There is no chair. They stay on the bare floor in the dirt. They are not tied but they don't come outside at all.

The third type is also above the ground but the prisoners are brought outside to do hard labor. That is their only activity. They stay in a very limited area.

It is hard to understand why some people go to one type of jail and other people go to another type. It is whatever is ordered by the Central Political Bureau of the Party. In the Lao Communist system they don't have any kind of court. They don't respect any rights. They can just be ordered to jail or to seminar camp by the Politburo. It is a system of persecution.

The way of killing in the Lao system is not the same as it was in Cambodia. In Laos the system is first to imprison and then to let the people die little by little of starvation and hard labor. They kill some in the open to let the people see and be afraid but killings have to be by order of the Politburo.

In the Savannakhet area alone there must have been two thousand senior and junior officers in seminar camps and there were three prisons. The only way people got out was by paying bribes.

I was in the Sepone camp, my first one, for three years — from 1975 to 1978. During that time ten people were accused and put in jail because the Communists had found out about their backgrounds. Some were colonels so they knew they had been battalion commanders fighting against the Communists. They accused them of being CIA or American spies. I don't know what happened to them. They were put in prison and there was no news at all after that. We had no contact with them any more. Even their families could not contact them.

In 1978 the Communists decided to change the camp I was in from Sepone to Tong Luang [also known as Senekheuane or Senekheune]. The main reason was because four groups of people had escaped [see page 260 for a list]. They went on trying even after two men were shot before us all. These two were majors — Major Inthasone and Major Nuck. They were killed in the open and all the people in the seminar camp had to come and see in order to make them afraid so that they would obey the regulations of the Communists.

Tong Luang is farther northeast in a more remote area closer to the Vietnamese border. This camp was the same as the first one. The system of working was exactly the same. I was there for one year but people were still attempting to escape so they decided to move us farther away again.

This time we were sent to Willko, or Lako as it is on the map. It is north of Route 9 near the Ho Chi Minh Trail. After each transfer we had to rebuild the camp — chop wood, carry wood and build the buildings. They didn't allow us to take our plants or our chickens. They took them for the Party. And so we had to go with empty hands and start again.

They would not allow us to talk to the people around the Willko camp for one year. Then they let us have a little contact and we exchanged our clothes for chickens. The guards watched to see if the local people were too friendly with the seminar people. If they thought they were they would separate us.

In 1981, while I was living in Lako, I was sent fishing in an area known as Battlefield 719. In this region, I came across the wreck of a helicopter and the remains of a crew that I believe were American. I can't be sure of the exact point but it lies in a ten square kilometer area between Baan KaLouai and Baan Ta-a

(Tasang Lako) in the subprovince of Sepone. It is in a stream in a depression between two hills in a heavily forested area. Father Mun and Father Ma Louie of Lako Village and Asoie Mun of Baan Ka Louie know the place of the wreck and can lead you to it [see page 266 for a map].

The Willko camp was right on the border of Savannakhet Province and Vietnam and sometimes, when we were out working, we would meet men from the mountains. In 1982 I met a mountain man who told me that there were Americans— POWs—in Dong Ha, a town in Bincetian Province, which is about the middle of Vietnam. He gave me three names: Rihs Chner, S.B. 2309.802A U.S. M.D.M., Jewish; Man, C.M.A. 2336737, U.S. M.D.M., Lutheran; Edwin J. Pearce, 192387.175, A.POS., Methodist. Later, in 1985, a United States official came to the Philippine refugee camp asking people about POW sightings. I do not know his name but I think he was from Washington. He seemed to be military in civilian clothes. He had a tattoo on his left arm and a military watch. I was interviewed but I go so nervous I forgot to give him the names.

Altogether I was in seminar camp for eight years—from 1975 to late 1983. Three years I was in Sepone, one year in Tong Luang and four years in Willko. During most of this time in the camps my wife and two of my children were with me. I was alone at first but in 1977, when I was in Sepone, my wife made a request to visit me. The Political Bureau gave her permission to come and then they made her stay. Most of the people in my camp had their families with them.

The Communists' tactic was this: They spread propaganda to the families who wanted to go visit their husbands and fathers in the camp. Then they gave permission to one or two women to come and see their husbands. They let them go again and these women added to the propaganda by spreading the word that it was OK to visit the camp.

Then the second time many people, maybe fifty or sixty, went. They let them go again and again they spread the word that it was OK. Then the third time these people collected most of the families and the Communists let them come again. But when these people tried to leave they stood together and stopped them from going out of the camp again. It was not the same in all camps but in ours that is what they did and that is how I came to have my wife and two children with me.

The women had to be equal to the men. They had to work as men — chop wood, carry it on their backs and build the camp. My wife and I were both forced to dig the earth and plant potatoes — cassava. It was hard work, even for a man.

For the children it was the same. When my children came to see me in the camp the oldest was nine years and the other one was eight. They were just little children but there was no study for them. They had to work carrying wood on their backs like everyone else.

Now, east of Savannakhet, straddling the Se Thamouk River on both sides of Route 9, is Soviet Command Post 923. Here they have about one hundred and eighty Soviets, Czechs and Hungarians. They pass themselves off as technicians but in reality they are soldiers. They are supervising the widening and improvement of the road to make it into a strategic route so that aircraft can use it as a runway. They started in 1975, using Lao manpower. The work is still not finished.

In that camp there is a hospital and when my wife became very sick with a uterine infection I asked for her to go there. She was sent but that hospital didn't have any kind of medicine and there were no Soviet doctors to treat her, only Lao nurses. So one day she went quietly out of the hospital and escaped to Savannakhet City.

She arrived angry and distressed, determined to try to get me freed. She wanted to go to the top so she went to the house of Mae-Dock, the mother of Communist Prime Minister Kaisone Phomvihane, and asked her to speak to her son about freeing me.

Mae-Dock agreed to do this but when my wife returned to her house with the wives of some other seminarists, they were told that their husbands were lucky not to have been executed as this had been the original plan for us.

This was borne out by what I myself was told by the Communist head of the Sepone camp, Thong Leuane Luangvisa. He told me that before the Treaty of Vientiane and the formation of the coalition government, the seven members of the Lao Politburo* had held a meeting at the leftist headquarters in Viengxay. Souphanouvong was there but the meeting was led by Kaisone. (Although Souphanouvong was the titular head of the Lao Communist Party, Kaisone, who was half Vietnamese and the puppet of North Vietnam, was the real power.)

Kaisone and Souphanouvong were plotting together to take over the coalition government — one from the inside (Souphanouvong), one from the outside (Kaisone). The matters they discussed were: how to undermine and overthrow the old regime, how to rid the nation of all vestiges of Western influence, and the fate of the Royal Lao Army officers and the political leaders.

During the meeting, a document was submitted to Souphanouvong recommending that all officers, including NCOs, be executed. Enlisted men were to be secured in concentration camps. Women and children were to be separated from their husbands and fathers and sent to separate camps. There was discussion and it was finally decided that killing all the officers outright was not a good idea as it would inflame world opinion against the regime. So it was decided to send them to "seminar" camps and let them die little by little.

And so it was all agreed before the coalition government was formed. The Communists had no intention of ever working as part of a tripartite government. They had no intention of ever abiding by the Eighteen Articles of the Coalition Government. Their real plan was to take over the country and they had people planted on the inside inciting strikes and labor unrest.

Then, in December of 1975, Kaisone went to Vientiane. Two days later the situation peaked. The coalition government was overthrown, the Communists took over, and they sent us all to hell.

Finally my wife paid a bribe to Mr. Savaeng, the bureaucrat in Savannakhet responsible for the camp, and had me and the chil-

---

*Kaisone Phomvihane, Nouhak Phoumsavanh, Souphanouvong, Phoumy Vongvichith, Khamtay Siphandone, Phoun Sripraseuth, and Sisomphone Lovansay. — Speaker.

dren released from Willko. We joined her in Savannakhet City and stayed there for three days while I looked for a way to flee to Thailand.

I found an old boat, just a small one, which I agreed to buy and we left from Pong Kham village in the district of Mukdaharn and sailed to freedom across the Mekong River. It was January 28, 1984, when we crossed the river. It was the dry season and the water was only about eight hundred meters wide.

In Thailand we were taken into the Na Pho camp and stayed there for eighteen months before coming to the Philippines in September of 1985.

I hope to go to the United States in February of 1986. That is my schedule but I am hoping that the paperwork will come through faster than that. I am going to Los Angeles where I have two other sons, a mother-in-law and a sister-in-law. I also have a twenty-three-year-old daughter in Paris. In 1976, when her mother was trapped in the seminar camp she decided to flee to Thailand. While she was waiting she lived with her two brothers and her grandmother. They were all looking for a way to escape and she was the first one to get a chance. She went alone. She was fifteen years old at the time.

My two boys escaped in 1978. They were about thirteen and fourteen years old. My mother-in-law escaped with my sister-in-law in 1980. I am very happy to be going to see them all again.

I would have tried to escape in 1975 if I had known what was in store for me and my friends and family. Even when we were first sent to the seminars we did not realize. The Communists had announced that the seminars for the army, the police and officials of the former government would last only three months. We believed them but it was a lie.

Since then, human rights violations in Laos have increased drastically. Thousands have been imprisoned without trial for holding beliefs not in accordance with those of the Communist government. Many prisoners have been systematically tortured and killed. Others have vanished without a trace. Prisoners are held incommunicado and years can pass without relatives knowing if their loved ones are alive or dead.

The Vientiane Agreement, a tripartite agreement signed by the national coalition government on February 21, 1973, has been ignored. What the Communists say and what they do are quite contrary.

For instance, the Vientiane Agreement guaranteed the promotion of peace, national independence, neutrality and nonalignment. But many more Lao people die now than during wartime. Where is the peace? More than seventy thousand Vietnamese troops occupy Laos and the government officials fraternize openly with them. Where is the independence? In 1977, the Communist government in Vientiane signed a twenty-five year military pact with the Soviet Union and Vietnam. Where is the neutrality and nonalignment?

The Vientiane Agreement made a commitment to social progress, to the encouragement and development of interrelations among all the Lao people, all ethnic groups, all religions, all classes of society. But the government actually promotes disunity. Under the Marxist/Leninist "new way," which the Communists claim is a period of transition to a full-fledged Communist state, the traditional system of village life has been altered. People are forced to relocate against their wills. Work groups of three families each have been formed. These families are forced to live in close proximity and do most things communally. They are encouraged to spy on each other and report any "infraction" in word or deed to the Communists officials.

Every Friday the families meet, sit in a circle and recite in turn a litany of self-criticism dealing with transgressions like bourgeois thoughts, desiring bourgeois food, and so on. Any deviation from the rules puts one at risk of being denounced as a reactionary and severely punished.

Travel is strictly controlled. Permission must be obtained to go anywhere. And a person from one family must always be accompanied by people from the other two families or risk punishment. This is not just for travel, but even for simply walking in the fields.

(It is not like this in Vientiane because the diplomatic corps is there and the Communists want to deceive them about the true state of the country. Diplomats from Communist bloc countries are the only ones allowed to travel in the countryside. The rest they allow to move only short distances outside Vientiane.)

The Vientiane Agreement guarantees economic equality and the promotion of prosperity. What they gave us is state economic planning. The economy is controlled and managed by the Politburo. Trade is not free. The movement of goods is severely limited. The country lives under a system of rationing.

The Vientiane Agreement guaranteed political and socio-cultural equality. What they did was suppress and root out all classes of society. They completely changed our way of life. They suppressed all our ancient customs. They suppressed our religions. The doctrines of Marx and Lenin have taken the place of the old and new testaments and the Buddhist precepts. The new "equality," rather than fostering unity, has bred suspicion and contempt. Such ingrained Lao traditions as showing respect to the elderly have broken down. People are isolated from each other. The country is divided and the Politburo is corrupt. While the people are starving, they live in big houses with televisions, they drive modern American cars, they wear European clothes, their wives wear expensive jewelry and they drink vodka. Kaisone is reputed to be very fond of Johnny Walker whisky. The wives of Nouhak and Kaisone traffic in Laotian gold with Vietnam.

The Vientiane Agreement guarantees such basic rights as freedom of speech, freedom of the press and freedom of assembly. But in fact speech and the press are strictly controlled. Ordinary Lao citizens cannot even use cameras publicly. And as for freedom of assembly, a gathering of two or three people is enough to attract official attention. Then there are demands for IDs and motives for the meeting. Even freedom of thought is curtailed. In self-criticism sessions, people are expected to reveal and critique the innermost workings of their minds.

The Vientiane Agreement guaranteed to respect and protect the throne. But on December 2, 1975, the Communists forced King Sri Savang Vatthanna to abdicate, thus ending the 622-year-old monarchy. And in March of 1977 the Politburo reported that it had arrested the sixty-nine-year-old king, his wife and children, and was sending them to reeducation camp.

Their treatment was like the Nazi concentration camps of Adolf Hitler. The Red cadre took them by force, hitting them about the head and face with the butt-ends of their A.K. muskets. The Prince Royal had barely arrived at the camp when he died. His Majesty was forced to walk barefoot from Sam Neua to the prison camp.* There, during his two years in captivity, the King was kept in an underground cell where sunlight and fresh air never penetrated. His foot, injured during the trek to the prison camp, became gangrenous. At last he died in despair.

Her Majesty, the Queen of Laos, died in the same camp. She took her own life in agony of mind over the fate of her husband.

The Vientiane Agreement guaranteed liberty and democratic elections. But there are no democratic elections in the Communist bloc. Elections are a farce, merely a ratification of government appointed officials. There is no campaign electioneering. Positions within the government are appointive. The Politburo screens the list of candidates and the voter must comply with this list or die. The only democracy in Laos is at the end of a gun.

Who is the number one enemy for the Socialist revolution, the greatest threat to Kaisone's Socialist Utopia? It isn't the imperalist American or the capitalist regime or the reactionaries within the country, as Kaisone claims all the time on the radio and in the newspapers. He himself is enemy number one to the "Socialist Revolution" and to all the Lao people. He is a despot and an oppressor in the history of the Lao nation.†

---

*I don't know exactly where the prison camp was that the king was sent to. I was told this story by my cousin who was told it by Thao Mon, who was a prisoner in the same camp as the king and is now a resettled refugee in Australia. I asked my cousin for the name of the camp but he didn't know. I gather it was a small one in the Viengxay area. I also heard some of this story from the Red guards in the Tong Luang camp. — Speaker.

†Kaisone Phomvihane was born of a Lao mother and a Vietnamese father in Savannakhet Province. As quite a young child he was sent by his father to Hanoi in North Vietnam where he began learning Marxist/Leninist dogma under the tutelage of "the Communist Party of Indochina." He became the

He claims to be a nationalist but he brought Vietnamese troops in to occupy my homeland. What is this? He is all talk. He talks all the time. He is constantly accusing the "imperialist Americans" of opposing the revolution. He says the Americans are colonialist, enemy number one for the Socialist revolution. He talks like this all the time to this very day.

From 1975 until now, 1986, seventy thousand Vietnamese troops have occupied Laos. What has been their mission? To protect the might of Kaisone. We of Laos would like to know what is old colonialism and what is new colonialism? Who is the imperialist aggressor? Who is the expansionist power? When Kaisone sent Lao troops to aid Vietnam in its 1979 conquest of Cambodia, was he observing nonalignment in international affairs?

What did Kaisone do with the financial support which the right-wing administration of Souvanna Phouma had secured from the Asian Development Bank? The intention had been to use it for the completion of the Nam Ngum River hydroelectric project. When the money came through in 1976, Kaisone gave it to Vietnam to help them in Cambodia.

It is difficult to criticize and censure the Communist "Utopia" because they don't recognize their misdeeds and mistakes. Maybe they did have some sort of unrealistic dream of a castle in the air but I know from experience that Communists are instinctively cheats and liars.

It is deplorable and disgraceful to hear them proclaim over and over, "Now the Lao people have been liberated."

Did the Pathet Lao liberate the Lao people? Or have the Communists put a yoke on their shoulders? [PRPC, October 24, 1985.]

loyal slave of the Communist regime under the guidance of Ho Chi Minh himself.

The French had left Indochina at the end of World War II. They reoccupied Vietnam in 1945 and Laos in May of 1946. In 1945, from Vietnam, the twenty-one-year-old Kaisone began his anticolonialist struggle against the French army. He liked the new colonialism no more than the old. I think it was he who created the Lao National Liberation Front in 1956. Now there are neither French nor American troops in Laos but the world wonders about him and his much-vaunted nationalism. — Speaker.

*   *   *

The following lists I compiled in collaboration with the Lao community in the PRPC. — Speaker.

Escapees from Sepone Camp

First Group: 1976

1. Lt. Colonel Soupanh (escaped; now in United States)
2. Major Champathong (escaped; now in United States)

Second Group: 1977

1. Major One Sy (killed in forest)
2. Lt. Colonel Kenavanh (killed in forest)
3. Lt. Colonel Phane (killed in forest)
4. Lt. Colonel Noukene (killed in forest)
5. Major Khambang (killed in forest)
6. Major Nouanesy (killed in forest)
7. Major Inthasone (shot in camp)
8. Major Nuck (shot in camp)

Third group: 1977

1. Colonel Thong Sy (escaped; now in France)
2. Lt. Colonel Noukanh (escaped; now in United States)
3. Colonel Vang-Thanadabouth (escaped; now in France)

Fourth Group: 1977

1. Lt. Colonel Khamsy Insisiengmay (escaped; now in San Diego)
2. Major Sing (escaped; now fighting the Communists from Thailand)

Escapees from Tong Luang (Senekheuane) Camp

First Group: 1978 (all shot in front of the people)

1. Lt. Colonel Paul Minh
2. Lt. Colonel Boune Kouang
3. Lt. Colonel Boune Nhem
4. Major Sopha
5. Major Khamphong

Second group: 1978

1. Major Inpeng (now in United States)
2. Lt. Colonel Chanthabank (now in United States)
3. Major Somphou (now in United States)

Escapees from Lako (Willko) Camp — 1982

Major Chommany Sanabounheuang (now in United States)

* * *

The following lists represent officers whose fates I know of personally. They may not be complete.

Still Detained in Ban Phadaeng Seminar Camp
(about 120 kilometers northeast of Sepone)

1. Colonel Khamsouk Insisiengmay
2. Colonel Manh Phravisaid
3. Lt. Colonel Tong Savanh
4. Major Thong Vonh
5. Major Leuth
6. Major Kato
7. Major Song
8. Major Sone Virabouth
9. Lt. Colonel Lith
10. Lt. Colonel Siboune Rasphone
11. Lt. Colonel Phoma
12. Major Inphong
13. Major Phoukhao
14. Major Kong-Keo
15. Major Vong-Keo

Still Detained in Ban Bhout Seminar Camp
(about 15 kilometers from Lako, northeast of Sepone)

1. Lt. Colonel Leng Lathanavongsa
2. Lt. Colonel Inpone Boungnaseng
3. Lt. Colonel Khamlianh
4. Lt. Colonel Champy Matmanivong
5. Lt. Colonel Chanthale Douangnali
6. Lt. Colonel Se

7. Lt. Colonel Keng Bouaphanh
8. Lt. Colonel Khoune Kham
9. Lt. Colonel Phanphaly
10. Colonel Pho Lathavongsa
11. Colonel Phou Sakda
12. Colonel Nouphanh Sihavong
13. Major Khamphong Khompasouk
14. Major Thong Khoune Nanthavong
15. Major Khambeo Kounnoulath
16. Major Thavonh Chelaka
17. Major Soubinh Phomphengdy
18. Major Nouane Sy
19. Major Kongkham Khamsouktavong
20. Major Noukane Rasvong
21. Major Polo Chandany
22. Major Phommakot Souvanheuane
23. Major Sithane Vongdara
24. Major Cham Katignavong
25. Major Tiane Phommathep
26. Major Lamleut Sanichanh
27. Major Khamphiou Keoborith
28. Major Phone Vongsouthi
29. Major Dam
30. Major Vath Lasat

Killed By Bombs Exploding in Minefields
(Forced to work the soil, they hit the bombs with their picks)

Sepone Camp: Major Moune

Tong Luang Camp (Senekheuane): Lt. Colonel Khamphanh

Willko Camp:
1. Lt. Colonel Lam Kham
2. Lt. Colonel Hang
3. Lt. Colonel Bounthone
4. Nang Keo (wife of a seminarist)
5. Thao Khoune (sixteen-year-old son of a seminarist)
6. Thao Khet Keo (eighteen-year-old son of a seminarist)

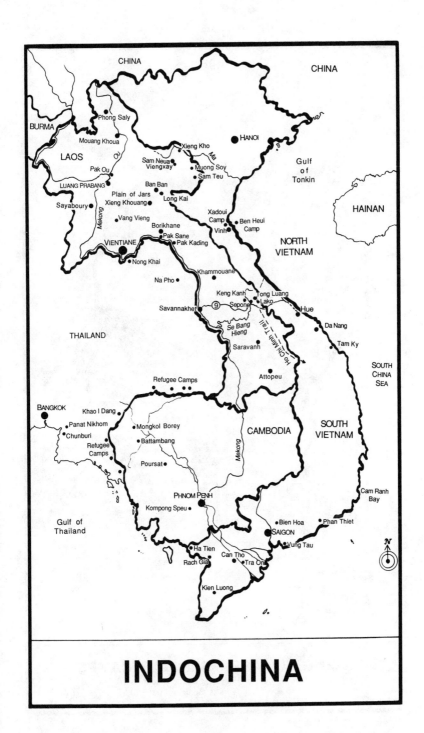

INDOCHINA

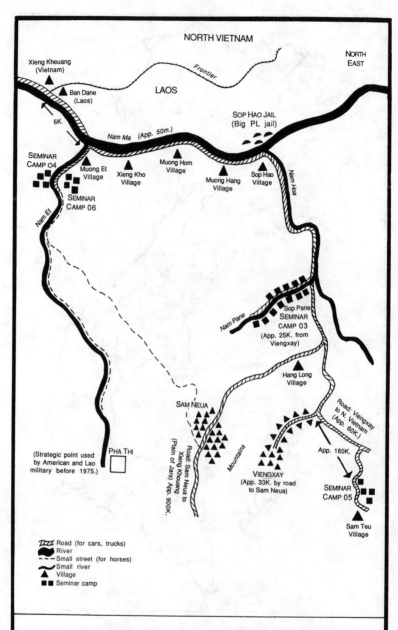

NORTH VIETNAM

NORTH EAST

Xieng Kheuang
(Vietnam)

Ban Dane
(Laos)

LAOS

Frontier

6K.

Nam Ma (App. 50m.)

SOP HAO JAIL
(Big PL jail)

SEMINAR
CAMP 04

Muong Et
Village

Xieng Kho
Village

Muong Hom
Village

Muong Hang
Village

Sop Hao
Village

SEMINAR
CAMP 06

Nam Et

Nam Hoa

Nam Pane

Sop Pane
SEMINAR
CAMP 03
(App. 25K. from
Viengxay)

Hang Long
Village

Road: Viengxay
to N. Vietnam
(App. 60k.)

SAM NEUA

App. 160K.

(Strategic point used
by American and Lao
military before 1975.)

PHA THI

Road: Sam Neua to
Xieng Kheuang
(Plain of Jars) App. 900K.

Mountains

VIENGXAY
(App. 33K. by road
to Sam Neua)

SEMINAR
CAMP 05

Sam Teu
Village

Road (for cars, trucks)
River
Small street (for horses)
Small river
Village
Seminar camp

VIENGXAY AREA SEMINAR CAMPS

Drawn from memory by Samly Khamphouy,
who spent ten years in Seminar Camp 06.

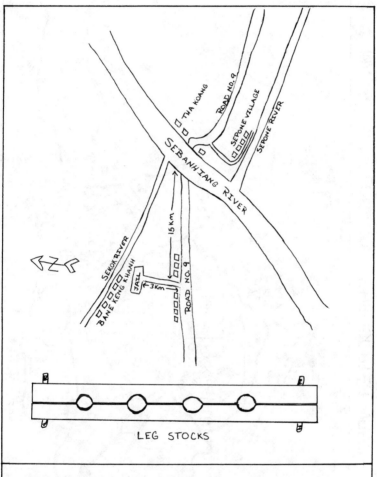

LEG STOCKS

SKETCH SHOWING LOCATION OF KENG KANH
JAIL AND LEG STOCKS USED AT THE JAIL

MAP SHOWING LOCATION OF HELICOPTER WRECK

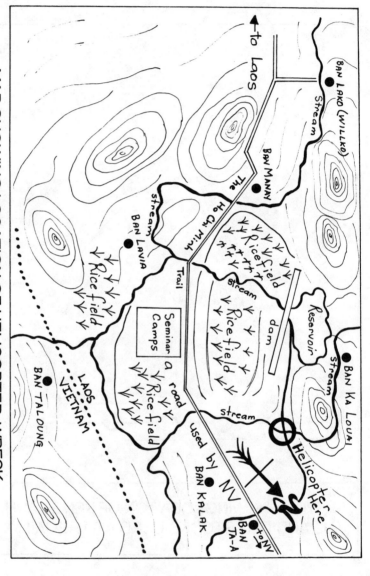

Appendix: Viengxay
Area Seminarists

Following is a set of four lists. These are the names of seminarists incarcerated in Camps 03, 04, 05 and 06 in the Viengxay area in the extreme eastern part of nothern Laos, close to the border with Vietnam. It was to these camps that many of the highest level military and civilians were sent after the Communist takeover in 1975.

The lists were compiled from memory by ex-seminarists in these camps after they had fled Laos as refugees. These are living documents, as accurate as possible at the time of publication.

The names are listed in alphabetical order by given name, as some family names are not remembered. "Tiao" or "Tchiao" before a name indicates royalty. Where the fate of the seminarist is known, it is provided.

These lists are a memorial, maybe the only one the seminarists will ever have, and the compilers are anxious to complete them accurately. Lao refugees who have information to add are encouraged to contact Joanna Scott through the publishers.

Seminarists of Camp 03 —
Viengxay Area

1. Maj. Bounchanh Heuanmisavat
2. Police Capt. Bounkham Sonethasack
3. Police Maj. Bounleuane Oudomsinh
4. Maj. Bounleuang Inthasane
5. Police Lt. Col. Bounnhong Vongphachanh
6. Police Major Bounphet Pradichit
7. Maj. Bounsom Thamountha (escaped Laos; migrated to U.S., 1986)
8. Lt. Col. Bounsouane Khounsombat
9. Police Maj. Bounta Phetnhothinh
10. Police Maj. Bounthanh Nhotsanga (escaped Laos, 1984; migrated to U.S.)
11. Maj. Bounthanh Siathone
12. Lt. Col. Bounthanh Sirisombat
13. Lt. Col. Bounthanh Sirivong
14. 1st. Lt. Chane Chanhtha
15. 1st. Lt. Chanhdy _____
16. Maj. Chanhthy Siphanhthong (escaped Laos; migrated to U.S., 1986)
17. Lt. Col. Tiao Chanthavong Rasvong (royal family)
18. Maj. Deng Sensavang (escaped Laos; migrated to U.S., 1986)
19. Maj. Deth Thongkhouha
20. 1st. Lt. Deune _____
21. Maj. Dioe Vannavong (escaped Laos; migrated to U.S., 1986)
22. Lt. Col. Do Thengthongsy
23. 1st. Lt. Hongkham Sayakham
24. Maj. Houmphanh Bounyasiri (escaped Laos; migrated to U.S., 1981)
25. Police Lt. Col. Houmphanh Chareunsy
26. Police Major Houmphanh Manikhong
27. Police Major Houmphanh Soukthavone
28. Lt. Col. Houmpheng Phounsavat (died in captivity, 1977)
29. Lt. Col. Houmpheng Sisopha
30. Maj. Inpeng _____ (died in captivity, 1977)
31. Maj. Kenechanh Meksavanh
32. 1st. Lt. Kenesy _____
33. Maj. Khambay Sirimanotham (escaped Laos; migrated to U.S., 1981)
34. Maj. Khamkhieng Thongsavat
35. Lt. Col. Khammonh Souvannaphalom
36. 1st. Lt. Tiao Khamphanh Rasvong (royal family)
37. Lt. Col. Khamphao Phayboune (escaped Laos, 1981; migrated to New Zealand)
38. Air Force Maj. Khamphao Phoummavong

39. Police Major Khamphay Bounsavat
40. 1st Lt. Khamphay Kaseumsouk
41. 1st Lt. Khampheui _____
42. 1st Lt. Khamphone _____
43. Air Force Lt. Col. Khampong Thongpane (released to Vientiane, 1987)
44. Maj. Khampoune Khammongkhoun
45. Lt. Col. Khamsay Singharath
46. Maj. Khamsene Keodara
47. Maj. Khamsop _____
48. Maj. Khamsy Thongvatsa
49. Maj. Khamtiene Keovilay
50. Lt. Col. Khunh _____
51. Maj. Ko Inthakoummane
52. Police Major Kongmy Sattasinh
53. Police Lt. Col. Lackthong Bounyavong (escaped Laos; migrated to U.S., 1986; now lives in Vancouver, Washington)
54. Maj. Lao Chomsavanh
55. Police Major Leum Sithixay
56. Police Maj. Leun Phetthasa
57. Maj. Mang Khamone
58. Maj. Na Thavat
59. 2nd Lt. Nane Inh
60. Maj. Nhane Khounthikoumane
61. Maj. No Sihamagna
62. Maj. Noi Muongsida
63. Lt. Col. Onechanh Sihamano
64. Police Maj. Onechanh Soukhaphonh
65. Lt. Col. Onesy Khaysavang (a medical doctor; died in captivity, 1976)
66. Police Maj. Onh Rithiphong
67. Lt. Col. Ounheuane Chittaphone (escaped Laos; migrated to U.S., 1981)
68. Lt. Col. Ounheuane Oudommongkhoun
69. Maj. Ounheuane Sipraseuth
70. Maj. Ounkeo Thamphya
71. Maj. Tiao Ounneua Phengsavat (royal family)
72. Lt. Col. Pane Siphanhthong
73. Maj. Phailoth Xoumpholphakdy
74. Maj. Phanh Anolak (escaped Laos; migrated to France, 1981)
75. Maj. Phanh Chanhthavatdy
76. 1st. Lt. Tiao Phanh Rasvong (royal family)
77. Police Col. Phanh Vandarak
78. Police Maj. Phao Bounlyaphonh (escaped Laos; migrated to U.S., 1986)
79. 1st. Lt. Phay Kaseumsouk
80. Lt. Col. Phay Phengchanh
81. Police Lt. Col. Pheng Savatdymao
82. Maj. Pheng Vongsonephet
83. 1st Lt. Phengsy _____
84. Police Maj. Phettharangsy _____

85. Maj. Pheui Bounyasiri
86. Maj. Pheui Mangkhala
87. 1st Lt. Pheung _____
88. Police Maj. Phomma Phommathet
89. Maj. Phouangphot Songvilay
90. Maj. Phoui Chanhthadara
91. Maj. Phoui Soutthidara
92. Maj. Phoumi Chanhthalekha
93. Maj. Phoumi Inthavanh (escaped Laos; last known whereabouts, Na Pho refugee camp, Thailand, 1986)
94. 1st Lt. Phya Sythong
95. Maj. Tiao Ratsmy Sayasane (royal family)
96. Maj. Sangthong Settharajxomphou (escaped Laos; last known whereabouts, Na Pho refugee camp, Thailand, 1985)
97. Police Maj. Sengpha Afhit Sisamouth (escaped Laos, 1985; last known whereabouts, Na Pho refugee camp, Thailand, 1985)
98. Lt. Col. Tiao Sing Rattana (royal family)
99. Maj. Sing Sourya
100. Maj. Singkham _____
101. 1st Lt. Singkham Maykeo
102. Maj. Siphanh Salika
103. Police Maj. Sisamouth Sengphaathit
104. Maj. Tiao Sisavath Bounkhong (royal family)
105. Lt. Col. Sisavath Phetxomphou
106. Lt. Col. Sisouphanh Phengsavat
107. Lt. Col. Sivixay Sackpraseuth
108. Lt. Col. Tiao Somchanh Sayasane (royal family)
109. Maj. Tiao Somchit Sayasane (royal family)
110. Police Major Somdy Chanhthavong (died in captivity, 1984)
111. Maj. Somdy Mixayboua
112. Maj. Sommano _____
113. NCO Sommay Somchit (escaped Laos; migrated to U.S., 1983)
114. Police Maj. Somphou Monthitay
115. Maj. Somsavat Souryo
116. Maj. Sopha Sisengrath
117. Maj. Tiao Souk Phatthanak (royal family)
118. Lt. Col. Soukthivong _____
119. Maj. Souvanh Sithideth
120. Lt. Col. Tiao Souvanna Settha (royal family; died in captivity, 1983)
121. Lt. Col. Tiao Tanh Soukthala (royal family; escaped Laos, 1985, migrated to Canada)
122. 1st Lt. Thongchanh Soukhaphonh
123. Capt. Thongdy _____
124. Lt. Col. Thongphanh Simmasing
125. Maj. Thongphet Bounyavong
126. Police Maj. Thongsouk Phonhphiboun
127. Maj. Vanhkham Phyasakha

128. Maj. Vanhna Sisengvong
129. Maj. Tiao Vanhthalangsy (royal family)
130. Capt. Xiengchanh Thammagno
131. Maj. Xiengmanh Sirisouk
132. Maj. Xom _____
133. Maj. Xomphou _____

Seminarists of Camp 04 —
Viengxay Area

1. Police Maj. Ai Thepnava
2. Col. Aksone Manotham (transferred to Camp 05; died there in 1984)
3. Maj. Alom Keopraseuth
4. Maj. Alom Misomphane
5. Civilian Ang Khammanivongsa
6. Civilian Angkham Manivong
7. Lt. Col. Angkham Senesanith (escaped Laos; migrated to U.S., 1981)
8. Lt. Col. Anouvong _____
9. Air Force Major Attachanh _____ (died in captivity, 1984)
10. Director Baliene Khamdaranikone (died in captivity, 1984)
11. Lt. Col. Ban Manivong
12. Police Major Bannavong Sisavanh
13. Air Force Maj. Belo Phomsavatdy (escaped Laos; migrated to Australia, 1980)
14. Maj. Bene _____
15. Maj. Benh _____ (escaped Laos; migrated to U.S., 1983)
16. Lt. Col. Beui Luangsouphom
17. Maj. Bida _____
18. Maj. Bou _____
19. Maj. Boua Sichamphone (died in captivity, 1985)
20. Maj. Boualay Muonghane (escaped Laos; migrated to U.S., now lives in Denver, Colorado. He gave these lists in their original form to Samly Khamphouy — Camp 06, #292, now of Connecticut — who gave them to me.)
21. Lt. Col. Boualay Vorarath (escaped Laos; migrated to U.S., 1981)
22. Maj. Boualoy Muonghane (escaped Laos, 1985; migrated to U.S., 1987)
23. Bouapha Sihanath (died in captivity, 1981)
24. Lt. Col. Bouapha Taxay
25. Police Major Bouaphanh _____
26. Maj. Bouaphanh Phonethip
27. Lt. Col. Bon Dejvongsa
28. Director Bosaykham Bouasy
29. Maj. Bouathep Khothisen
30. Maj. Bouathong Bounphaxaysonh
31. Lt. Col. Bouathong Chemdasack
32. Maj. Bouathong Vongsathiene
33. Maj. Bouchom Xouykeomixay (transferred to Camp 06)
34. Civilian Bounchanh _____
35. Lt. Col. Bouneua Sayakham (died in captivity, 1980)

36. Maj. Bounfeng Thirakoun
37. Lt. Col. Bounhom Phandanouvong (died in captivity, 1982)
38. Maj. Bounkeua Kongsayasack (escaped Laos; migrated to U.S., lives in Seattle, Washington)
39. Lt. Col. Bounkhong Phonthachack
40. Lt. Col. Bounkouang Insixiengmay
41. Civilian Bounleui _____
42. Lt. Col. Bounlith Manikham
43. Police Maj. Bounlouane Nouankhamchanh
44. Lt. Col. Bounmy Bouphataxay
45. Police Maj. Bounmy Chanthavong (escaped Laos; migrated to U.S., 1986)
46. Maj. Bounmy Phengkhamphat
47. Lt. Col. Bounnhang Insixiengmay
48. Maj. Bounnho _____
49. Maj. Bounnhou _____
50. Police Maj. Bounnhouat _____
51. Police Maj. Bounoua Soukasen
52. Maj. Bounoum _____
53. Maj. Bounphama Thanasouk (escaped Laos; migrated to U.S., 1986)
54. Police Maj. Bounpheng _____
55. Police Maj. Bounpheng Phanphila
56. Civilian Bounpheng S. Phabmixay
57. Maj. Bounpheng Siharath
58. Police Col. Bounpheng Sivoraphonh
59. Police Col. Bounpheng Thatsaphone
60. Civilian Bounsom _____
61. Maj. Bounsong Phouminh (escaped Laos; migrated to U.S., 1981)
62. Lt. Col. Bounsouane Simoukda
63. Lt. Col. Bounsong _____
64. Civilian Bounthai _____
65. Lt. Col. Bounthanh _____
66. Director Bounthanh _____
67. Lt. Col. Bounthanh _____ (escaped Laos; migrated to U.S., 1981)
68. Civilian Bountheung K. Pheng Nhavong (escaped Laos; migrated to U.S., 1981)
69. Maj. Bountheung _____
70. Civilian Bountheung Keuthla
71. Lt. Col. Bountheung Oudom
72. Lt. Col. Bountheung Phanhvongsa
73. Lt. Col. Bounthone _____
74. Maj. Bountiem Souryavong
75. Lt. Col. Bounxieng Souaymany
76. Police Maj. Boutdy _____
77. Civilian Chanhtha Insixiengmay (escaped Laos; last known whereabouts, Na Pho refugee camp, Thailand, 1981)
78. Police Maj. Chanhny Phengdara

79. Police Lt. Col. Chanhpheng Chittaphong
80. Police Maj. Chanpheng _____
81. Police Maj. Chansom S. Sengsirivanh
82. Lt. Col. Chansamouth _____
83. Lt. Col. Chansouk _____
84. Maj. Chansouk Douangvongsa
85. Maj. Chanthakhat Sivoravong
86. Maj. Chantho _____
87. Director Chiengchanpheng Sinbanhdit
88. Lt. Col. Chindavong _____
89. Maj. Chit _____
90. Police Maj. Chommuang Mahachay
91. Lt. Col. Choum _____
92. Maj. Chiam _____
93. Lt. Col. Daovong Kinpatthoum
94. Lt. Col. Daovong Phanpathoum
95. Air Force Lt. Col. Day Vinavong
96. Police Maj. Done Keopaseuth (died in captivity, 1980)
97. Maj. Done Ratavong
98. Maj. Dy Sengsouvanh (escaped Laos; migrated to U.S., 1981)
99. Maj. Eunh Phothirath
100. Air Force Maj. Fongsamouth _____
101. Maj. Hatsady Luangrath
102. Lt. Col. Hem D. Phaysouvanh
103. Civilian Heuang Choundara
104. Lt. Col. Heung Insixiengmay (escaped Laos; migrated to U.S., 1981)
105. Lt. Col. Hom Rasphone (escaped Laos; migrated to U.S., 1986)
106. Maj. Hom Savatdy
107. Police Maj. Hot Southalath
108. Lt. Col Houan _____
109. Maj. Houane Somrasmy
110. Lt. Col. Houi Pholsena
111. Civilian Houmpheng Phongsavanh
112. Maj. Houmpheng Souksavath
113. Police Lt. Col. Infeng Sengkyavong
114. Maj. Inh _____
115. Lt. Col. Inpeng _____
116. Maj. Inpeng _____
117. Police Maj. Inpeng Vongphouthone
118. Maj. Inta Phixayavong
119. Director Kayphet Chanthrathip (escaped Laos; last known where-
     abouts, Na Pho refugee camp, Thailand, 1986)
120. Civilian Kaysone Thepmany
121. Maj. Keng _____
122. Lt. Col. Keng Pathammavong
123. Maj. Kenethong _____
124. Police Maj. Keo _____

125. Maj. Keo Phavongsay
126. Maj. Keua _____
127. Maj. Keuth _____
128. Police Major Khaisy S. Salakham (escaped Laos; migrated to U.S.)
129. Civilian Kham Ouan _____
130. Maj. Khambeng Pathammovong
131. Maj. Khambot Nakhiengchanh
132. Maj. Khambou Sananikone (died in captivity, 1982)
133. Air Force Maj. Khamchanh Sisounol
134. Maj. Khamdy _____
135. Lt. Col. Khamfong Keomany (died in captivity, 1980)
136. Maj. Khamkeuth Sayarath
137. Maj. Khamkhiene Vongchanh (escaped Laos; migrated to U.S., 1983)
138. Lt. Col. Khamky Khounsombath (escaped Laos; migrated to Canada, 1983)
139. Maj. Khamla Bounlutay
140. Civilian Khamleck Phanvongsa
141. Maj. Khamliene Sanaviseth (escaped Laos; last known whereabouts, Na Pho refugee camp, Thailand, 1984)
142. Maj. Khamlom Xoumpholphakdy
143. Police Maj. Khammao _____
144. Maj. Khammone _____
145. Maj. Khammone Chanthavong
146. Maj. Khammone Dejvongsa
147. Maj. Khammoune _____
148. Maj. Khammy _____
149. Lt. Col. Khamnhot Luangrath
150. Civilian Khamphanh _____
151. Police Maj. Khamphanh Chanthalath
152. Civilian Khamphanh Sayasith
153. Police Lt. Col. Khamphanh Vongsamphanh (escaped Laos; migrated to France, 1981)
154. Maj. Khamphat Singharath
155. Police Lt. Col. Khamphay _____
156. Lt. Col. Khamphet Moukdarat
157. Maj. Khamphou Sackpraseuth (escaped Laos; migrated to U.S., 1986)
158. Civilian Khamphoui _____
159. Police Major Khamphoui Somchanthavong
160. Civilian Khamphoui Phanthavong
161. Maj. Khamphout _____
162. Maj. Khamphy _____
163. Director Khampine Phanhdamaly
164. Police Maj. Khamsene Thamabanvong
165. Police Maj. Khamseng S. Phabmixay
166. Civilian Khamsing Khammanivong (escaped Laos; migrated to Australia, 1983)
167. Maj. Khamsone _____

168. Civilian Khamsone Noudaranouvong (escaped Laos, migrated to U.S., 1981)
169. Police Maj. Khamsop _____
170. Maj. Khamsouk S. Phabmixay (escaped Laos; migrated to U.S., 1986)
171. Maj. Khamsy Luangkhot
172. Maj. Khamsy Soukaseum (escaped Laos; migrated to U.S., 1983)
173. Maj. Khamta Sirimanotham
174. Civilian Khamtanh Lithamalay
175. Maj. Khamtanh Malaythong
176. Police Maj. Khamtanh Naovarangsy (died in captivity, 1980)
177. Civilian Khamtanh Phengsaya
178. Police Maj. Khamteum Sanouban (escaped Laos; migrated to U.S., 1986)
179. Maj. Khamthong Chanphianamvong
180. Lt. Col. Khamtoui Phachansithi
181. Civilian Khamxay Phoumivong (escaped Laos; migrated to U.S., 1980)
182. Maj. Khamxy Soukaseum (escaped Laos; last known whereabouts, Na Pho refugee camp, Thailand)
183. Director Khanhthong Thammavong (escaped Laos; migrated to France, 1984)
184. Maj. Khao _____
185. Maj. Khaysy Sisanakham
186. Maj. Khen Anouvong
187. Maj. Khen Sangboutsady
188. Khen Souryavong
189. Maj. Kheuane Phanhthathirath
190. Lt. Col. Khom Phasavath
191. Lt. Col. Khoun Phavorabouth (escaped Laos; migrated to U.S., 1986; see his story, beginning on page 201)
192. Civilian Khoune _____
193. Maj. Khoune Vongsa
194. Maj. Khounmy Rajsombat (escaped Laos; last known whereabouts, Na Pho refugee camp, Thailand, 1985)
195. Police Lt. Col. Kingkeo Souksavat
196. Maj. Kisouy _____
197. Maj. Kongkham Sirivongxay
198. Police Maj. Kongmoun _____
199. Police Lt. Col. Kongmoun Thanavady
200. Police Maj. Kongpheng _____
201. Police Maj. Kongpheng Vongdara
202. Maj. Kongsinh Phetxomphou
203. Maj. Kongsin Xoumpholphakdy
204. Lt. Col. Kongty _____
205. Maj. Kongty Sinakhone
206. Director Kossadary Phimmasone (escaped Laos; migrated to U.S., 1986)
207. Maj. Koum Vongsanith
208. Maj. La Kaosana

209. Police Maj. La Keoninh
210. Maj. La Phommaphavanh
211. Maj. Lack Thepmany (escaped Laos; migrated to U.S., 1986)
212. Police Maj. Lackthay Bounyavong (escaped Laos; migrated to U.S., 1986)
213. Civilian Lamlakhone Insixiengmay (escaped Laos; migrated to U.S., 1986)
214. Lt. Col. Lamngeun Sounthonevichith
215. Civilian Lamthong Hangla
216. Police Maj. Langsy Vannavongkot (escaped Laos; migrated to Belgium, 1986)
217. Lt. Col. Lanh Rajphangthong
218. Maj. Lay _____ (escaped Laos; last known whereabouts: Na Pho refugee camp, Thailand, 1984.)
219. Maj. Leck Bouromavong (escaped Laos; migrated to U.S., 1983)
220. Maj. Leek Sengsourichanh
221. Maj. Leuane _____
222. Maj. Lith Panyanouvong
223. Maj. Leuth Thavone
224. Lt. Col. Lithi Luangnikone
225. Maj. Lo Van Heuang
226. Maj. Lom Bounlom Phouangphet
227. Maj. Louane Nouankhamchanh
228. Maj. Mahachay Chommuang
229. Lt. Col. Mak _____
230. Maj. Manh Sourinhosack
231. Civilian Mit Nilandone
232. Maj. Mok Somphithak
233. Police Maj. Mone Singvilay
234. Maj. Moune _____
235. Maj. My _____
236. Lt. Col. Nhanh Manivong
237. Maj. Ngone Sayarath (escaped Laos; last known whereabouts: Na Pho refugee camp, Thailand, 1986)
238. Civilian Nheth Khounxamnane
239. Police Maj. Nhot _____
240. Maj. Nhot Koumphol
241. Maj. Nhot Chanthaphon
242. Police Maj. Nilanh Sirisane
243. Lt. Col. Tiao No Sayasane (royal family)
244. Director Noi Sihavong
245. Police Maj. Nou Souvannavong (escaped Laos; migrated to U.S., 1986)
246. Maj. Nouane _____
247. Civilian Nouanedeng Silaphone (escaped Laos; migrated to U.S., 1983)
248. Capt. Noudam _____
249. Maj. Noukay Xoumpholphakdy (escaped Laos; migrated to Australia, 1983)

250. Maj. Noukiem _____
251. Maj. One Vongsa
252. Civilian Onechanh Thammavong
253. Maj. Onechanh Thomvong
254. Maj. Oneta Homesombath
255. Maj. Oua Soukaseum
256. Director Oubonh S. Sanavongsa
257. Lt. Col. Oudom Bountheung
258. Lt. Col. Oudom Vongkingkeo (died in captivity, 1982)
259. Maj. Oui Boulom
260. Police Maj. Oumma Thepharack
261. Maj. Oupatham Luangrath
262. Director Outama _____
263. Civilian Outy Khamvongsa
264. Maj. Pahonh Soundara
265. Lt. Col. Pane Thiphasouk
266. Police Maj. Panh Bounyasith (escaped Laos; last known whereabouts:
     Na Pho refugee camp, Thailand, 1985)
267. Maj. Pattha _____
268. Police Lt. Col. Pha Nounenelady (died in captivity, 1976)
269. Civilian Pha Paseuth
270. Maj. Phan Inthasolith
271. Maj. Phao Southiphong
272. Lt. Col. Phay Mixayphonh
273. Lt. Col. Pheng Boualay
274. Maj. Pheng Boupha
275. Police Maj. Pheng Latxanithone
276. Lt. Col. Pheng Oudomvilay
277. Maj. Pheng Phetsakhone
278. Police Maj. Pheng Thatsaphone
279. Lt. Col. Phengsy Phouminh (escaped Laos; migrated to U.S., 1986)
280. Police Maj. Phet Silaso
281. Maj. Phila _____
282. Maj. Phila Silavong
283. Civilian Phimpha Thepsimuang
284. Lt. Col. Phimpho Phomsouvanh
285. Lt. Col. Pho Phoukhongsy
286. Lt. Col. Pho Souvannasane
287. Police Maj. Phokham Phengkhamhack
288. Maj. Phomma Daovannavong
289. Police Maj. Phomma Kiattisack
290. Civilian Phomma Thepsimuang
291. Maj. Phone Inthasoroth
292. Police Maj. Phone Phaly
293. Police Maj. Phone Phavannorath (escaped Laos; last known where-
     abouts: Na Pho refugee camp, Thailand, 1985)
294. Police Maj. Phoui Ulavanh (escaped Laos; migrated to U.S., 1986)

295. Air Force Maj. Phoui Uplavanh
296. Civilian Phoumi Phommachack
297. Maj. Phouvieng _____
298. Police Maj. Phouvinh Chanthavongsa
299. Civilian Phoxay Rajasack
300. Lt. Col. Piam Chantharath
301. Lt. Col. Piene Soulinouanchanh
302. Director Prachith Sourisack
303. Governor Praseuth Bounyavong
304. Lt. Col. Prasith Bouavong (escaped Laos; migrated to U.S., 1987)
305. Civilian Prasith Senelaluk (died in captivity, 1980)
306. Police Lt. Col. Pravet Sourisack
307. Maj. Sae Inthiphab (escaped Laos; last known whereabouts: Na Pho refugee camp, Thailand)
308. Police Maj. Saly Khamvongsa
309. Air Force Maj. Sam Bouaphanh
310. Air Force Maj. Samane Vilaylack
311. Police Maj. Sanga Thammavongsa
312. Maj. Savay Chanthepha
313. Maj. Savay Xaysavanh
314. Police Maj. Saykham Southammavong
315. Lt. Col. Saysamone Naovarath
316. Lt. Col. Seng Naoluangrath
317. Lt. Col. Sengkeo Kingsada
318. Director Seomanivong Insixiengmay (escaped Laos; migrated to U.S., 1986; now lives in Vancouver, Washington)
319. Maj. Seumphanh Mahathirath (escaped Laos; migrated to U.S., 1986)
320. Maj. Seumphanh Phommavong (escaped Laos; migrated to U.S., 1986)
321. Maj. Siaosavath Sirimanotham
322. Lt. Col. Sideune Douangdara
323. Police Maj. Signa Rasphone (died in captivity, 1985)
324. Maj. Sika _____
325. Maj. Sila Phaxay
326. Governor Silome Nachampassack (escaped Laos; migrated to France, 1985)
327. Director Simek Sihavong
328. Maj. Simone Antoine
329. Maj. Simoune Kingkittisack
330. Maj. Singkham _____
331. Police Maj. Singthong _____
332. Civilian Singto _____ (escaped Laos; migrated to U.S., 1981)
333. Maj. Sinong _____
334. Lt. Col. Sinong Mingmalychanh
335. Maj. Siphay Chaypha
336. Police Maj. Sisavanh Bannavong (died in captivity, 1985)
337. Maj. Sisavath _____
338. Maj. Sisavay Saysavanh

339. Lt. Col. Sisoumang _____
340. Lt. Col. Tiao Sisouphanh _____ (royal family)
341. Director Tiao Sisouphanh Manoroth (royal family, escaped Laos; migrated to U.S., 1986)
342. Director Tial Sisouphanouvong _____ (royal family)
343. Maj. Sisouphit Kittirath (escaped Laos; migrated to U.S., 1981)
344. Maj. Sisouvanh Siphay
345. Lt. Col. Sith Saysi
346. Maj. Sombath S. Phabmixay
347. Police Lt. Col. Somboune Salinhthone
348. Police Maj. Somchine Bandith
349. Maj. Somchith Soulivong
350. Maj. Somchith Vixaysouk
351. Maj. Somkham Sirattanakoul
352. Lt. Col. Somkhit Vanisavath (died in captivity, 1978)
353. Police Maj. Somlit Phanhnavong (died in captivity, 1981)
354. Civilian Somlit Youansamouth (died in captivity, 1978)
355. Air Force Lt. Col. Somlith Vannarath (escaped Laos, 1985; migrated to U.S. Now lives in Wisconsin. He and Viliam Phraxayavong — Camp 05, #315 — were the original compilers of these lists.)
356. Lt. Col. Sommay Phanthavong
357. Civilian Somnuk Vongsavanh
358. Maj. Somphanh Mahathirath
359. Police Maj. Sompheng S. Phabmixay
360. Maj. Somphone _____
361. Civilian Somvang Vilayvanh (escaped Laos; migrated to France, 1981)
362. Civilian Sone _____
363. Maj. Sopha Vongphachanh
364. Police Maj. Soubanh Arounsavath
365. Police Maj. Soubinh _____
366. Police Maj. Soui Phimmasane
367. Lt. Col. Souk Latthamone (escaped Laos; migrated to U.S., 1988)
368. Maj. Souk Oudomphong
369. Lt. Col. Soulenh Phetxomphou
370. Lt. Col. Soulika _____
371. Police Maj. Soulinh Souvannasing
372. Civilian Souphat _____
373. Maj. Souphat _____
374. Lt. Col. Souphot _____
375. Lt. Col. Sourika _____
376. Police Maj. Sourinh Souvannasing
377. Maj. Soutchay _____
378. Maj. South Sounantha
379. Police Maj. Southanh _____
380. Maj. Souvanh Philavong
381. Police Maj. Souvanthong Thammavongsa
382. Police Maj. Souvath Thongdara

383. Maj. Subsack Nachampassack (escaped Laos; migrated to U.S., 1987)
384. Maj. Sy _____
385. Police Maj. Sychanh Phyathep
386. Maj. Symoune _____
387. Maj. Ta Thaodara
388. Governor Tanh Avong Vorabout (escaped Laos; last known whereabouts: Na Pho refugee camp, Thailand, 1985)
389. Police Maj. Tanh Malaythong
390. Lt. Col. Tiao Tanh Patthanak (royal family, escaped Laos; migrated to Australia, 1981)
391. Maj. Tao _____
392. Lt. Col. Taxay Sopha
393. Maj. Thai _____
394. Maj. Tham Sananikone
395. Civilian Thanh Phomsavanh
396. Police Maj. Thanom Khamvath (escaped Laos; migrated to U.S., 1986)
397. Police Maj. Thavisath Songvilay
398. Civilian The Intharajvongsy
399. Lt. Col. Theung Phanvongsa
400. Lt. Col. Theung Siharath
401. Maj. Thone Rattanasavanh
402. Maj. Thonechanh Luangrath (escaped Laos; migrated to U.S., 1983)
403. Civilian Thong _____
404. Maj. Thongdam
405. Maj. Thongdy Vongmahatham (escaped Laos; last known whereabouts: Na Pho refugee camp, Thailand, 1986)
406. Lt. Col. Thongkham Daranouvong
407. Police Maj. Thongkhanh _____
408. Maj. Thongna _____ (died in captivity, 1986)
409. Civilian Thongphanh Vannasy
410. Maj. Thongphat _____
411. Maj. Thongphat Siharath
412. Lt. Col. Thongthep Chantharatry
413. Civilian Thongthip S. Phabmixay
414. Police Maj. Thongvanh Panya
415. Lt. Col. Thot Nhouyvanisvong (died in captivity, 1970)
416. Lt. Col. Thouane Panyanouvong
417. Police Maj. Thoum _____
418. Maj. Thoune Phommahaxay
419. Maj. Tiam _____
420. Police Maj. Tom _____
421. Civilian Toulong Lyfoung
422. Police Maj. Triem Souryavong (escaped Laos; migrated to U.S., 1986; now lives in Vancouver, Washington)
423. Police Maj. Ty Sengkhane
424. Police Maj. Vandy Chittarath
425. Lt. Col. Vandy Thongprachanh (died in captivity, 1984)

426. Police Maj. Vang Xoumpholphakdy
427. Maj. Vanhsy S. Phabmixay
428. Maj. Vanhtheuang Mondokkham
429. Police Maj. Vanna _____
430. Police Maj. Vanhsong _____
431. Police Maj. Vanthong Sivankham (escaped Laos; migrated to U.S., 1986)
432. Director Vetsouvanh Kamkasomphou (escaped Laos; migrated to New Zealand, 1985)
433. Civilian Vixay _____
434. Maj. Xeuam Rajphangthong (died in captivity, 1984)
435. Lt. Col. Xieng Mathouchanh
436. Maj. Xiengkongsy Bounlutay

Seminarists of Camp 05 —
Viengxay Area

*Number following name shows age when sent to seminar camp in 1975.
Asterisks precede names of the twenty-seven accused of rebellion in the camp in
1977. (See Boukeo Bounnam's story, page 209.)*

1. *Col. Amkha Khanhthamixay, 43 (believed died in captivity, 1977,
   although some sources say he is still living)
2. Police Col. Arun Boupha, 44
3. *Gen. Atsaphangthong Pathammavong, 45 (asst. to commander, Region 5 — Vientiane sector; died in captivity, 1977)
4. Maj. Baccam Kouay, 32
5. Maj. Baccam Vien, 32
6. Col. Banouvong Panya, 40
7. Police Col. Bolibane Vongsarasinh, 38
8. Police Col. Bot Luangrath, 58
9. Governor Bouahom Souvanhdy, 49
10. Col. Bouakeo Nhoymani, 44
11. Boualy Sopha, 44 (member of 1975 political coalition; previously a high
    school teacher)
12. Police Col. Bouaphanh Southavilay, 40
13. Governor Bouathip Thongpane, 56
14. *Gen. Bounchanh Savatphayphane, 47 (operations — Armed Forces
    Headquarters; died in captivity, 1977)
15. Col. Bouchanh Thamvong, 47
16. Air Force Col. Boukeo Bounnam, 42 (escaped Laos; migrated to U.S.,
    1985. See history beginning on page 207.)
17. Police Col. Bounkan Saycocie, 47
18. Col. Bounkeung Nakepone, 44
19. *Gen. Bounleuth Sanichanh, 54 (inspector general, died in captivity, 1977)
20. Col. Bounleuth Philavong, 44 (died in captivity, 1984)
21. Col. Bounlouane Daoheuang, 45
22. Lt. Col. Bounlu Nammathao, 49
23. Gen. Bounma Vongphachanh, 51
24. Police Col. Bounmy Mounivong, 43
25. Col Bounmy Siharath, 42
26. Col. Bounnao Thirakoun, 42
27. Col. Bounpheng Sounthone, 45
28. Air ̗Force Col. Bounphou Sanichanh, 40 (escaped Laos, 1987; mi-
    grated to U.S.; now lives in Arizona)
29. *Gen. Bounpone Marthepharack, 53 (Armed Forces Commander-in-
    Chief; died in captivity, 1977)
30. Police Col. Bountem Phanhthavong, 40

31. Lt. Col. Bounthanh Keophanhboua, 37
32. Col. Bounthanh Oudomphong, 43
33. Col. Bounthavy Phouisangiem, 37
34. *Gen. Bounthieng Venevongsoth, 51 (International Control Committee; died in captivity, 1977)
35. Col. Bounxou Bouakhasit, 45
36. Civilian Bounyasit Marthepharack, 30
37. Col. Bounyavet _____, 48
38. Police Col. Bounxou Silalack, 45
39. Col. Champa Phengpasack, 42
40. Police Col. Changvat Vilayhong, 50 (died in captivity, 1983)
41. Police Col. Chanh Sirimath, 42
42. Police Col. Chanhpheng Philaphonh, 40
43. Col. Chanhpheng Phongsavat, 38
44. Air Force Col. Chanhpheng Sadettan, 40
45. Police Col. Chanhpheng Xoumpholphakdy, 51
46. Director Chansamone Voravong, 44 (escaped Laos; migrated to France)
47. Police General Chanthala Sihachack, 48
48. Police Col. Dao Phachareun, 48
49. Col. Dok Luangkoumphol, 48
50. Col. Douangpy Phanakhone, 42
51. Police Col. Eng _____, 42
52. Police Maj. Feuy _____, 54
53. Police Col. Fone Phakaysone, 54
54. Gen. _____ Hayasane (released to Vientiane, 1980–81; sent back to 05 a week or two later for talking)
55. *Heng Saythavy, 43 (member of political coalition; died in captivity, 1977)
56. Police Col. Heuang Intravong, 43
57. Col. Hom Niravong, 48
58. Col. Hongkeo Sadettan, 46
59. Col. Hongkham Sadettan, 50
60. Police Col. Houmphamh Kingsave, 41 (one of four colonels [and see #80, #125, #153] who escaped in 1978, was recaptured about two weeks later and killed; see page 211)
61. Gen. Houmphanh Norasing, 52 (released to Vientiane, 1980–81; sent back to 05 a week or two later for talking; see page 224)
62. Col. Houmpheng Bounlyaphol, 42
63. Police Col. Houmpheng Souksavat, 41
64. Police Col. Houn Ratananongsy, 47
65. Col. Inpanh Luangrath, 45
66. Police Col. Inpanh Savanhkham, 46
67. Police Gen. Inpeng Thammavongsa
68. Police Lt. Col. Insadet Rajphangthong, 45
69. *Director Issara Katay Don Sasorith, 38 (died in captivity, 1977)
70. *Gen. Kane Insixiengmay, 50 (logistics — Armed Forces Headquarters; died in captivity, 1977)

71. Col. Kanh Keohavong, 44
72. Police Col. Kathong Don Sasorith, 44
73. *Police Col. Kavin Keonakhone, 46 (died in captivity, 1977)
74. Col. Kene Phomvidone, 55 (escaped, 1983; recaptured and killed)
75. Lt. Col. Keuth Sirivongxay, 44
76. Director Kham Ouane Rattanavong, 51 (escaped Laos; migrated to France, 1982)
77. Col. Khambouane Phommabout, 44
78. Col. Khamchanh Phanouvong, 40
79. *Ambassador Khamchanh Pradith, 45 (died in captivity, 1977)
80. Col. Khamdeng Boulom, 44 (One of four colonels [and see #60, #130, #153] who attempted escape in 1978)
81. Col. Khamdeng S. Praseuth, 44
82. Khamfanh Nouanesavanh, 48 (Was a member of the 1975 political coalition. Escaped Laos; migrated to U.S., 1986. Now lives in Fresno, Calif.)
83. Col. Khamfong Phommata, 42 (escaped Laos; last known whereabouts: Na Pho refugee camp, Thailand, 1986)
84. Lt. Col. Khamheuang Sounanthavong, 40 (escaped Laos, 1986; migrated to the U.S.)
85. Director Khamkhing Souvanlasy, 46
86. Col. Khamko Boutmuongnong, 43
87. Col. Khamlane Chanhthryasack, 49
88. Gen. Khamlom Thongphanh, 46
89. Police Col. Khamlouang Nokham, 37 (escaped Laos, migrated to U.S., 1986)
90. Col. Khammanh Koumphol, 45 (escaped Laos; was visiting his children in Anaheim, Calif., at this writing)
91. Air Force Col. Khammay V. Bouxasinh, 43
92. Col. Khammet Luangviseth, 47
93. *Police Col. Khammouk Phengsiaroun, 42 (died in captivity, 1977)
94. Col. Khamphanh Bounsavath, 45
95. Director Khamphanh Phaxaysithideth, 35
96. Col. Khamphanh Phoummavong, 43
97. Governor Khamphanh Pradith, 40
98. Col. Khamphanh Raxaseuk, 49
99. *Col. Khamphanh Thammakhanhti, 44 (was still alive in captivity in 1984; in January 1988 his wife reported to Boukeo Bounnam that he had since died; she lives in Portland, Oregon)
100. Col. Khamphanh Ulavanh, 44
101. Police Maj. Khamphao Thongkham, 38
102. Col. Khamphatboua _____, 42 (died in captivity, 1986)
103. Col. Khamphay Ratsvongthong, 46
104. Col. Khamphay Sayasith, 45 (escaped Laos; migrated to U.S., 1981)
105. Police Col. Khampheng S. Phabmixay, 38
106. Col. Khamphet Douangdara, 47
107. Police Col. Khamphone _____, 49

108. Police Col. Khamphou Sengdeuanepheng, 42 (died in captivity, 1978)
109. Police Col. Khamphoui Bounsavath, 40
110. Police Col. Khamphoui Luangrath, 41
111. Col. Khamphoui Phanouvong, 43
112. Police Col. Khamsavang Chanhthryasack, 41
113. Police Col. Khamsene Keomanideth, 42
114. Police Col. Khamsene Phimphachanh, 42
115. Col. Khamsene Sayavong, 42
116. Police Gen. Khamseng Vorosane, 47
117. Director Khamsing Ngonvorarath, 48
118. Police Col. Khamsone Boutchantharath, 41
119. Col. Khamsouane Ngonvorarath, 44
120. Police Col. Khamsouang Sihalathavong, 43
121. Col. Khamsouk S. Rajphak, 46
122. Police Col. Khamsouk Virachit, 51
123. Director Khamtanh Kanhalikham, 43
124. Col. Khamtanh Thirakoun, 43
125. Director Khamtou Boulom, 39 (Was one of four colonels [and see #60, #80, #153] who attempted to escape in 1978.
126. Col. Khamveui _____, 45
127. Col. Khamxay Phommavong, 45
128. Col. Khanhkham Bouphasavanh, 45 (escaped Laos; migrated to Australia, 1986)
129. Police Col. Khatha Khanhthamixay, 39
130. Col. Kheuang Pathammavong, 45
131. Police Col. Khongxay Baphavanh, 42
132. Khoun Praseut (student; sent to Phadaeng jail near Viengxay; escaped Laos, 1984; last known whereabouts: Na Pho refugee camp, Thailand)
133. Police Gen. Kolakanh Kamkaxomphou, 47
134. Police Gen. Kom Nhoybouakong, 56
135. Police Gen. Kong Sengsouryachanh, 59 (escaped Laos; migrated to France)
136. Col. Kongkeo Songvilay, 44
137. Air Force Col. Kongsana Koumpholpakdy, 45 (escaped Laos, 1987; migrated to U.S.; now lives in Seattle, Washington)
138. Police Col. Ky Senesouvanh, 43
139. Col. Lamkeo Uprajai, 44 (escaped Laos; migrated to U.S., 1987; now lives in Houston, Texas)
140. Col. Lammathou Bouphanouvong, 44
141. Police Col. Leuth Phet-Asa
142. *Ambassador Lian Phavongviengkham, 47 (ambassador to PRC; died in captivity, 1977)
143. Col. Liemphakhaythong Xoumpholphakdy, 44
144. Col. Liep Outhay, 48
145. Police Col. Lot Khounsaphaothong, 46
146. Lt. Col. Lot Kovin, 42
147. Police Col. Lot Siluxa, 46

148. Police Col. Luk Pasatthong, 45
149. *Gen. Thao Ly Lithiluxa, 46 (intelligence—Armed Forced Head-quarters; died in captivity, 1977)
150. Col. Maloun Phommavong, 49
151. Col. Mang Indara, 44 (escaped Laos; migrated to U.S., 1987; now lives in California)
152. Col. Manh Opma, 50 (escaped Laos; migrated to U.S., 1986)
153. Col. Maykhamphanh Banhdasack, 46 (one of four colonels [and see #60, #80, #125] who attempted escape in 1978)
154. Police Col. Ming Manivong, 41 (died in captivity, 1985)
155. Col. Mok Khouvongsavanh, 48
156. Gen. Tiao Monivong Kindavong, 47 (member of royal family, a nephew of Souvanna and Souphanouvong. It is believed he is still in captivity in the Viengxay area. His younger brother, Colonel Sintha-novong Kindavong was also in Camp 05. See #250)
157. Col. Mounthala Chanhthalusi, 44
158. Police Col. Nakhonekham Bouphanouvong, 46
159. Police Col. Ngeunsamlit D. Sasorit, 39
160. Police Col. Nhay Sengsavanh, 47
161. Police Col. Nhon K. Rajpu, 42 (escaped to Laos 1987 with his family and four other families to join Liberation Front. All were arrested by Lao Communists in Nong Khai and sent back to Laos.)
162. Police Col. Nhon Phomvongsa, 48
163. Col. Nhouat Kongdara, 42
164. Police Col. Nikhom Linthong, 40
165. Police Capt. Niphonh Thavonekham, 40
166. *Gen. Nouphet Daoheuang, 46 (commander, Region 3—Savannakhet; died in captivity, 1977)
167. Civilian Okham Anoulack, 60
168. Police Col. One Phakhounthong, 44
169. Police Col. Onechanh Keosavang, 42
170. Col. Onh Bounphaxayxon, 43
171. Police Maj. Onh Mahasena, 38
172. Col. Op Soukaseum, 44
173. Police Col. Ouan Dara, 40
174. Police Col. Ouane Phanhphengdy, 44
175. *Gen. Ouane Ratikoun, 54 (retired as Armed Forces commander about 1972 and became member of 1975 political coalition; died in captivity, 1977)
176. Police Col. Ouansy Southidara, 48
177. Minister Ouday Souvannavong, 56 (minister of information; escaped Laos; migrated to France, 1981, with his brother, Oudong; see # 181)
178. Col. Oudom Phanhthavong, 42
179. Police Col. Oudom Sourintha, 40
180. Air Force Col. Oudone Manibod, 44
181. Minister Oudong Souvannavong, 59 (escaped Laos; migrated to France, 1981, with brother Ouday; see #177)

182. Col. Ounheuane Chittasi, 40
183. Police Gen. Ounheuane Sinhbanhdit, 50
184. Air Force Col. Outama Thongsithavong, 42
185. Col. Padap _____, 50
186. Police Maj. Pakaykeo S. Phabmixay, 38
187. Director Pane Rassavong, 42 (was a classmate of Boukeo Bounnam from 1948; when Boukeo was released in 1984, he was working at Sam Teu [Camp 05]; reported to be still alive)
188. Maj. Pangthong Chokbengboun, 42
189. Col. Nai Pany, 44
190. Police Maj. Paphot Phommathet, 41
191. Police Col. Pasong Sommay, 46
192. Civilian Pha Phonseya, 52
193. Maj. Pha Praseuth, 49
194. Director Phak Savanh, 50
195. Col. Phanh Inthavong, 49
196. Col. Phanh Nola, 43
197. Police Gen. Phao Abhay, 52
198. Col. Phao Soutthi, 47
199. *Gen. Phasouk S. Rajsaphak, 47 (chief of staff; died in captivity, 1977)
200. Col. Phay Malavong, 44
201. Police Col. Phay Souksavong, 40
202. *Minister Pheng Phongsavanh, 56 (defense minister; died in captivity, 1977)
203. Police Col. Pheng Misomphane, 41
204. Col. Phengkeo _____, 47
205. Police Col. Pheo Khouphongsy, 47
206. Police Col. Phet Khouphongsy, 47
207. Police Col. Pheui Chittaphong, 42
208. Gen. Pheui Mixayphonh, 50
209. Col. Phimpha Rattanakosol, 46
210. Police Col. Phimpha Sinhbanhdit, 57 (died in captivity, 1985)
211. Police Col. Phimphone Panyanouvong, 39
212. Police Col. Phokhay Vilayhong, 40
213. Phom Bounlutay, 43 (member of 1975 political coalition)
214. *Col. Phom Phanhthavong, 52 (accused of rebellion and arrested in August, 1977, one month before the twenty-six others; sources report that he is still alive in captivity; previously battalion commander, Ban Keun area, north of Vientiane)
215. Police Col. Phomma Sokhanhthong, 53
216. Police Col. Phomma Soukaseum, 55
217. Police Col. Phonethip Chindavong, 42 (died in captivity, 1985)
218. Col. Phongprasansack Insixiengmay, 39
219. Director Phoui Phouthasack, 55 (escaped Laos; migrated to France, 1981)
220. Air Force Col. Phoui Siriphong, 42 (escaped Laos; migrated to U.S., 1981)

221. Police Col. Phoui Souksavath, 42
222. Col. Phoukhong Saysanith, 43
223. Police Col. Poun Sananikone, 44 (died in captivity, 1981)
224. Col. Phouthasenh Phanekham, 44
225. Police Gen. Phouvang Saysithideth, 49
226. Col. Praseuth Khamphoui, 40
227. Col. Praseuth Mounsourisack, 45
228. Col. Praseuth Soundara, 46 (died in captivity, 1984)
229. *Gen. Rattanabanhleung Chounlamountri, 45 (died in captivity, 1977;
      previously General Security Commander)
230. Col. Salao Signavong, 46
231. Police Col. Salat Raxasack, 42 (member of 1975 political coalition)
232. Col. Samlane S. Rajphack, 43
233. Director Samlith Ratsphong, 50
234. Lt. Col. Savat Chanthavong, 42
235. Gen. Tiao Sayavong, 47 (brother of the late king of Laos, was still in
      captivity when Boukeo Bounnam left in 1984; believed to be still
      there)
236. Gen. Tiao Sengsouvanh Souvannarath, 45 (member of royal family, a
      nephew of Souvanna and Souphanouvong; was still in Camp 05 when
      Boukeo Bounnam left in 1984; as of now, April 1988, there are
      reported to be seven military generals as well as an unknown number
      of police generals left in captivity in the Viengxay area)
237. *Capt. Sery Sayakham, 39 (died in captivity, 1977)
238. Col. Seumsack Chatouxay, 47 (died in captivity, 1985)
239. Police Col. Sichanh Chitdamrong, 37
240. Col. Sichanh Kayavong, 45
241. Col. Sichanh Thamvong, 45
242. Col. Sida Sinamonti, 42
243. Police Gen. Tiao Siharath Phasouk, 38 (member of royal family, a
      nephew of Souvanna; was still in captivity in 1984; believed still there,
      1988)
244. Col. Sing Chanhthakouman, 44
245. Police Lt. Col. Sing Rajphangthong, 42
246. Police Col. Sing Vetmany, 56
247. Maj. Singkapo Nouhouang, 34 (escaped Laos; migrated to France,
      1986)
248. Col. Singkeo Sinhbanhdith, 43
249. *Gen. Tiao Sinh Saysana, 43 (member of royal family; assistant to
      commander, Region 1—Luang Prabang; died in captivity, 1977)
250. Col. Tiao Sinthanavong Kindavong, 44 (royal family; a nephew of Sou-
      vanna and Souphanouvong and younger brother of Gen. Monivong
      Kindavong, also in Camp 05, #156; was released at the same time as
      Boukeo Bounnam, December of 1984; escaped Laos; migrated to
      France, 1985)
251. Col. Sisamouth Sananikone, 46
252. Col. Sisavath Mekdarasouk, 45

253. Col. Sisavat Vongkhamheuang, 48
254. Col. Sisoumang Kounlavouth, 43
255. Tiao Sisoumang Sisaleumsack, 60 (royal family; Minister for Tele-
     communications in Souvanna Phouma administration; became a
     member of 1975 political coalition; still in captivity in Viengxay area)
256. Col. Sisouphanh Vanhnachit, 42
257. Police Col. Tiao Sisouvanh Phanhthavong, 40 (royal family)
258. Col. Sith Soutthichack, 41
259. Police Col. Sitheua Bongnasith, 43
260. Police Col. Sitho Inthavong, 46
261. Col. Sithonh Vongphachanh, 39
262. *Police Col. Sivilay Phichith, 35 (died in captivity, 1977)
263. Police Gen. Som Rajphangthong, 49
264. Col. Somboun Khennavong, 44 (died in captivity, 1984)
265. Police Col. Somboun Ounkeo, 48
266. Col. Somboun Thammavongsa, 49 (died in captivity, 1984)
267. Col. Somboun Vixaysouk, 46 (died in captivity, 1981)
268. Police Gen. Somchine Phouthakhanhty, 51
269. Police Col. Somdy Somsavath, 45 (died in captivity, 1984)
270. Police Gen. Somnuk Thongphanith, 45
271. Police Col. Somphet Vongsouvanh, 50
272. Col. Somphone Phommachanh, 44
273. Col. Somphong Soukaseum, 45
274. Police Col. Somsouk Banouvong, 43
275. Col. Song Douangphachanh, 42
276. Police Col. Soui Inthavong, 44
277. *Minister Sukan Vilaysane, 58 (Minister for Veteran Affairs; died in
     captivity, 1977)
278. Col. Souk Darik, 46
279. Col. Soukanh Phachanhsiri, 42
280. Police Col. Sounthone Douangchack, 42
281. Col. Sounthone Keomanikhot, 43
282. Police Col. Sounthone Soundara, 38
283. Police Col. Souphanh Rattanasamay, 45
284. Col. Souphannavong Bouavong, 45
285. Gen. Sourith Don Sasorith, 53 (died in captivity, 1978)
286. Lt. Col. Southep Vongphet, 53
287. Souvanh Sananikhom, 43 (member of 1975 political coalition)
288. Col. Souvanh Signavong, 42 (died in captivity, 1985)
289. Col. Souvanhphansy Muanhhane, 44
290. Police Gen. Souvanny Phomphakdy, 49
291. Col. Tanh Luangrath, 32 (died in captivity, 1984)
292. Than Praseut (student; sent to Phadaeng jail with brother, Khoun,
     #132; escaped Laos, 1984; last known whereabouts: Na Pho refugee
     camp, Thailand)
293. Col. Thanom Phakhim, 48
294. Police Col. Thanomsack Sunxom, 39

295. Col. Thone Khomsarasin, 44
296. Col. Thongphanh Chanthamalin, 42
297. *Gen. Thongphanh Knoksi, 44 (Information Officer; died in captivity, 1977)
298. Col. Thongphanh Soukaseu, 42 (escaped Laos; migrated to U.S., 1986)
299. Col. Thongsy Souphab, 57
300. Col. Thoun _____, 41
301. *Minister Toubi Lifoung, 56 (Head Buddhist Monk—a government position; died in captivity, 1977)
302. Governor Thuk Chokbengboun, 49
303. Col. Vanh Sisouvong, 44 (released to Vientiane, 1980–81, and escaped Laos; reported to be third-in-command of Lao Liberation Front in Thailand. The leader is General Thonglit Chokbengboun who was Commander of the Fifth Military Region, Vientiane Province, and escaped to Thailand in 1975. His second-in-command, Colonel Loun Sisounon, escaped to France in 1975, returning to Thailand circa 1987.)
304. Col. Vanhthong Chitananonh, 41
305. Police Col. Vanhsy _____, 41
306. Gen. Vannaseng Sayasane, 47
307. Vannavong Lescure, 42 (member of 1975 political coalition; still in captivity in Viengxay area)
308. Col. VAnnivong Xoumpholphakdy, 39
309. Director Vannothone S. Thongsit, 30
310. Police Col. Vatthaboun Boupharath, 42
311. Viboun Abhay, 36 (member of 1975 political coalition)
312. Col. Viengkhone Nokeo, 47
313. Maj. Viengthong Viravouth, 38
314. Col. Vikorn Bilavarn, 43
315. Director Viliam Phraxayavong, 41 (escaped Laos, 1985; migrated to Australia. He and Somlith Vannarath—Camp 04, #355—were the original compilers of these lists)
316. Col. Visith Khamphounvong, 49

CAMP

6

VIENGXAY

Seminarists of Camp 06 —
Viengxay Area

1. Maj. Amma Koumphon (still in captivity in Viengxay area; a relative of Boukeo Bounnam; see page 207)
2. Police Lt. Col. Ammone Vimonphanh (escaped Laos; migrated to U.S.)
3. Police Maj. Anh Vongsamphanh (last known whereabouts: Vientiane)
4. Director Anorath Voravong (died in captivity, 1985)
5. Anouram Vilaythong (escaped Laos; last known whereabouts: Na Pho refugee camp, Thailand)
6. Lt. Col. Ba Ot Phakhin (still in captivity in Viengxay area)
7. Police Maj. Ba Sayabanha (escaped Laos; last known whereabouts: Na Pho refugee camp, Thailand)
8. Civilian Bakanh Boulom (still in captivity in Viengxay area)
9. Governor Bane Phetxomphou (died in captivity, 1983)
10. Capt. Banh Douangchanh (died in captivity, 1981)
11. Lt. Col. Blonthao Yonlu (still in captivity in Viengxay area)
12. Maj. Bong Phanhthalath (still in captivity in Viengxay area)
13. Air Force Maj. Bong Phanhthavong
14. Maj. Bou _____ (died in captivity, 1982)
15. Capt. Boua _____ (died in captivity, 1984)
16. Capt. Bouachanh Somsacksy (still in captivity in Viengxay area)
17. Air Force Lt. Col. Bouaket Bounthavalang (released to Vientiane, his last known whereabouts as of May, 1988)
18. Maj. Bouaket Sotsavanh (still in captivity in Viengxay area)
19. Maj. Boualinh Chanthavilay (escaped Laos; migrated to U.S., 1981)
20. Capt. Boualith Khamluxa (still in captivity in Viengxay area)
21. Maj. Bouasy Kalaya (escaped Laos; migrated to U.S., 1981; sponsored Samly Khamphouy; see page 191)
22. Lt. Col. Bouasy Sihanath (released to Vientiane, his last known whereabouts as of May, 1988; nephew-in-law of Boukeo Bounnam)
23. Lt. Col. Boun Eua (committed suicide by poison in camp; see page 197)
24. Maj. Boun Phommachack (still in captivity in Viengxay area)
25. Maj. Boun Phoualavanh (still in captivity in Viengxay area)
26. Police Maj. Bounchanh _____
27. Police Maj. Bounchom Soykeomixay (still in captivity in Viengxay area)
28. Capt. Bounchouane Kanhlaya (still in captivity in Viengxay area)
29. Maj. Bounkeo Kongphavong (still in captivity in Viengxay area)
30. Maj. Bounkham _____ (still in captivity in Viengxay area)
31. Lt. Col. Bounkham Kongsayasack (still in captivity in Viengxay area)
32. Police Maj. Bounkham Sihapanya (still in captivity in Viengxay area)
33. Maj. Bounkham Sourinhosack (still in captivity in Viengxay area)

34. Maj. Bounlam Mounchanhthabout (escaped Laos; migrated to U.S., 1986)
35. Police Lt. Col. Bounleua Souvannasing
36. Maj. Bounleuth Panyasiri (died in captivity, 1976)
37. Col. Bounleuth Philavong (died in captivity, 1985)
38. Director Bounlieng Philavong (escaped Laos; migrated to U.S., 1986)
39. Police Lt. Col. Bounloth Bounyavong (escaped Laos; last known whereabouts: Na Pho refugee camp, Thailand, 1985)
40. Maj. Bounma Chanhthavong (escaped Laos; last known whereabouts: Na Pho refugee camp, Thailand)
41. Lt. Col. Bounmak Arounlangsy
42. Capt. Bounmak Phommala
43. Police Capt. Bounmak Songmixay (died in captivity, 1979)
44. Police Lt. Col. Bounmy Dengmanivanh
45. Lt. Col. Bounmy Khammanithong
46. Director Bounnhon Khamhoung (escaped Laos; migrated to U.S., 1981)
47. Lt. Col. Bounnhong Homsombat
48. Police Maj. Bounnhot Sisouphon
49. Maj. Bounnhou Mixaysouk
50. Maj. Bounniem Chanhsombath (escaped Laos; migrated to U.S., 1986)
51. Maj. Bounniem Chanhthalangsy
52. Lt. Col. Bounpheng Bounphathy
53. Director Bounpheng Phenglamphanh
54. Lt. Col. Bounpheum Phommahaxay
55. Civilian Bounsana Oudanonh (escaped Laos; migrated to France, 1981)
56. Civilian Bounseng Soulivong
57. Air Force Lt. Col. Bounsot Phenglamphanh (escaped Laos; migrated to U.S., 1988; now lives in Maryland)
58. Police Maj. Bounsouane Thirath
59. Lt. Col. Bounsouei S. Prasong
60. Lt. Col. Bounsy Thirakoun
61. Police Maj. Bounta _____
62. Lt. Col. Bountang Insixiengmay
63. Police Lt. Col. Bounthanh Sirikoun
64. Bounthene _____ (escaped Laos; last known whereabouts: Na Pho refugee camp, Thailand, 1986)
65. Maj. Bountheuang Vongphachanh (died in captivity, 1980)
66. Governor Bountheung _____ (escaped Laos; migrated to U.S.)
67. Lt. Col. Bountheung Phanhvongsa
68. Police Maj. Bountoum Chanhthamath
69. Maj. Bounxom Luangphixay
70. Maj. Boury Chindavong
71. Capt. Chaleunsack Nachampassack
72. Air Force Maj. Chamleune Phetsomphone (released to Vientiane, his last known whereabouts as of May, 1988)
73. Director Champathongphet Banhthrongsack (escaped Laos; migrated to France, 1986)

74. Maj. Chang Paoyang
75. Police Maj. Chanh Bounnhong (escaped Laos; migrated to U.S., 1981)
76. Maj. Chantho Vorasane (escaped Laos; migrated to U.S., 1987)
77. Police 2nd. Lt. Chansamone Ratsphone (escaped Laos; migrated to U.S., 1983)
78. Col. Chansom Pakdimanivong
79. Police Lt. Col. Chanthaboun Vilaysane
80. Air Force Lt. Col. Chanthala Chounlamany
81. Maj. Chanthalay Hanevichith
82. Governor Chanthy Phitsamay
83. Capt. Chath Xoumpholphakdy
84. Dr. _____ Chiampa (medical doctor)
85. Lt. Col. Chouangchanh Anyamany
86. Maj. Choummany Rajasack (still in captivity in Viengxay area)
87. Lt. Col. Domone Bilavarn (still in captivity in Viengxay area)
88. Maj. Douangchanh Sanouvong (still in captivity in Viengxay area)
89. Maj. Douangchanh Siharath (still in captivity in Viengxay area)
90. Air Force Maj. Douangdy Hemmavanh (escaped Laos; migrated to U.S., 1981)
91. Civilian Douangsy Nouanephanhthakoun (escaped Laos; last known whereabouts: Na Pho refugee camp, Thailand, 1985)
92. Maj. Douangsy Oudomsouk (escaped Laos; migrated to Canada, 1981)
93. Cap. Dy Sisomvang (escaped Laos; migrated to U.S., 1986)
94. Lt. Col. Eng Amphavanasouk (Last known whereabouts: Vientiane)
95. Lt. Col. Eunh Traymany (escaped Laos; last known whereabouts: Na Pho refugee camp, Thailand, 1986)
96. Col. Fongsamouth Arounpradith (escaped Laos; migrated to U.S., 1981)
97. Maj. Heuxong _____ (died in captivity, 1980)
98. Police Maj. Hom _____
99. Maj. Hongkham Mekdarasouk
100. Director Hongsa Chanthavong (escaped Laos; migrated to U.S., 1981)
101. Civilian Houmphanh Simmasing (died in captivity, 1978)
102. Police Maj. Houmpheng Phongsavanh (escaped Laos; migrated to Australia, 1985)
103. Police Capt. Houmpheng Pradichith
104. Lt. Col. Houmpheng Vongpradith (died in captivity, 1977)
105. Maj. I Trayouran (still in captivity in Viengxay area)
106. Maj. Intong Inthivong (died in captivity, 1986)
107. Maj. Intong Thammavongsa
108. Civilian Inthy Kosanouvong (escaped Laos; migrated to U.S., 1981)
109. Maj. Intong Thiravong (still in captivity in Viengxay area)
110. Civilian Keng Vetthana
111. Police Capt. Keo Manisoth
112. Police Lt. Col. Keo Manivong
113. Keo Phommahaxay
114. Civilian Keoviengkot

115. 1st Lt. Ket _____
116. Civilian Khambay Dorabout
117. Maj. Khambay Phothirath (escaped Laos; migrated to Canada, 1981)
118. Maj. Khambou Insixiengmay
119. Lt. Col. Khamchanh Chanthany
120. Maj. Khamchanh Vongkabkeo
121. Maj. Khamdeng _____
122. Maj. Khamfong Sananikone
123. Police Maj. Khamfong Saythavy (escaped Laos; migrated to Australia, 1981)
124. Lt. Col. Khamhaksone _____ (died in captivity, 1984)
125. 1st. Lt. Khamhou Phachanhpheng
126. Lt. Col. Khamhoung Phounsavath
127. Maj. Khamkeo Vongphasouk
128. Police Maj. Khamkhong Samountry
129. Lt. Col. Khamkip Phommachanh
130. Lt. Col. Khamkone Thepsombandith
131. Maj. Khamkong Lanephouthakoun
132. Police Lt. Col. Khamla Boutdara
133. Maj. Khamla Souvannakhot (escaped Laos; migrated to U.S., 1981)
134. Civilian Khamlay _____
135. Civilian Khamlay Khanthavixab (escaped Laos; migrated to U.S., 1979)
136. Police Lt. Col. Khamlu Koumpholpakdy
137. Maj. Khammanh Sihapanya (escaped Laos; migrated to U.S., 1987)
138. Police Lt. Col. Khammao Phommaseng
139. Maj. Khammay Baochanh
140. Maj. Khammoune Liemphimmasane
141. Capt. Khammoung Phothirath
142. Police Lt. Col. Khammy Virachith
143. Lt. Col. Khamouane Douangphachanh (escaped Laos; migrated to U.S., 1981)
144. Air Force Maj. Khampane Voranout (died in captivity, 1978)
145. Director Khampha Sackda (died in captivity, 1978)
146. Maj. Khamphanh Chanminhavong
147. Air Force Lt. Col. Khamphay Thongkham
148. Director Khamphone Khounthapanya
149. Lt. Col. Khamphone Simuong (escaped Laos; migrated to U.S., 1981)
150. Lt. Col. Khamphong Sourignosack
151. Police Lt. Col. Khamphou Abhay
152. Lt. Col. Khamphouang Philavanh (died in captivity, 1984)
153. Governor Khamphoui Douangphouxay (escaped Laos; migrated to U.S., 1981)
154. Governor Khamphoui Souydarai (escaped Laos; migrated to France)
155. Maj. Khamphout _____
156. Police Maj. Khamphou Baobounmy
157. Maj. Khampiene _____

158. Air Force Lt. Col. Khampoune Phanhthavong
159. Maj. Khamsamongdy Saycocie
160. Capt. Khamsamouth _____
161. Lt. Col. Khamsay Kiettavong
162. Police Maj. Khamseng S. Phabmixay (escaped Laos; migrated to U.S., 1986)
163. Maj. Khamsing Pathammavong
164. Police Lt. Col. Khamsom Inthavong
165. Director Khamsouk Singharath (died in captivity, 1984)
166. Lt. Col. Khamthanom Soulivong
167. Khamtou Sackda (member of 1975 coalition; died in captivity, 1978)
168. Lt. Col. Khamtoune Luangrath
169. Police Capt. Khamvene Phanhthavong
170. Lt. Col. Khamvong Chanhthalasy
171. Police Lt. Col. Khang Thinavongsy (escaped Laos; migrated to U.S., 1988)
172. Police Lt. Col. Khanhthaly Sisouvong
173. Lt. Col. Khaophone Simmavong (escaped Laos; last known whereabouts: Na Pho refugee camp, Thailand)
174. Police Lt. Col. Khaykham Komkaysone
175. Maj. Khene Sangboutsady
176. Mil. Police Maj. Khene Tuy (sent to Sop Hao jail)
177. Maj. Khenmay Baochanh
178. Police Lt. Col. Khenkhili _____ (escaped Laos; migrated to France, 1984)
179. Maj. Khentoui S. Phabmixay (escaped Laos to Thailand, 1987)
180. Lt. Col. Khom Phasavat
181. Maj. Kheuap Khonesavanh
182. Lt. Col. Kheuap Koumphol
183. Air Force Capt. Khom Bounyasith
184. Air Force Lt. Col. Khouang Sounthavong (escaped Laos; migrated to U.S., 1981)
185. Police NCO Khoune Lakhonekham
186. Lt. Col. Kongkeo Thirakoun
187. Lt. Col. Kongsinh Keorajvongxay (escaped Laos; migrated to U.S., 1981)
188. Maj. Koukham Douangdara
189. Governor Koukham Vixayvong (escaped Laos; migrated to U.S., 1981)
190. Lt. Col. Koum Phouvanh
191. Col. Kynonh _____
192. Civilian La Dariphone
193. Maj. La Thirakoun (died in captivity, 1980)
194. Capt. La Viengxay
195. Police Maj. Lam Rattanatrai (died in captivity, 1980)
196. Lt. Col. Langsanh Souvannasoth (escaped Laos; migrated to U.S., 1986)
197. Director Lapphoune Khamvongsa (escaped Laos; migrated to Australia, 1981)
198. Lt. Col. Lenou _____ (died in captivity, 1980)

199. Maj. Leuthavone Douangsavanh
200. Director Linh Sourinho
201. Police Capt. Lom Sisomphone
202. Director Lyteck Nhyavu (attempted escape in 1976, was recaptured and killed)
203. Lt. Col. Lyteng _____
204. Maj. Mahosot Borihane
205. Maj. Mang Chanhsamouth
206. Lt. Col. Manh Ounalom
207. Police Lt. Col. Manh Sisounthone (died in captivity, 1979)
208. Maj. Manh Sourynhosack
209. Lt. Col. Maysouk Bounlutay (escaped Laos; migrated to U.S., 1986)
210. Air Force Lt. Col. Meui Boriboun
211. Maj. Mouapao (died in captivity, 1976)
212. 1st Lt. Moung Phothirath
213. Police Capt. Nack Sananikone
214. Maj. Nenekeo Manivong (escaped Laos; migrated to France, 1986)
215. Lt. Col. Neng Yingyang (died in captivity, 1976)
216. Police Lt. Col. Ngamdy Siharath
217. Maj. Ngon Sayarath (escaped Laos; last known whereabouts: Na Pho refugee camp, Thailand, 1985)
218. Police Maj. Ngone Ngaoluangrath
219. Maj. Nhomband Sourinhphoumi
220. Lt. Col. Nim Teso
221. Lt. Col. Nou Dabanhdon
222. Maj. Nouane _____
223. Maj. Nouanedy Douangxay (died in captivity, 1983)
224. Director Nouanethong _____
225. Cap. Noukham Phongsi
226. Lt. Col. Noukone Thetmasith
227. Lt. Col. Noy Manivong
228. Governor Noysay Chanhphianamvong
229. Civilian O Xoumpholphakdy
230. Police Maj. One Khamphilom
231. Police Maj. One Norasing
232. Civilian Onechanh Dara
233. Police Lt. Col. Onechanh Phongsavanh
234. Maj. Onechanh Thammavongsa
235. Lt. Col. Ouane Phenephom
236. Maj. Oudom Sisomxune
237. Capt. Oudom Thanadabout
238. Director Oudone Kongsayasack
239. Maj. Ouneheuane Thongphet (died in captivity, 1982)
240. Lt. Col. Ounheuane Phounsavath (escaped Laos; last known whereabouts: Na Pho refugee camp, Thailand, 1986)
241. Police Lt. Col. Ounkham Maovilay (escaped Laos; migrated to France, 1981)

242. Police Capt. Ouphonh Silalack
243. Director Oute Khamvongsa
244. Maj. Pane Mixaysouk
245. Lt. Col. Pany Somvong
246. Police Lt. Col. Phanh Aryavong
247. Capt. Phanhpheng Dara (escaped Laos; last known whereabouts: Na Pho refugee camp, Thailand, 1986)
248. Civilian Phanhthourath _____
249. Civilian Phao Panyatheung
250. Lt. Col. Phao Rattanakone
251. Police Capt. Phat Philavanh
252. Police Capt. Phatsone Ouanesenesy
253. Maj. Phay Banouvong
254. Police Lt. Col. Pheng Phakhinh (died in captivity, 1976)
255. Maj. Pheng Phommaphavanh
256. Maj. Pheng Sengdara
257. Lt. Col. Pheng Sirichanhtho
258. Police Lt. Col. Pheng Thatsaniphone
259. Lt. Col. Phengdy Phanhnaphet
260. Maj. Phengphat Sananikone
261. Maj. Phet Soundara (escaped Laos; migrated to Canada, 1983)
262. Maj. Phetsanakanh Daranouvong
263. Lt. Col. Phoi Soidara
264. Maj. Phomma Bounkham (escaped Laos; migrated to U.S., 1986)
265. Civilian Phomma Sayarath
266. Lt. Col. Phomma Simmalaychanh (escaped Laos; migrated to U.S., 1981)
267. Phommadeth Thammachitto
268. Lt. Col. Phommathat _____
269. Lt. Col. Phone Phouthakesone
270. Police Maj. Phou Baobounmy
271. Lt. Col. Phoui Sananikone
272. Police Lt. Col. Phouk Thonglivong
273. Lt. Col. Phoukhong Kamkasomphou
274. Police Lt. Col. Phoumi Nouanelahong
275. Police Lt. Col. Phoumi Sourivong (escaped Laos; migrated to U.S., 1986)
276. Civilian Phouphane Khamphaphongphane (died in captivity, 1977)
277. Maj. Phouphet Phommachanh (escaped Laos; migrated to U.S., 1986)
278. Director Phouthone Virasack
279. Police Col. Phouttha Chandara
280. Lt. Col. Phouvieng Chanhsina
281. Director Phouvong Vilaythong
282. Police Lt. Col. Phy Phamuong
283. Civilian Pieng Mounnarath
284. Maj. Piengkham Siharath
285. Air Force Capt. Pine Sayarath (died in captivity, 1983)

286. Maj. Pramay Philavanh
287. Maj. Prasob Sihaphom (escaped Laos; migrated to U.S., 1981)
288. Maj. Sa Keophoxay
289. Lt. Col. Salabe Issaraphab
290. Governor Saly Boutsadachanh
291. Maj. Samay Phongsa
292. Maj. Samly Khamphouy (escaped Laos; migrated to U.S., 1986; see his story beginning on page 191)
293. Police Lt. Col. Samphanh Phonephetrath (escaped Laos; migrated to France, 1981)
294. Amb. Samrit Lasaphong (died in captivity)
295. Police 2nd. Lt. Sangouane Khamsomphou
296. Police Maj. Sangouane Vorachack
297. Maj. Saveui Sananikhom
298. Maj. Saysamone Noudaranouvong
299. Maj. Seng Paomanivong
300. Civilian Seng Souliving
301. Capt. Sengkeo Leuthsongkham (escaped Laos; migrated to U.S., 1986)
302. Police Lt. Col. Sengphachanh (escaped Laos; migrated to U.S., 1980)
303. Police Lt. Col. Seumkham Frichittavong (escaped Laos; migrated to U.S., 1986)
304. Maj. Seuth Sengphachanh
305. Maj. Tiao Sichanthavong Kindavong (royal family)
306. Air Force Lt. Col. Siheuane Sourichack (died in captivity, 1979)
307. Governor Siloloth Nachampassack
308. Police Lt. Col. Sing Saysettha (died in captivity, 1981)
309. Police Maj. Sing Sisamouth
310. Civilian Singkhamxay Choummanivong
311. Maj. Singnoy Kethkeo
312. Lt. Col. Singthong Inthavong (escaped Laos; migrated to U.S., 1981)
313. Maj. Sinouane Sonesaksith (escaped Laos; last known whereabouts: Na Pho refugee camp, Thailand, 1986)
314. Maj. Sipha Khannara (escaped Laos; migrated to Australia, 1986)
315. Police Lt. Col. Siphanh Chanthalanonh
316. Maj. Sisouphouay Kitthirath
317. Governor Sisouvanh _____ (died in captivity, 1980)
318. Police Maj. Sisouvanh Keophomma (escaped Laos; last known whereabouts: Na Pho refugee camp, Thailand, 1981)
319. Lt. Col. Sith Kingkittisack
320. Lt. Col. Sith Nachampassack (escaped Laos; last known whereabouts: Na Pho refugee camp, Thailand, 1981)
321. Maj. Sithanh Khammanivong (escaped Laos; migrated to U.S., 1981)
322. Civilian Sithonh Phonpradith
323. Maj. Sithuk Boutthasay (died in captivity, 1984)
324. Capt. Som Khounlavong
325. Lt. Col. Sombat Singharath
326. Air Force Lt. Col. Somboune Vilaysane

327. Lt. Col. Somboune Phannouvong
328. Civilian Somlith Youansamout (died in captivity, 1976)
329. Capt. Somnuk Thai-Outharath
330. Police Lt. Col. Somphamit Sounnarath
331. Civilian Somphao Chanthavisith
332. Maj. Somsakoun Soundara
333. Maj. Somsanouk Phanhnouphonh
334. Civilian Samsanouk Singharath
335. Maj. Somsy Vandisirisack (escaped Laos; migrated to France, 1981)
336. Maj. Somthuk Thongphanith (died in captivity, 1979)
337. 1st Lt. Somvang Insixiengmay
338. Air Force Maj. Sonephet Vongnarath (escaped Laos; migrated to U.S., 1981)
339. Police Lt. Col. Songkane Phiathep
340. Maj. Sopha Sithisaribout
341. Lt. Col. Soubanh Sithiphanh
342. Civilian Soube Southivongnorath (died in captivity, 1976)
343. Police Maj. Souk Ratthamone
344. Civilian Soukan Vignavong (escaped Laos; migrated to U.S., 1986; see his story, beginning on page 175)
345. Civilian Soukane Kongvongxay
346. Maj. Soukaseum S. Sanavongsa
347. Director Soukpraseuth Sithimolada
348. Lt. Col. Soulat Thirakoun
349. Maj. Soulinheuang K. Rajpu
350. Civilian Soulivanh Philivanh (escaped Laos; last known whereabouts: Na Pho refugee camp, Thailand, 1981)
351. Lt. Col. Souloth Kittikul
352. Police Capt. Sounay Kenemy (escaped Laos; migrated to U.S., 1981)
353. Maj. Sounthone Phommasourinh
354. Lt. Col. Sounthone Vongpradith
355. Maj. Souphanh Sisounthone
356. Police Lt. Col. Souphat Phetchareun (escaped Laos; last known whereabouts: Na Pho refugee camp, Thailand, 1985)
357. Police Lt. Col. Souphot Sengsourichanh
358. Police Lt. Col. Souvanny Siboriboune
359. 1st Lt. Soutanh _____
360. Air Force Maj. Soutchay Boutkasca
361. Police Lt. Col. Southaboune Boupharath
362. Police Lt. Col. Southanou Phoumivong
363. Police Maj. Soutta Sonesitthideth
364. Police Lt. Col. Souvanh Borihane
365. Lt. Col. Souvanh Sourinho (escaped Laos; migrated to U.S., 1981)
366. Lt. Col. Souvanh Virivong (died in captivity, 1985)
367. Lt. Col. Souvankham Douangsithi
368. Police Lt. Col. Souvanno Tavinnhal
369. Maj. Sy Simmala

370. Civilian Syfong Choummanivong
371. Police Maj. Sylay Phommala
372. Capt. Tack Sirivong (escaped Laos, 1983; migrated to Australia, 1987)
373. Capt. Tanh Ratsavanh
374. NCO Thao Manivong (escaped Laos; migrated to U.S., 1980)
375. Lt. Col. Thaviseuth Songvilay (died in captivity, 1979)
376. Police Maj. Thit Nantha
377. Police Maj. Thone Vilalay (escaped Laos; migrated to U.S., 1986)
378. Air Force Maj. Thongchanh Phengsavanh
379. Lt. Col. Thongcheua Phothivongsa
380. Lt. Col. Thongkhamchanh Phommasy (escaped Laos; migrated to U.S., 1981)
381. Police Maj. Thongkhoune Dhengnarath
382. Lt. Col. Thongphanh Patthasinh (died in captivity, 1985)
383. Maj. Thongsa Khanhtiyavong
384. Maj. Thongsa Thavivanh
385. Maj. Thongthavone _____
386. Police Maj. Thongthep Mouksavanh
387. Police Maj. Thongthep Senesith
388. Police Lt. Col. Thongthep Viraphanh
389. Maj. Thongvanh Douangphatmalay
390. Lt. Col. Thongvanh Manivong
391. Police Maj. Thongvanh Panya
392. Police Lt. Col. Thotsakanh Kosol
393. Maj. Tong Paosong
394. Air Force Maj. Touane Norinh
395. Police Lt. Col. Toui Phongsa
396. Civilian Tu Laysoulivong
397. Lt. Col. Va Sayarath
398. Maj. Vandy Vongdara (escaped Laos; migrated to U.S., 1986)
399. 1st. Lt. Vane Sipraseuth
400. Civilian Vanhthong
401. Police Lt. Col. Vanhpheng Phanouvong
402. Lt. Col. Vanhsy Srivannara (escaped Laos; migrated to U.S., 1986)
403. Police Maj. Vanna _____
404. Maj. Tiao Vatthana Nokham (royal family)
405. Police Lt. Col. Vone Vorabout
406. Civilian Vong Sengphaket
407. Air Force Lt. Col. Vongsouli Panya
408. 1st Lt. Xieng Singharath
409. Xieng Soymani
410. Police Lt. Col. Xom Michaleun
411. Maj. Xoum Manivong
412. Maj. Y Trai Ouran
413. Maj. Ya Vang
414. Maj. Yong Yethao

Index